Business Foresight

Business Foresight

Scenarios for Managing Uncertainty Strategically

Tony Grundy

BEP

BUSINESS EXPERT PRESS

Leader in applied, concise business books

First published in 2023 by
Business Expert Press, LLC
222 East 46th Street, New York, NY 10017
www.businessexpertpress.com

ISBN-13: 978-1-63742-463-6 (paperback)
ISBN-13: 978-1-63742-464-3 (e-book)

Business Expert Press Human Resource Management and Organizational Behavior Collection

First edition: 2023

10 9 8 7 6 5 4 3 2 1

Description

Turbulence in recent years has become unprecedentedly wicked. Uncertainty has become a dense fog for business leaders, difficult to tackle. This book uses scenario and other methods like systems thinking to look ahead and time travel to the future. Written by an extremely experienced consultant who has in parallel been a strategy academic at leading business schools for over 30 years, it is a practical toolkit grounded in theory. There are many practical experiences to illustrate "How to Do It" to complement theory.

There are many exercises for the interested reader to try out and many fascinating case studies to take the reader beyond "what happened and why?" to "how the process was managed and tips for applying it for yourself."

This is a must-read for business leaders who are finding uncertainties a difficult problem to deal with. For MBA students, it will give them a different dimension for thinking about their course work and projects and provide a real edge over those trapped within a single view of the future, not just a journey but a new way of thinking.

Keywords

uncertainty; scenarios; strategy; future; turbulence; innovation; disruptive; disruption

Contents

Testimonials

"Tony once again pushes the field of management to account for increasing uncertainty. His work should be required reading for both management students as well as corporate leaders. Using the tools and techniques, Tony presents in this book, will help any leader address the future in a proactive versus a reactive way. Uncertainty is a certainty, Tony helps his readers strategically and practically see around corners and into the future."—**James Berry, PhD, Director of the UCL MBA**

"Tony Grundy helps us unpack uncertainty. He develops novel frameworks and techniques, blends these with tried and tested scenario planning processes and illustrates them by applying them to current challenges facing us all. His style is lively, irreverent and very thought provoking. This book will help strategic leaders find ways of both understanding the sources of uncertainty and coping with them."—**Professor Cliff Bowman, Professor of Strategic Management, Cranfield School of Management**

"This book takes a very fresh, 'Alien Perspective' on Uncertainty. I love the way you are always being told what is coming next so that you can pick and choose and don't necessarily have to grind through the whole text. All this is done in a challenging, lively and practical way. Terms such as the strategic subconscious mind appeal (or 'sleep on it'). 'The Uncertainty Grid' and 'a weak signal that something may be going wrong' and 'scenario storytelling and strategic options going hand in hand' all appeal too and urge me to use the book in my work. Storytelling is critical in getting people on board and a great way to communicate. This book is ultra relevant to these uncertain times."—**Sir Philip Craven Director, Toyota Motor Corporation 2018–present. Also, former President, International Paralympic Committee 2002–2017—responsible for the staging of the Paralympic Summer and Winter Games**

"Tony is a seasoned, serious, clear and challenging communicator, particularly when unravelling the strategic options and risks of allocating resources in alternative futures Years ago he advised all planners 'not to drive your car on a motorway by using the rear view mirror-' but in this latest book he takes that far beyond into mental time travelling through pictorial tools that stretch thinking. For instance we see a circle representing customers, employees, suppliers and shareholders. This enables discussions of the impact of changing the allocation of resources e.g. through artificial intelligence. Scenario thinking like e.g. for AI is critical to reducing strategic uncertainty in a wickedly changing world- where demand for finance, leading edge technical skills, new products and services is outstripping supply. Tony is the master in ensuring you not only look ahead when driving but round corners, over hills, and can ride all the strategic bumps."—**David Bishop, retired Senior Partner, KPMG, Chairman Infrastructure and Government Consultancy**

*"*Business Foresight *is an invaluable tool for executives and MBA students, especially those facing the challenges of unprecedented turbulence and uncertainty in the business world. It is a practical toolkit that offers a unique approach to managing uncertainty and provides solid tools for navigating complex business environments. One of the book's standout features is its use of scenario planning and systems thinking to explore possible futures and help readers navigate the complexities of an uncertain business environment. By encouraging readers to 'time travel' into the future, Dr. Tony Grundy encourages them to think ahead and provides them with the skills necessary to anticipate and adapt to different scenarios. Dr. Grundy's extensive practical experience comes through in the pages as he seamlessly blends theory and real-life examples. The inclusion of numerous practical experiences and case studies not only explains 'what happened and why,' but also delves into the intricacies of 'how the process was managed and how you can apply it for yourself.' These insights add depth and authenticity to the concepts discussed and make the book relatable and actionable.* Business Foresight *challenges readers to embrace uncertainty as an opportunity for growth and offers a new dimension to strategic thinking. Dr. Grundy's accessible writing style and expertise make the book a must-read for anyone seeking to navigate a complex, ever-changing business world."*
—**Dino Mariutti, Head of EU, Damon Motors**

Acknowledgments

I would like to express my huge thanks to Nicky Burton; Stuart Reed; Matthew Harris, CEO of Fitness for Less; and Dr. Jim Berry, Director at UCL for the help on this book. Thanks too to my wife and delightful minder Dr. Carolina Yepes for her strategic companionship.

Prelude

… I can hear the marching feet
They're moving into the street
Now did you read the news today?
They say the danger's gone away
But I can see the fires still alight
They're burning into the night

There are too many men, too many people
Making too many problems
And not much love to go 'round
Can't you see this is a land of confusion?

Oh, Superman, where are you now
When everything's gone wrong somehow?
The men of steel, the men of power
Are losing control by the hour

This is the time; this is the place
So we look for the future
But there's not much love to go 'round
Tell me why this is a land of confusion
                    —"A Land of Confusion," by Genesis, 1986

One of the very biggest challenges organizations and managers grapple with today is *managing* uncertainty, which in the last few years has become a wicked problem to deal with.

Few would not recognize the escalation and increased volatility of uncertainty—the credit crunch, Brexit, and COVID-19, racial tensions, and climatic change.

As I was writing this book, a Genesis YouTube concert was playing: "The Land of Confusion." With the present conflagration of COVID-19 and post-COVID uncertainty, a war in Ukraine undermining geostability, a surge of inflation squeezing incomes, turbulence in Financial markets and massive energy price rises slowing measures to control climate change, we do seem to be in a huge uncertainty pickle.

The words of Phil Collins of Genesis, penned in 1986, 36 years ago, do seem prophetic. He even weaves into his story the rather inept leadership of great figures or "Supermen" failing to rescue us. One figure stands out: Volodymyr Zelensky, the President of Ukraine. Formerly a comedian who moved not only his own people to display unbelievable courage but carried much of the world with his vision, within the limitations, he admirably cut through uncertainty and ambiguity.

On a maybe at a less intense level, managers are surrounded by unprecedented lifetime's uncertainty. While it may be less dramatic than world turbulence at present, uncertainty is still extremely stressful and apart from things like risk registers that fundamentally do little more than log things that can go wrong, there is a scarcity of coherent and practical frameworks to deal very effectively with uncertainty.

This is not without consequence: the incidence and impact of uncertainty can lead to managers throwing strategy and long-term planning out of the window. But by using scenarios, there is huge potential for using mental time traveling and storytelling to dissolve much of what we label "uncertainty."

Many people have dimly heard of the word *scenarios*, but only a few know that they are a lot more than forecasts and are living stories about the future. They believe forecasts to be shrouded in mystery resembling the "black boxes" in an aircraft. We know there are insights inside, but who knows what they are?

In this book, I will demonstrate that they are actually processes supported by visual tools that allow both individuals and groups to visualize and to sense business future(s). Scenarios are capable of dissolving many of the problems of strategy and dealing with uncertainty.

The main focus of this book is demystifying what we call "uncertainty," which is often thought of as too difficult or scary to think about. The primary audience for this book is CEOs or those aspiring to become CEOs: those who are, or might be in future, challenged to be the early warning systems that detect, qualify, and diagnose scarier uncertainties.

The book is also immensely helpful at a practical level for business and management students, for entrepreneurs in new or existing ventures, or for corporate managers or consultants.

Readers can use it to get a grip on uncertainty through a flexible repertoire of tools, models, and processes. In addition, the book is energized by strategic mindfulness (acting as an observer, detached but fascinated by complexity). Through scenario storytelling, structured investigation, and conversations about the possible and the unlikely, the book opens up a new world about uncertainty. *Finally, it is channeled through asking probing questions that open up "lines of enquiry."*

It is as much relevant to everyday life as it is to business, the planet, and our survival and to business life.

A quick story of scenarios in everyday life:

As a lifelong Genesis fan, one of my regrets was "I have never seen them perform live." So, when they embarked on what was likely to be their very last live tour during 2021 to 2022, I bought two tickets at a considerable cost. The show got canceled due to COVID-19 in 2021 and then the venue, the O2, was damaged by a storm in early 2022. But after a chunk was blown off the roof, amazingly it was repaired in a month!

But in the week of the concert, I began to sneeze (hay fever/cold?) and after a day got a lingering headache; it was a heavy laptop screen week and my two lateral flow tests were negative. These symptoms were, however, "weak signals" of maybe something bigger. On the day of the concert, I had a bit of a dry cough and then tested positive. So, I missed the last Genesis ever!

Unlike some top politicians who by nature would do "what's in it for me and just go," we canceled.

I and my wife made our own light show instead and watched the YouTube version of the concert on our big TV and speakers, but still it was not quite the real thing! Maybe there's a parallel world where I botched the test and went anyway (as many politicians would do). Had I delayed by a day in coming out as COVID positive, we would have gone to the concert, but probably I would have spread it to ten people, which might have led to the death of some old and vulnerable persons.

The "hay fever" was a precursor to a very major and upsetting disruption that with twist and turns could have infected an elderly tourist and killed them! The world is uncertain and that uncertainty is variable and part predictable—uncertainty is uncertain. But this book argues that it isn't all deterministic and we can have many tools and processes for navigating through uncertainty.

So, futures crystallize out of various events and causal streams. It is precarious and has mechanics of complex causes and effects, which might not be easily predicted but could be sensed. At the time there were over 100,000 reported cases of the Omicron virus a day—in reality, the underlying number was probably 200,000 including nonreported ones. So I might have just hidden indoors for the week before and avoided it. So, we can often do something about future possible events even if we are faced with uncertainty.

Similarly, then British Prime Minister Boris Johnson must surely have realized that attending all those parties at number 10 Downing Street at the same time as advising the country that we should all practice social distancing and isolation might rebound at some stage in the future. The tools in this book, even if just only sampled a bit, would have screamed to the user "Don't go!" Even Rishi Sunak, the then UK Chancellor of the Exchequer, who would have been in pole position to lead the government had Boris resigned, got a fixed penalty notice for attending one of those Downing Street parties.

I have tried, over the period, to get Boris to think more systematically about the future through 2021 to 2022 (six long letters; see Case Study 5 for the last), but all efforts seem to flounder on reactivity by the British. Managing uncertainty is not a discretionary game; it is something we need to do strategically. This book provides you with a set of tools for doing just that.

So just a quick word on what this book is and how its frameworks have been compiled. While this book is not meant as a dry academic text but meant for top and senior executives and also for MBAs and MBA students, it has rigor and is not splattered with references. The frameworks are born out of my 30 years or more of consulting and facilitation experience and academic research and teaching.

I have often asked what I call my "strategic unconscious mind" to help me out for inspiration at times—by asking your subconscious for a strategic insight that can often serve it up for you on a plate! Figure P.1

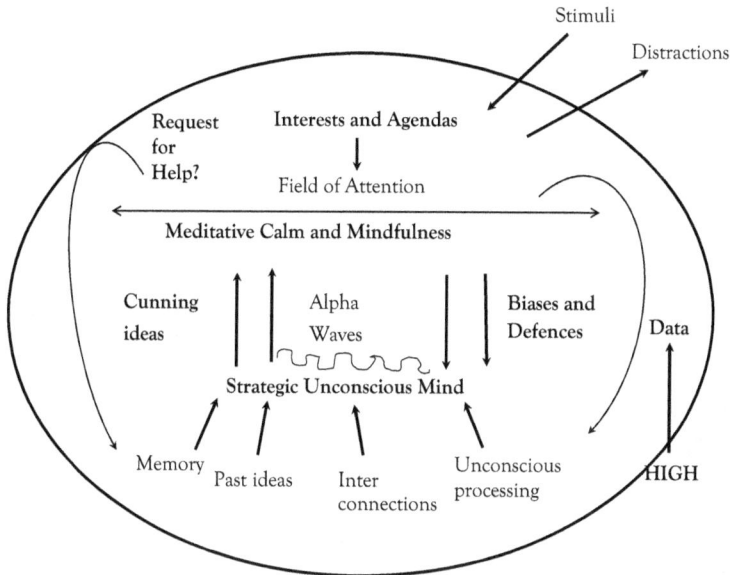

Figure P.1 *Cognitive dynamics and the strategic unconscious mind*
Source: Inputs from Dr. Carolina Yepes and Dr. Tony Grundy.

depicts how that works showing the iteration between the conscious and the unconscious mind.

Finally, I drew my studies way back from existentialism that suggests we should reflect on how we construct our social world to discern how it is created as a reality, "what could be really going on here," and its sister, "phenomenology." Phenomenology is how we take a phenomenon like uncertainty and try to see it as something strange. Then we try to characterize it afresh based on our encounters—what goes into it and what come out of it, and how does it behave and how do we get around it?

Police detectives do this with crimes, crimes scenes, and suspects so they widen their field of awareness and pick up patterns and clues.

Hence, I opted to merge mindfulness, existentialism, and phenomenology in navigating this exploration of uncertainty because they act as guides at a practical level to look at uncertainty from all kinds of angles yet in a subtle but not a heavy way.

CHAPTER 1

Introduction

Exploring the World of Scenarios

Introduction

This book is aimed at future and aspiring CEOs who wish to develop their skills in dealing with uncertainty. They will learn how to manage attendant emotions like anxiety and fear, and maybe dread and panic. Besides causing sluggishness and paralysis, these emotions can also severely erode the cognitive ability of individuals to deal with the ambiguity that surrounds "wicked uncertainty."

Uncertainty can be a very funny thing to deal with. Indeed. I encountered "uncertainty" when I was studying strategic investment decisions for my PhD. When I interviewed senior managers making very big decisions, they made frequent references to uncertainty, but they seemed curiously reluctant in doing any "deep dives" into why something was uncertain. This led me to assume that, in large part, "uncertainty" was a convenient label for things that were too difficult or scary to deal with. Around that time, I was a consultant at KPMG. We were doing sensitivity analysis for our clients—playing with positive or negative percentages on key variables to do a rough sanity check on business plans and business cases. These were very crude calculations. I am inclined to believe that what we did was something similar to taking some paracetamols to reduce the pain of a broken leg.

I now define uncertainty as "an unquantified possible variance from a default view of the future, or futures"—or call it ambiguity.

"Foresight" has been defined by the *Oxford English Dictionary* as "to be able to predict what is likely to happen or will be needed in the future." Maybe a better definition would be "to be able to predict what will happen or not happen, or be needed or not needed in future."

Foresight, in this context, means the ability to sense a whole range of outcomes rather than getting hung up on a diet of "likely," "optimistic," and "pessimistic" scenarios.

"Business" is our main focus, and uncertainty is more pronounced in the public and not-for-profit sectors.

"Managing" uncertainty may not find favor with some on the grounds that uncertainty is something inherently slippery. And believing that it can be managed is therefore untenable for them. I would disagree.

"Scenarios" are self-consistent stories and pictures of the future.

So why this book?

1. We have lived through perhaps the most uncertain times between 2020 and 2022, caused by COVID-19, since World War II with the possible exception of the credit crunch; there has to be an unequivocal need for a book on business foresight and scenarios as a way of dealing with uncertainty.

2. Strategic planning desperately needs to be reenergized as it is perceived to be too mechanistic and inflexible and, for sure, ill-equipped to deal with uncertainty.

3. Having enriched and extended of managing uncertainty strategically through developing the new Capstone Futures MBA project at UCL School of Management in London, I would like to share that process with the CEOs, directors, and others involved in strategy making and execution, as well as with MBA students globally.

4. I also wish to say that the process achieved success with clients like Amerada Petroleum, HSCC, National Iranian Oil Company, PepsiCo, Standard Life, Tesco Express, Direct and Non-Foods, and Zurich Life.

5. I have read a number of books on scenarios and have enjoyed the theory part in them. But they tend to be written in a sort of neo-religious vein, encouraging us to believe in the process. But they are generally rather thin on *how to actually do it*, which is what this book is all about.

   This chapter covers the following:

   - Basic forecasting—its strengths and weaknesses
   - Shell case study—original interview material
   - Storytelling—the trajectory of COVID-19

- Structure of the book
- Summary and key concluding insights

For brevity, a number of rich case studies are provided in appendixes online. Our first one is on Russia as it was threatening to invade Ukraine. This provides insights into the experience of the initial formulation of some future views that are embedded in stakeholder and behavioral analysis. Coming from a virtually very basic understanding of Russian president Vladimir Putin, they do yield some insights on possible future states of the world. The reader is encouraged to go through these case studies.

Reader Exercise

Have you ever had the experience of picking up a "weak signal" (Ansoff 1975) that something might be going wrong and discounted it because you felt it was something you can't influence? For example, you take a Vauxhall from the garage and everywhere you go there is smoke billowing behind you. Did you initially think it must surely be another car? How long did it take for you to accept that something might be wrong with your car and a diagnosis has to be made?

The Russia–Ukraine situation was something similar. Until mid-February 2022, it was on my radar screen, but I had assumed it was mainly posturing by Putin, but it wasn't going away. When I took up the challenge of structuring possible scenarios, quite quickly after the Russia–Ukraine conflict began to take shape, it was emotionally not just satisfying, especially when the insight that uncertainty sneaks up on you came into play but also because there was a greater sense of manageability. *The wind of fear had been stemmed and I felt reassured that there would now be less chance of a huge surprise or shock—all very interesting!*

Uncertainty becomes more amenable to managing when it is approached strategically. This is achieved through a structured but agile approach, in this case organized around:

- Stakeholder agenda analysis;
- Strategic options generation and evaluation; and
- Initial gaming of what moves the parties might make.

Basic Forecasting: Strengths and Weaknesses

Forecasting became trendy in the 1960s, partially because of macroeconomic forecasting of growth, inflation, the effect of government borrowing and spending and taxation, and the impact of monetary growth. Economists vied with each other for the high ground but rarely agreed, despite sophisticated models becoming feasible now thanks to giant computers.

Meanwhile as computers became more powerful, corporate planners attempted to see into the future through scaled down models of corporate sales demand and profit to support growth strategies. By the latter part of the 1970s, long-range planning was in vogue coincidentally around the rise of intercontinental ballistic missiles (ICBMs) as long-range nuclear rockets. Fueled by scientific management, forecasting offered a "white coat" solution to the problem of uncertainty.

Long-range forecasting was plausible as markets and growth were relatively stable save for political and economic shocks. But even so, uncertainty, like the weather, has compounding effects limiting forecasting. Indeed, theorists and practitioners turned to softer, more intuitive types of modeling like scenario storytelling as instigated by Shell in the 1970s to which we will turn very soon.

In sum, the strengths of forecasting, such as using correlation equations, were that:

- It enabled flexing of assumptions to reflect change in or changing market and other economic conditions; and
- Where relationships between variables and the variables themselves could be well defined, there could be quite good estimates of the short-term and long-term results, assuming quite stable markets.

In contrast, the weaknesses were as follows:

- The data demands could be quite high and it would be time-consuming to target, collect, clean, analyze, and evaluate data.
- Over the more recent decades, particularly since 2000, markets have become increasingly unstable. So it is simply not much use to rely on relatively well-structured models.

- Senior managers and directors, even if trained in engineering and science, were often still not very comfortable with statistics and preferred use of intuitive judgment.

So, the conclusion is that long-range forecasting is well balanced but can sometimes still have a role to play and is probably best after the application of more intuitive methods like those that are proposed in this book.

Before we get into an introduction to the scenario process, let me just clear up any possible confusion between scenarios and forecasts. These terms are often used interchangeably, but they have distinct meanings. I defined "forecast" in *Dynamic Competitive Strategy—Turning Strategy Upside Down* (Grundy 2018) as

a set of quantitative assumed outcomes that are the end product of interacting variables and then extrapolations of various trends that will affect certain decisions.

So, a forecast is expressed in some numbers and has input and output variables plus some process or model for dealing with interdependencies and so on. It is determinate and "hard," and the answers can be accurate or inaccurate, right or wrong.

An example of a forecast would be the business and financial plans we used to do long ago at KPMG. We derived sales from volumes and prices (and thus market demand) and costs (fixed, variable, and semivariable) for a business plan, a buyout, an acquisition, or a turnaround. Another would be the business valuations I did with my then MBA students at Henley Business School with similar assumptions plus ones on the investment needed, the tax payments, cash flows, and finally the NPVs (net present values). This was done to put an economic value on a business or strategic decision.

Typically, in such exercises, uncertainty tends to get pushed to the periphery as the focus is on more easily identified risks. These types of calculations usually boil down to some crude playing around with the variance resulting from plus or minus 5 percent or 10 percent upside and downside, each done very separately. Such manipulations often fail to achieve their purpose of doing really thorough stress testing as the calculations are very limited and may not reflect worse cases. Even more concerning, if these models get into the hands of overly enthusiastic number crunchers, then they may forget to factor in any reasonably well thought through picture of the market and of the competitive environment. The result then is all too often "GIGO" (garbage in–garbage out).

"Scenarios" differ completely from pure forecasts. I defined "scenario" as being "a coherent and consistent series of events and actions that are set against a backdrop or environment" (Grundy 2018).

So in scenarios, we emphasize the softer aspects of interpreting the softer interplay of factors that are embedded: the present, changes in the pipeline, emergent new trends and events as well as the more random and disruptive stuff that may shift the system to a new equilibrium. Scenarios are best done either before doing hardcore forecasting as characterized above or in parallel to inform the forecasts.

Indeed, at the heart of scenario storytelling is the process of *surfacing causality*, where some patterns in the chains of events are beginning to become visible and offer the choice as to whether you take much notice of them. Surfacing causality is "the systematic identification of causes and effects within a system and data collection and analysis in different ways from different sources to get a better fix on all of that."

There will always be a lag between the recognition of a new or notable phenomenon and determining it as warranting attention, and between actually investigating it and finally doing something about it. Scenario storytelling reduces the time lags for understanding phenomena, decisions, and actions, increasing the effectiveness of the process and also the chances of some action or decisions being taken, thus making change happen. We actually show that as a picture (Figure 9.6).

Consider these things carefully when deep-diving (highly recommended!) into Case Study 2 on "COVID-19 and the Initial UK Pandemic."

This brings us to how intuitive modeling might work, which takes us back to the efforts that Shell kicked off in the 1970s. Originally, Shell used the scenario process for anticipating the threefold price hike in oil prices allegedly not foreseen by the other oil majors. In the next section, we will get a glimpse of just how different this approach is from a more primarily forecasting-based one.

Shell Case Study—Original Interview Material

Years ago, I was doing research into how companies developed scenarios. I got lucky and interviewed Graham Galer of Shell Group Planning (Grundy 1995). That interview shaped my thinking about scenarios, my work over the years in facilitating and doing *scenario storytelling*, and this book considerably. Graham was clear, crisp, and structured. He explained:

> In the late 1970s, Scenario Planning started duly as a response to the increasingly turbulent environment with oil shocks, political uncertainty, and economic turbulence.
>
> It was only in 1981 that the methodology we made was more coherent ... when a major review of Shell's planning systems was undertaken. This, in effect, institutionalized scenario thinking... You can't go for long within Shell before you hear the word "scenario."
>
> The principal use of scenario thinking is in strategic planning. We tend to regard that as separate from business planning, which is more concerned with allocating resources needed to implement agreed strategies and is typically not numerically based.
>
> Broadly speaking, we do a major review of our global scenarios every two or three years. We put a lot of our work into that but that's not all our work.

(He goes on to describe later the work on "focused scenarios" on a specific issue.)

The Potential and the Pitfalls of Scenarios

Basically, we wanted to move forward from single views of the future environment and this meant that we had to explore uncertainty in much greater depth, but we faced problems. First, we tended to carry out a study, go away and come back with the result, and involve the management on it. This gave rise to big problems of ownership.

A second problem that we also had was "groupthink" (Janis 1982) (convergence of views)

Focused Scenarios

"Focused scenarios" deal with more localized or specific issues. First of all, we start by drawing a bare skeleton—if you like, a quick and dirty version of the scenario.

Imagine we are one of Shell's Opcos. So, we might begin by getting the managers to think individually about the factors in the business environment that are important. We would then take a look at the existing trends in order to explore the continuities and any possible discontinuities.

The other things that we would focus on are those factors which would appear to be particularly uncertain.

At this point I remember thinking, "This is getting interesting. Graham seems to be implicitly using the uncertainty grid, which also rates assumptions in terms of their importance as well as their uncertainty." Indeed, he was.

We then build up the scenario around the key uncertainties… We would follow up the work of managers individually and we rely upon workshops to provide some structure and a learning opportunity to support scenario development.

This whole theory of importance and uncertainty is of some significance. We get managers to think about the relative importance (and also the (relative) degree of uncertainty) of all the key factors. This helps identify the factors with the greatest impact in shaping a different world to the one prevailing at present.

To support the process, we use devices such as Post-its in the form of magnetic, hexagonal shapes. We then write the appropriate factor on each shape and position each one on a magnetic board. This allows managers to play with what they see as the relative importance and uncertainty relative to one another.

We might also, at that point, draw the axis of a matrix in four quadrants to frame the factors of particular interest. But the really important bit is the moving around of the factors relative to each other.

This, of course, is the uncertainty grid (see Figure 2.4) that I could see him inching toward, exactly the same grid which I had discovered myself in papers and a book (*The Unbounded Mind* by Mitroff et al. 1993) and which I have used for 27 years.

So far, I have described how we break down the future environment, but we also need to build up to create a scenario. Based on the earlier analysis of key factors, we would then explore the underlying driving forces in greater depth, focusing on the most important and most uncertain factor.

Besides the driving forces, we would be particularly interested in any special events that might lead the world to develop in a new and different ways.

We call these in this book (as does Shell) "transitional events."

It is also helpful to then look at the dynamic paths that might lead from the present to the future world as described in the scenario. This is quite a creative point as you need to imagine what sort of events (and knock-on events) might occur and what these might do to the overall scenario.

We visualize them (the events) in this book mainly with the uncertainty tunnel (see Figure 3.10) by picturing specific chains of causality and by looking at the impact of events coming later or sooner and changes beginning later or sooner too.

Global Scenarios

With our global scenarios, we obviously have to consider an array of events, especially a combinations of events. We sometimes write these events on cards and look at particularly interesting dynamic sequences.

This is very interesting too as it emphasizes the playful aspect as well as the possibility of actively creating possible and plausible futures—a far cry from the basic forecasting techniques that we saw in the last section.

Building scenarios into strategic management also raises the question of "can we do anything to shape or influence that chain of events?" I once worked with BP and it was clear to me that BP was not necessarily "hands off" in terms of what went on in its territories of operation vis-a-vis government.... But my main point here is that formation of scenarios and the formulation and evaluation of strategic options need to go "hand in hand."

We don't necessarily look just at two or three (scenarios), although we usually end up with three.

He then moves on to some broader reflections:

We do find more difficulty in encouraging managers to work up scenarios for major strategic decisions or (investment) projects. But I can understand the reluctance of the champion who has an awful lot of energy to make a project happen, but not to want it tested vigorously against scenarios. We already have enough hurdles without posing more. But on the other hand, there is an argument that the project should be tested against scenarios to get a better discussion of the risks.

I did then share my own views with Graham that scenarios were essential as vehicles for developing and testing strategic investment decisions, which was the subject of my then recent PhD and which resonated with him.

I would like to add the following specific comments on this fascinating interview:

- The need to kick off with an initial sketch of a scenario mirrors very closely the work I did in around an hour on scenarios for Russia versus the UK (discussed earlier).

- It is interesting that Graham emphasized the need for a structured process, the bare bones of which were scenario skeleton, the analysis of the main "factors" or variables, their evaluation, the exploration of driving forces, and transitional events with appreciation of potential dynamics and timings, and finally the creation of a plausible storyline.

But he did emphasize that the structure really shouldn't drive out the creativity:

Scenario planning is very much an art and not a science. It is a creative and qualitative exercise in analysis. It is a mental modeling, but you really couldn't map the mental processes at work. They are just too complex.

Before we leave Shell, I want to clarify the following. Comparing the Shell process with that in my scenario structure of Russia versus Ukraine, the reason why I didn't use the uncertainty grid at that stage was not just because it was too detailed at that early stage, but that it was obvious that the issue was both very important but also extremely uncertain!

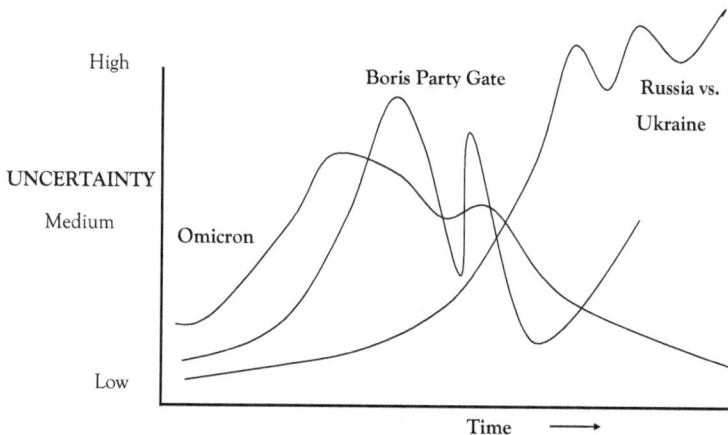

Figure 1.1 Uncertainty Waves—UK November 2021–March 2022

A bigger picture and a more "systemic" model of what might happen is necessary first to get the overview. Over the years, I have learned to devise a more tailored process that is then applied to the issue rather than as a set piece process. At that stage, the process is fluid—there are many options.

This systemic view is also dynamic and in this book we will be showing this as: "Waves of Uncertainty."

Reader Exercise

For possible numerical forecasts, like sales growth of your company, the growth of a market, or of the economy (stripping out seasonality (the variation of demand over the annual cycle), ask:

- What has the past growth been (by percent) over a period?
- What is likely to drive future growth (more/less)?
- What is likely to reduce it (less/more severely)?
- What new concrete factors might kick in (upside and downside)?
- Are there any other psychological factors to factor in?
- Based on all these factors, what might your growth curve look like? (Avoid a straight line.)

As this is a practical book, I am keen to engage you as a reader. I do sprinkle a bit of humor here and there. But I do stress that there is a serious point put in a lighthearted way. Humor after all lightens some of the impact of uncertainty. I am also enthused as I have seen how this works too.

Structure of the Book

Chapter 2: Figuring Out Uncertainty

In this chapter, we look at the key ingredients of uncertainty including the Arrow of Time. Uncertainty drivers, the uncertainty grid and the uncertainty tunnel, and charting the dynamic variables over time curves are covered in the chapter. We then deal with an art of storytelling with the case study of the War in the Pacific.

Chapter 3: Scenario Building Tools, Concepts, and Process

In this chapter, the scenario process is explained in detail with an introduction to the background tools like the Strategic Onion and the Business Value System for understanding the economic dimension. Next, we show different aspects of the scenario process such as system pictures and transitional events with the oil industry and other cases.

Chapter 4: Step-by-Step Scenario Tools and Process

Next, we go deeper into the scenario tools and process, particularly with the help of the process, amplifier and dampeners, accelerators and retarders, and slicing the future into phases. Finally, we link the scenario back to strategy to deal with futures in a proactive and inventive way through the Cunning Plan, using which we can perform the actual storytelling of favorable pathways from present to future.

Chapter 5: Managing Organizational Change Scenarios

Scenarios are associated with the external environment, but they are equally applicable to the internal environment as well, particularly in change management situations. Here we see a small number of specialist tools in action such as fishbone analysis, from–to (FT) analysis, and root cause systems.

Chapter 6: Decision-Specific Uncertainties and Scenarios

In this chapter, we take scenarios into the land of finance and tease out specifically some of the decision-specific aspects of applying them and use storytelling technique for explaining how scenarios can be applied to mergers and acquisitions (M&As), alliances, international strategy, and other investment decisions.

Chapter 7: Behavioral Scenarios and Role Playing

In this chapter, we look at the behavioral dimension to see how it drives much uncertainty and how insights can be gained by putting yourself in the minds of other stakeholders with a scenario case study of North Sea gas. In addition, we cover the role of cognition and cognitive bias in assessing uncertainty.

Chapter 8: Application to MBA and Case Study of Scenarios for the MBA Market

Uncertainty features highly not just in real projects on the job but also in MBA projects. Here we show how that can be dealt with much more effectively. There will also be a worked example with commentary on the thought and decision process.

Chapter 9: Conclusions

In our final chapter, we suggest how to use scenarios both in business and in everyday life, followed by key concluding insights for the whole book. We then stress on the role of resilience and fragility and the dynamics of response and delay in scenario planning.

There are also many practical and valuable exercises that you would find interesting and I encourage you not to skip them. This is a practical book and not a guide. There are useful references throughout and pointers in Chapter 9.

Finally, we have some hugely valuable appendixes available online:

- Appendix 1: Russia Invades the Ukraine and Putin's Motives (written in February 2022)
- Appendix 2: COVID-19—The Trajectory of COVID-19
- Appendix 3: Tesco Scenarios
- Appendix 4: International Strategy
- Appendix 5: BT and Behavioral Uncertainty
- Appendix 6: Boris Johnson Letter
- Appendix 7: The Random Weekend

Conclusions and Key Concluding Insights

The main purpose of this chapter was to explain the differences between conventional forecasting and scenarios, which are summarized below:

	Conventional Planning	Scenario Storytelling
Main Content	Financial projections	Dynamic pictures of the future
Key Outputs	Numbers	Patterns, events, stories, dynamic consequences
Key Processes	Financial modeling	Sensing, debate, gaming, role plays
Key Inputs	Past trends extrapolated	Disruptions, uncertainty grids and tunnel, agendas
Key Skills	Financial and statistical	Psychological, economic, imagination, innovation

We used three main case studies to illustrate the application of scenarios. The first was the scenario before and after the Russia–Ukraine conflict, the second was an account of how scenarios enabled Shell to think differently about a more turbulent future, and finally, how uncertainty around COVID-19 might have been managed better.

I will conclude with a long list of key concluding insights. The CEOs should get what a "key insight" is, but as most MBA students don't seem to know even by the end of their course, I will define key insight as:

a thought which makes sense of a set or data, observations, discussions, or ideas with potentially significant implications—it is an AHA moment.

The key concluding insights from Chapter 1 are as follows:

- Contrary to what some think, uncertainty can be managed.
- The first step is to do a scenario skeleton (a plan for the plan?), which can be done quickly and can yield rich insights.
- Central to such an exercise is looking at the stakeholder intention and the optional set of the players.
- Scenario processes should be tailored to the issue and context and are rarely "set piece."

- Successful scenario developers are more likely to have well-developed psychological and behavioral skills or economic analysis skills, or both.
- Central to the process is identifying the key factors, variables, or assumptions and evaluating their importance and uncertainty; by doing this, the areas of most volatility can be identified, which would act as a precursor to identifying transitional events and storytelling.
- While scenario planning is very intuitive, it can still be informed and guided by quantitative forecasting, targeting, and doing "what ifs."
- Scenarios don't necessarily have very long-term time horizons—for example, the COVID projections were done just for a month.
- Scenario storytelling can help reduce the emotional difficulties of dealing with acute anxiety, fear, or dread associated with deep uncertainty.
- Scenario storytelling can also help minimize the time lag to react.

CHAPTER 2

Figuring Out Uncertainty

Introduction

In this chapter, we cover the following topics:

- The nature of uncertainty
- The arrow of time
- Uncertainty drivers
- The uncertainty—importance grid
- The uncertainty-over-time curve
- Other variables over time (curves)
- Concluding insights

But before we plunge in, I would like to step back a little. When we think of the future, we often contemplate strategy and maybe do not visualize scenarios that will truly anchor ourselves in the future. Strategy to be sure is rooted in the present and the past. I have called it "T − 1 thinking" where thinking about the future is not only embedded in the present but even the past. Here T − 1 thinking means "earlier than the present."

My argument is not that no one ever really thinks about the future but that their approach is patchy, fragmented, and, if done at all, is linear and framed in extrapolating the past. But this book seeks to demonstrate that visualizing future could be done far better. *Indeed, the fact that it is done at all should be encouraging.*

Reader Exercise

How much of your time is spent on thinking about your business and your role focusing on

- The present—percent?
- The past—percent?
- The future—percent?

Is that the optimal balance and what are the options for shifting the focus?

But before we dive into uncertainty, let me emphasize that my interest in uncertainty and scenarios comes partly from strategy. My MBA was taught from an initial present perspective: it is how you journey from position to objectives. When I read *Competing for the Future* by Hamel and Prahalad (1994) 28 years ago, I observed that it stressed on:

- Future environmental attractiveness
- Future customers
- Future competitors
- Future competitive advantage
- Future value and cost base (added by me)

But we have something far more powerful.

We will indulge in some future time traveling and that means diving into more uncertainty. Given that conventional forecasts are extremely limited, we enter the world of scenarios, which maps the core premise of the book.

Time traveling is central to this book. In H.G. Wells' *Time Machine* (1885), the time traveler visits a graphic future of a postindustrial society. With hindsight, he did it probably 150 years before its time! It was absolutely astonishing as it senses for sure a plausible future. Anyone skeptical of scenario storytelling technology should read this book.

The Nature of Uncertainty

In this section, we try to make sense of uncertainty by defining it.

"Uncertainty" can be defined as:

(something that) arises when decisions have to be made about the future where it is not possible to assign probabilities to the various outcomes.

It is often synonymous with risk.

The hallmark of uncertainty is that future outcomes can't be estimated numerically. It makes uncertainty a fuzzy thing. Risks can be quantified.

While both uncertainty and risk are all about chance, risks are less anxiety provoking. Some use both these terms interchangeably, which is a bit unfortunate. When facilitating strategic thinking, I usually combine the two as "uncertainty and risk" for a strategic option evaluation criteria.

Uncertainty was one of the "three curses" of doing the economic valuation of strategies, and in my doctoral research *Exploring Strategic Financial Management* (Grundy 1998). The other two were interdependences and intangibles. Uncertainty was a curious phenomenon as it seemed to be a frequent label for strategic decisions that were particularly challenging. It seemed too often be used to depict something hard to think about and difficult to analyze and evaluate rather than an inherent property. Once this "label" was used, that seemed to let managers off the hook of investigating it.

Indeed, much of uncertainty seemed to me to be about putting things into the too hard "box," rather than exhibiting some inherently unknowable factor. I therefore conjectured that "all too often uncertainty is something that is too hard or just too threatening to even think about."

So, where does "uncertainty" reside in? Is it an outcome? Yes, but 'it's a consequence or effect in a causal process. So, to say "there could be a terrible war in the Ukraine" is obviously an uncertain outcome, but so too are the variables (inputs) that lead to the situation. So, uncertainty involves both outcome and inputs.

It is generally most helpful to frame these inputs as assumptions because it makes them very specific. If we were to apply assumptions to uncertainty generally, they might be broken down into different systems such as:

- The wider environment
- The economic environment
- Business variables
- Behaviors
- Intentions and agendas
- Mindsets

Notice that half of these—the last three—revolve around people and psychology. When evaluating business decisions, much of the modeling is done around deep diving into the harder business variables. Uncertainty revolves around these softer variables. The corollary of that is that "*if you understand the people and the psychological factors, you can get a grip over uncertainty.*"

Reader Exercise

For a business decision that seems relatively uncertain, what are the key risk drivers (perhaps using or drawing from the ones listed earlier)? (Be specific about the items in the list though.)

The Arrow of Time

The idea of arrow of time (see Figure 2.1) comes partly from modern physics where time is depicted as an arrow from past to the future with the embellishment of the idea of possible futures where the arrow goes off from a linear direction. (See the book "*The Arrow of Time*" in modern physics (Coveney and Highfield 1991).)

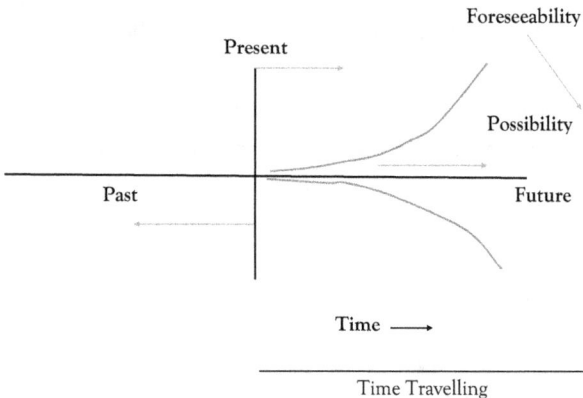

Figure 2.1 The arrow of time

Note: This picture is inspired by Modern Physics which plots trajectories of particles as "thought experiments"—our past trajectory through time conditions our thinking—as a singularity it conditions us to think in a linear way. Yet peering forward to the future we can foresee concave probability curves that allow wider and wider possibilities of change (like the weather) over time. By mental time travelling we are able to start visualizing much wider possibilities than linear planning.

So, what I am asking 'you, the reader, to do is to visualize that journey by locating yourself mindfully in the now, the present, and being carried along in the flow of time. You are able to see backward as a series of past events in a causal sequence and sensing forward into possible event sequences too.

That sensing forward captures an ever-widening set of possibilities. As you sense deeper into the future, these possibilities tend to broaden, except where uncertainty is low as there is convergence to a narrower range of possibilities. An example of this sensing would apply to market maturity, an election, or a latent financial crisis. What I find about this model is that it takes me further into the sense of latent potentials and away from a fixation on forecasts.

Some sources liken this form of sensing to a cone of possible future(s) or the "cone of plausibility" where more and more events are possible as one moves into the future with an ever opening up curved cone.

I also show Figure 2.2, which is a helicopter view as if we were transcending this perceived linear flow as it unexpectedly shoots into another direction or another trajectory. Examples we have already covered under this sensing are COVID-19, the variant Omicron, and the massive invasion of the Ukraine in February 2022 by Russia.

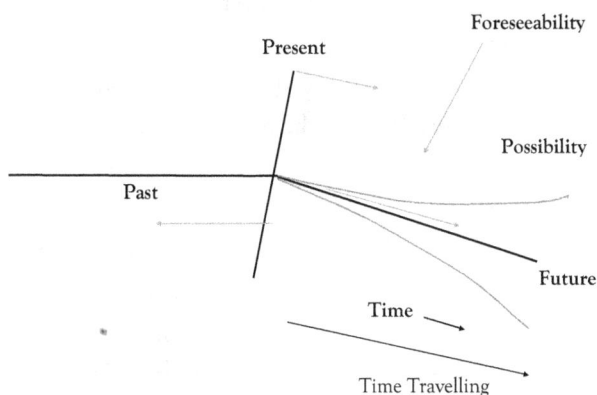

Figure 2.2 The arrow of time—with discontinuous change

Note: OOPS! What happens if the world shifts its trajectory? This can be both directional and also in terms of velocity too! What about the Credit Crunch 2008 which had a very near financial meltdown? Or of course COVID 19—all that was needed was a bat to snuggle up with a furry animal and hen get stroked by a human who wiped his nose with his/her hand! Hypothetically.

It is as if you are heading north from London Euston train station. You get to Crewe 160 miles away or you can stay on the train to Scotland, go to Manchester or Liverpool, or even North Wales to have very different experiences. These possible subworlds can crystallize as a result of choices—decisions the actor makes or events externally may be in charge of that outcome! A very memorable film that illustrates this well is *Sliding Doors* where in one version of the future, the protagonist gets on the tube as the doors are shutting and, in another world, she doesn't get into the tube, leading to different outcomes.

The arrow of time is thus a very useful model for preparing us to dive deeper into uncertainty. What's really interesting here is the use of pictures and diagrams to help us process the "uncertainty of uncertainty," which isn't about uncertainty itself but about the process for dealing with it, similar to the cone of plausibility (Taylor 1990 beyond "possibility").

The Uncertainty Drivers

An "uncertainty driver" is something that aggravates the degree of uncertainty in a specific context. Analyzing these variables can produce a greater vision of why something is particularly uncertain and can be done visually in five to ten minutes.

One way of getting behind uncertainty is therefore to break down the drivers of uncertainty. This can be depicted as a risk tree shape with a hierarchy of uncertainty with two levels of uncertainty—macro and micro as a top–down picture. Or the other shape is that of a fishbone analysis where the fish's head is "uncertainty" and the bones are the root causes of uncertainty (see Figure 2.3, which depicts the case of Russia versus Ukraine, which was explored in Chapter 1).

Figure 2.3 splits the symptom to the right as part of a chain of causality, and the "root causes" to the left. These would also be deep-dived to a further level, for instance, the scale of the conflict embraces the whole of the Ukraine and then threatens Eastern European countries formerly part of the Soviet Bloc, encompassing military conflict, cyber war, economic

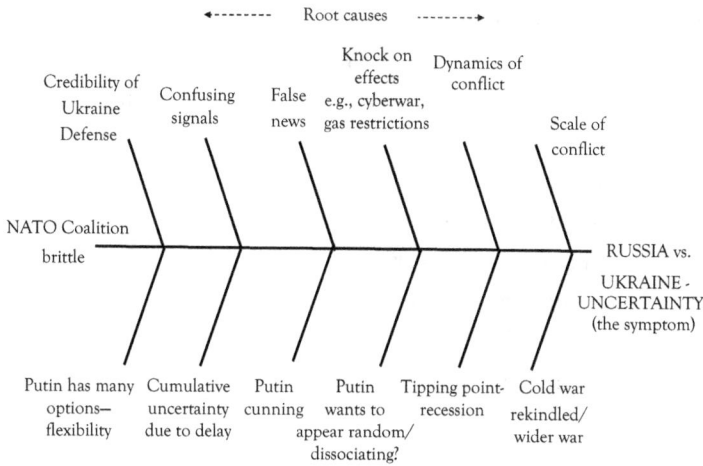

Figure 2.3 Fishbone analysis—why is the Russia versus Ukraine conflict uncertain

sanctions, and even the supply of gas from Russia to the West, plus the whole of Europe—that might invite a mini fishbone.

Here we see that the sheer scale of the conflict magnifies the uncertainty as well as the huge range of possible speeds with which the conflict could develop as of the time of writing (February 2022).

I found it difficult to squeeze onto the fishbone all the uncertainty drivers (see Figure 2.3) from the military to the deceptive communications to the state of mind and intent of Vladimir Putin. It did also capture some consequential uncertainty in the form of the cold war being rekindled, and even some air strikes to help counterbalance Russian war attacks (help! But that's what can happen in war!).

The implication of this fishbone is that it is clear that the uncertainty is very high and a myriad of trajectories are possible. Putin would seem to be much more resilient than the North Atlantic Treaty Organization (NATO) and the European Union (EU), and he enjoys all the attention and the confusion. Also, he is far more in control than we are, especially as he runs an autocratic state and militarily he is very much in charge of any bigger battles, although resistance might be a different matter.

If we asked the Rumelt's (2011) killer question of "What is really going on here?" Putin seems to be playing a conventional bullying game with Ukraine and a psychological bullying game with the West and EU. Right now he has had the time of his life or maybe he is suffering from the onset of dissociative identity disorder!(I am speaking here in 2022).

A "so what" from this scenario is the question, "what can we do to unsettle him—anything he hasn't thought about?" and another would be "what would throw him off balance?"

Another factor that needs to be investigated in understanding uncertainty is to decipher the compounding effects of uncertainty. The easiest way of thinking about this is to consider how weather forecasts operate and pan out. Forecasts of weather within the next day are typically very certain indeed, days 2 to 3 days are relatively probable, days 4 to 5 out are moderately probable, and a week out have a lower reliability.

To mitigate this difficulty, identify the most sensitive variables within the system—like in the UK, the influence and direction of the jet stream, which typically goes West to East and carries depressions over the UK.

In the world of business, monetary growth plays a similar role to the jet stream and can give a clue to economic dynamics. The economy is an important driver of business growth and competitive pressure so all CEO's and directors really need to have some training in macro and microeconomics so that they can anticipate shifts in demand over the short and medium timescales. I did my training in macroeconomics at the London University and it has proved to be so valuable throughout my career.

While compounding uncertainty can dampen or kill forecasting accuracy, it doesn't necessarily prevent one from sensing futures and the shifts that might take us on a particular direction. For instance, around 2016, I was running a strategy workshop in Dubai and at break time, I stared out of the window. I saw 99 percent petrol cars in my vision. I foresaw a huge shift to electric in 20 years. Probably 90 percent of these vehicles would be electric as UAE is an early adopter of technology. That seemed pretty clear and pretty certain even without doing a full uncertainty driver analysis.

But over the period 2022 to 2032, the shape of the technology diffusion curve rendered forecasts to be more "illustrative projections" that we couldn't attach such accuracy to. This suggested drawing an "uncertainty over time curve."

The Uncertainty and Importance Grid

The uncertainty and importance grid (Mitroff and Lindstone 1993) is a way of identifying the assumptions that would underpin the future. Typically, this grid would be used after the exploration of the trends and discontinuities that are either already happening, or that are emerging, or have the potential to occur. The grid is used before the actual structuring and definition of the scenarios particularly to identify them out of clusters of the most uncertain and important assumptions.

So, for example, at the time of writing (February 2022), the assumption that the increase in national insurance, energy prices, and declining real incomes due to inflation *will not trigger UK recession* is very important and very uncertain indeed. An equally volatile assumption is that a Ukrainian conflict along with the Organization of Petroleum Exporting Countries (OPEC) pushing up oil prices will also not trigger a broader recession. Also note that these two assumptions are interdependent and represent a dangerous amplifying dynamic.

Figure 2.4 illustrates the use of the grid including the arrows which express the directional shifts that may move the assumptions around like glasses on a Ouija Board in a séance. In the case study of Shell (Chapter 1), this was done using hexagonal magnetic shapes. I personally like to use a flipchart or whiteboard and Post-its.

With the framing of the assumptions, it is a best practice to define them with very clear and specific parameters such as the magnitude of something (e.g., a deep or shallow recession, six months, a year, or 18 months (its time), and its space (UK, EU, or global)). This will have a very big impact on the positioning of the assumptions on the uncertainty grid.

Note that the tool is used to frame the assumption relative to things going well in the world, rather than things going pear shaped. The first time people use the grid they often get it wrong or mix the two, resulting in a mess, which then needs to be sorted out. Such experimentation does

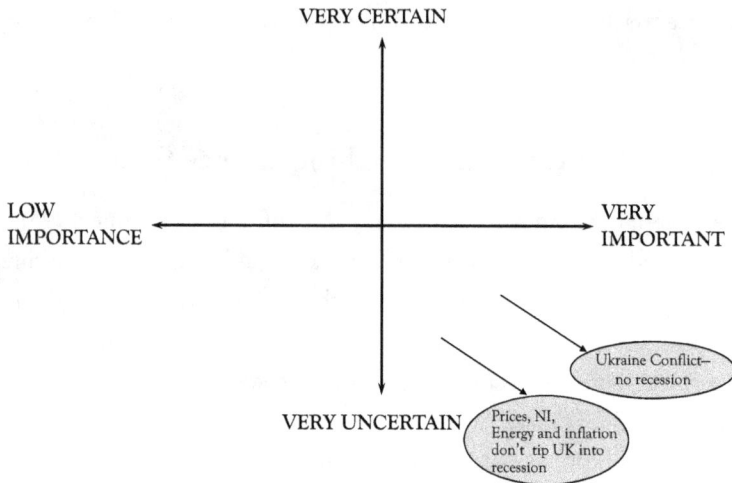

VERY CERTAIN

LOW
IMPORTANCE

VERY
IMPORTANT

Ukraine Conflict—
no recession

VERY UNCERTAIN

Prices, NI,
Energy and inflation
don't tip UK into
recession

Figure 2.4 The uncertainty–importance grid: Recession in the UK on the assumptions that all goes right

need a close facilitation at least on its first cycle. But when you understand how the grid is applied, you have truly got it for good!

The uncertainty and importance grid can be used as:

- A central tool for the initial generation of scenarios;
- For further refinement of these to flesh out a variety of self-consistent storylines—the scenario menu;
- As a standalone tool for investigating the uncertainties and risks within a specific decision;
- As a way generally of scanning incoming data on a project;
- Or as a part of scanning the environment for weak or perhaps stronger signals.

As an example of how incoming data can be scanned for a project, I use the following event. Recently I was driving out of London and headed south to meet a very old friend for lunch at a very posh golf course. I was doing okay on time, but on the penultimate turn I miscounted exits relative to what Google Maps was telling me. I was on the wrong road. Now Google Maps is rather too gentle and noncritical and proceeded to direct me around in a square shape so that I could turn around without doing a U-turn.

Please can someone up there in the Google universe just tell me, "You took the wrong turn, go back" and then recalibrate and reroute me. Is that asking too much?

So, I turned right down Jackass Road, which sounded dodgy. It seemed very narrow, but that was just the start. I went about 500 meters and it got narrower, dirtier, and bumpier. Clearly, I had gone wrong as this couldn't have possibly been the entrance road to a posh golf course! The assumption that "this is a sensible route" had gone out of the window.

I called up in my head the uncertainty grid and other assumptions while heading toward the danger zone, the South East (most important and most uncertain):

- A car won't be wanting to go the other way (there had been no passing places).
- I won't get a puncture (50 times more probable on Jackass than on the average road).
- If I break down, have a puncture, crash, or get wedged, I will still be able to get a signal to summon help (we were dropping down into a gully).

Or a combination of all three assumptions going wrong.

Finally, after 1,000 meters I found a main road and found my way back to the right junction. I went straight and found the ever so posh entrance to the golf club—that was more like it! I was on time and safe. The uncertainty grid made me far more mindful of what was going wrong and made me much more careful as well as ready to deal with the unexpected and thus agile.

When I told my friend the story and about the grid, he said to me: "Tony, don't you think you overthink sometimes?" to which I said:

Well, I have found the grid invaluable. I have survived missions like an adventure into the desert near the Red Sea, river rafting in a Colombian rain forest, a week on the island Kish off the coast of Iran to develop scenarios for the oil market, a race across Jeddah with taxi drivers that couldn't read street names nor speak English, to find which Banking Branch my workshop was at … It's not just luck to survive these but it's about sensitivity to possibly divergent signals. The uncertainty grid I visualize is one that is rich and detailed and dynamic. It also helps you to ask deeply probing questions that managers sometimes react to by feeding back for example, "That's a really an excellent question, how on earth did you get that?"

As well as a high-level analysis of the uncertainty of assumptions as seen in Figure 2.4, it is possible to do a breakdown of one of these into its subassumptions (see Figure 2.5). This can be crucial where the situation is complex and could be riddled with vulnerability. I often liken this type of detailing to exploring physical matter—there is level of the molecule, of the atom, the particle, and ultimately the subatomic particle.

The uncertainty grid is one of the most useful tools that I have ever come across, both as a formal one and on the hoof, every day. There are others kicking around like the impact–probability grid, which more commonly detects risks as it is framed probabilistically: *less the nonobvious.* Another one is the risk register, which seems mainly used as a brain dump for uncertainty.

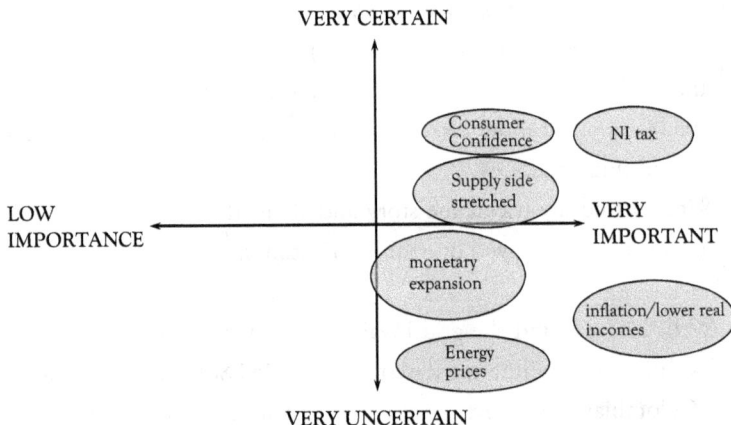

Figure 2.5 The uncertainty–importance grid—no UK recession: "subatomic" level

Reader Exercise

For an important decision or project, what are the key assumptions (make them specific and write them down on Post-its taking care to frame them in a positive world)? What is their importance and uncertainty? Place these assumptions on the uncertainty grid that you prepared earlier and debate their relative positionings.

- What does their distribution on the grid (Figure 2.5) look like and tell you?
- What can you do to reduce any more severe exposure?
- Is there a one big assumption you missed? A second big one?

The Uncertainty-Over-Time Curve

Uncertainty is never static as we can see from the directional arrows in the uncertainty grid. But to drill down into the dynamics further, we may need to tailor it, perhaps by drawing the way in which uncertainty varies over time.

I have been drawing the uncertainty-over-time curve for at least two decades. It is inspired by Cartesian geometry where you have an X- and a Y-axis. Actually, I understood mathematics as being a language of relationships that can not only be very useful but also rich and interesting! By plotting a variable over time like value or difficulty (my first ever two), you can capture dynamic change so graphically as well as being playful by visualizing what could happen and not just what is likely to happen by default.

To illustrate, in Figure 2.6, I drew what I saw back in 2016 a possible shape of an uncertainty-over-time curve for the electric car market in Dubai. This showed uncertainty high as there were many variances possible in their market penetration over 2020 to 2028. Then the variances began falling as by then electric cars would become cheaper in terms of life cycle costs and also mean a greater ethical value.

Having a broad shape of the longer view enabled me to feel much more confident at the back end of the picture and draw a declining uncertainty-over-time curve. A takeaway here is that uncertainty doesn't always

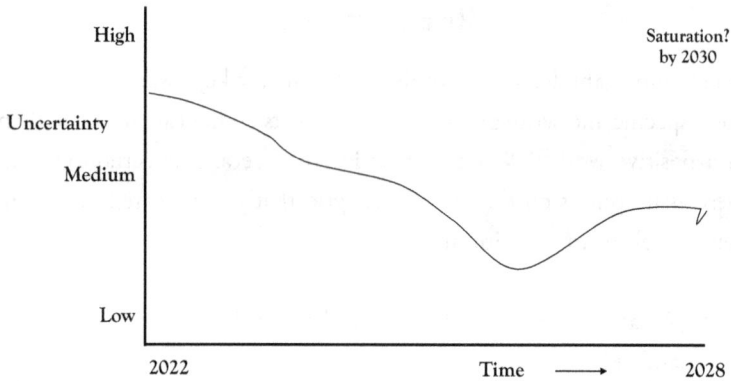

Figure 2.6 Uncertainty-over-time curve—the electric car market in the UAE: its ultimate dominance

keep going asymptotic and getting worse (vertical) but can either come down in its fundamentals or the fog we are peering through gets simply thinner.

Another graphical way of grasping this situation is to refer these oscillating curved shifts as "waves of uncertainty." This is just a series of curves of uncertainty that suggests that uncertainty itself is uncertain. Yet, that very feature can be still grasped by the mind as is the mission of this book. (This is not to be confused with Heisenberg's uncertainty principle, which is all about the fuzziness of position and velocity at a subatomic particle level—that would be a digression!)

Of course, if you to want to take this a step further, you might split the curves down into their main constituents and plot, say, up to three curves on top of each other with a summation of the total uncertainty over time. So, you might split up, for example, the uncertainty around COVID-19 as curves of:

- New strain—its transfer rate
- New strain—hospitalization and mortality rate
- Immunization effectiveness after 6 months

Reader Exercises

(a) For some project that you have done in the past, draw an uncertainty-over-time curve. What is it telling you?

(b) For a future project you are embarking on or that you are contemplating, what does its future uncertainty-over-time curve look
like, and what might you do to alleviate or avoid where uncertainty
is high?

Uncertainty and Interdependences

As we suggested in the last section, assumptions may be based on interdependent factors, which again invites some visualization. In this short section, we dip into this phenomenon through mapping interdependences
between uncertainties. To do this effectively, I have chosen the example
of the famous liner that sank, the *Titanic*. First of all, let's deep dive into
the causal factors (obviously after the event) that conspired to sink this
iconic ship. I was informed in this process by a TV documentary, which
was scathingly critical. See Figure 2.7 for the resulting fishbone analysis.
For instance, the binoculars that might have been used to see icebergs had
been locked away!

For brevity, I won't go into every single root cause, but it is clear
from this picture that it was not surprising that the *Titanic* sank on its
first crossing across the Atlantic (so many loose screws in Figure 2.7
(UK Channel 5)).

But now look at Figure 2.8 on the interdependences. We see here
the extent to which these uncertainties were reinforcing causally and

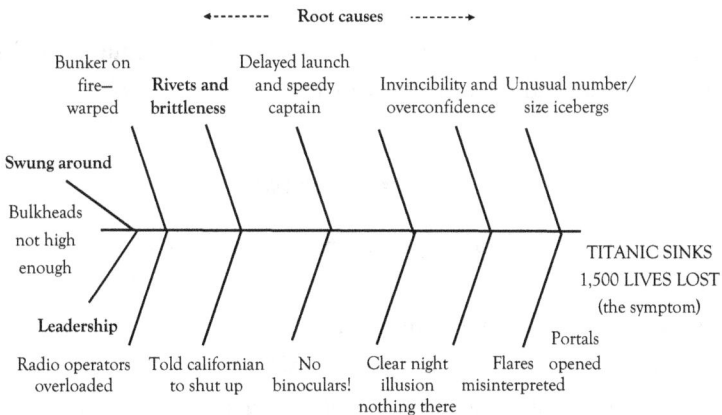

Figure 2.7 Fishbone analysis—why did the Titanic sink?

Bunker on fire   Rivets and brittleness   Swung
                                            around—last minute

Size of icebergs   DEVASTASTING
        Racy captain—   IMPACT
Invincibility/   flat out
Overconfidence   RAPID
                                                  SINKING
Delayed launch
            BAD   Portals
Leadership MANAGEMENT   opened   1,500 LIVES
                                                   LOST
                               radio
            DIDN'T SEE   California told   NO
            ICEBERG   "shut up"   RESCUE

Clear night—   No   Radio
illusion nothing there binoculars   operators   Flares
                                       overloaded   misinterpreted

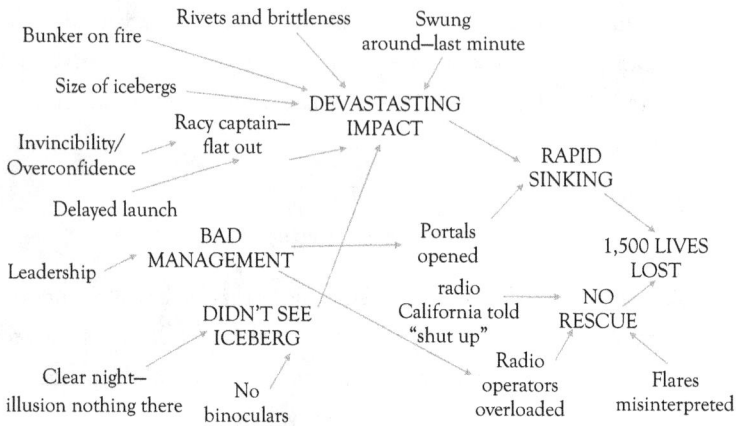

Figure 2.8 Root cause systems—the Titanic

magnifying uncertainty. Note that such visual pictures give us so much of a better and clearer bird's eye view of the context. I called them "root cause systems" in the past.

A particularly profound causal knot in this picture combines the following:

- Leadership
- Bad management
- Portals opened (by people to gaze at the disaster letting in water later on)
- Overwhelmed radio operators

Obviously, in our case, we are more interested in the future (unless you are doing an audit of something that went wrong).

Reader Exercise

For a future project, discuss the decision, issue, or situation:

- What could go really wrong (fishbone head)?
- What might be the future root causes for that?
- How might these be interdependent (causal chain analyst)?
- What are the insights from this analysis?

Other variables over time curves include:

The uncertainty-over-time curve (Figure 2.6) was just one of many curves that have been shown to be very useful over the years, some early ones being:

- The value-over-time curve for a strategy, a project, a relationship, or stand-alone experience;
- The difficulty-over-time curve for implementation, for change management, doing business in a market;
- An influence-over-time curve for particular' stakeholders or over an assumption.

For external scenarios, particularly useful ones are the following:

- Market attractiveness-over-time curve: the PEST (political, economic, social, and technological), factors, the growth drivers (Figure 2.9);
- Competitive forces-over-time curve (ditto);
- Relative competitive advantage-over time curve (ditto).

Finally, another resource we can draw from is to deploy an "event tree," which breaks down the effect of an event into its alternative pathways, which are the possible outcomes. This is done by identifying

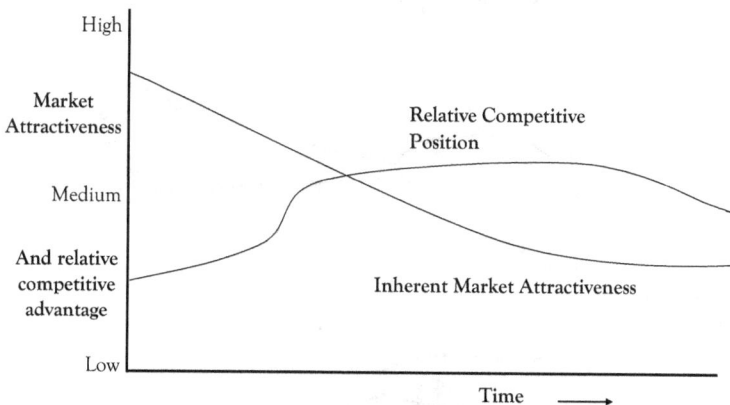

Figure 2.9 External market attractiveness over time curve and the relative competitive advantage curve

the interdependences as a mind map. This was inspired by a previous tool, the "decision tree analysis," often used in conjunction with probabilistic assessments of outcomes. (A refinement of this tree possibly is to assess their positive or negative pay-offs as part of an economic assessment.)

This is not an absolutely "must use" tool, but because it is something that I might well use myself intuitively for structuring either the range of possible scenarios from a transitional event (taking us into a new world) or for the storyline within an existing scenario. In Figure 2.10, a consequential event 2B actually has an impact on another consequence of an earlier event, so there is a cross-impact.

So, for instance in the earlier case study on Ukraine, I visualized the sequence of events that could have led to an active intervention by NATO; for example, war atrocities and other escalations maybe in extreme (setting off of a tactical nuclear weapon) to give NATO and the United States serious jitters. Or there might be damaging cyber-attacks as a response to sanctions (my time of writing was March 1, 2022). In the last week of April, Putin was pretty obviously threatening a nuclear attack. So I had to add a new bubble at the bottom for "nuke!" (see Figure 2.11).

Update to October 2022: Putin openly threatened the United States of the use of nuclear weapons, generating vague threats back from NATO. On October 20, there were suggestions of a tactical nuke might be detonated over the Black Sea.

Some of my thinking for Figure 2.10 was from game theory—looking at interdependent moves in a series.

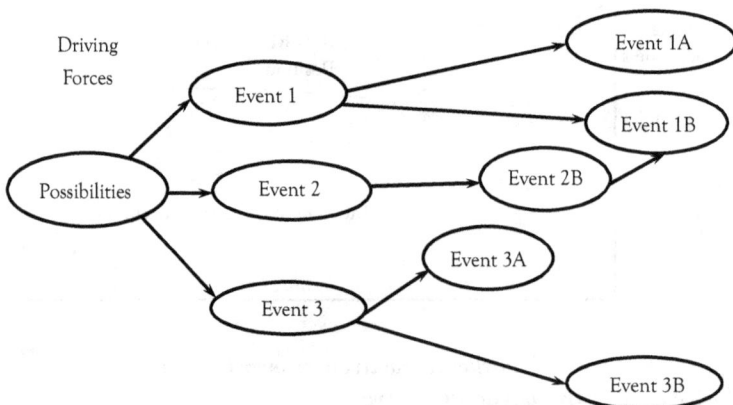

Figure 2.10 An event tree

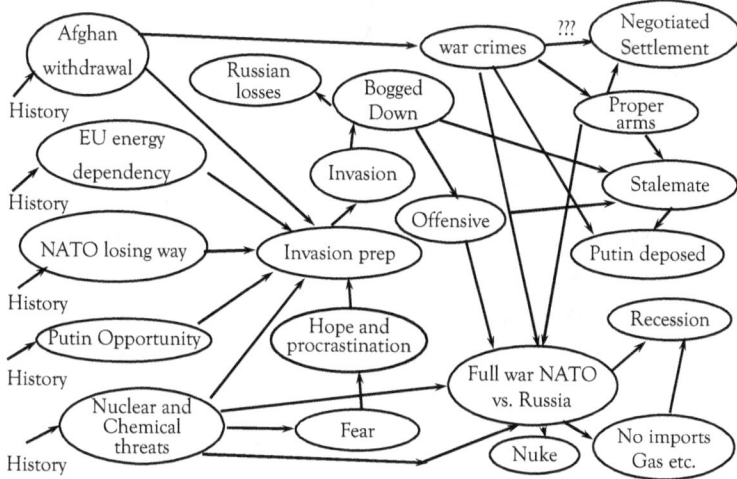

Figure 2.11 Example of an event chain—Ukraine invasion

There are many types of games. Often those in the literature are two-person games that are more easily structured and thus amenable to mathematics. Where there are more and/or where there could be different types of players, it is much harder to play around with maths. That is the norm in business, especially where there can be part clear rules, and some fuzzy, or where these might shift. That doesn't mean throwing the whole theory out, but we can take the principles, for example for estimating real and perceived "pay-offs" and their importance to stakeholders in a variety of circumstances. Some moves in the game may be real and some are just signals; these can be genuine or bluffs. There can also be deception.

As we will see in Chapter 7 (behaviors and scenarios), these players can be rational, part rational or nonrational, as in the following example of a collaborative game that I once used to characterize my opponent in a major legal case I had fought:

The Story of the Scorpion and the Frog

A frog was bathing in a river and caught sight of a scorpion. The scorpion also saw the frog and scuttled nearer. After a moment, the scorpion said "That's a lovely river but I really need to get across and I can't swim. Would you mind helping me, please?"

"I would love to help, but I fear you will sting me to death," said the frog.

Scorpion promised, "I won't sting you."

The frog agreed and the scorpion hopped on its back. The frog swam to the middle of the river laden with the scorpion and the scorpion stung it.

"Why on earth did you do that?" asked the frog.

"*Because it's my nature,*" replied the scorpion, and with those words they both began to drown.

Moral of the story: Some games aren't nice and while you might try to collaborate, this may not be the game at that time.

- You thus need to see the bigger picture, factor in history and understand the game, its constraints, and its dimensions of opportunity to manage uncertainty.

Now, let's go back to our discussions of Russia versus the Ukraine war. Catching up on the war nearly eight weeks later, based on that sketch, I drew up a similar picture depicting that process as a more open model with five key alignment factors (the precursors) so that we move through the "event chain" (here chains, plural), charting the postinvasion consequences and their causal flows including the possible outcomes, namely:

- Stalemate (highly likely as in North Korea versus South Korea);
- Negotiated settlement—made more likely with freer flow of arms including more offensive arms to Ukraine, including planes to prevent or severely curtail Russian success. Also, this would be less likely now that there is much war crime evidence in mid-April 2022, without Putin becoming deposed (a key insight);
- Of course, there is the very real possibility of escalation and even triggering a direct atomic war that may be precipitated by a nuclear or bio or chemical attack.

In the latter scenario, the NATO members and the EU would neither have the wish to nor the option of continuing to buy gas and oil from

Russia (*an insight*). This would have serious economic consequences, resulting in turbulence in the financial markets and recession and maybe stagflation (stagnation and high inflation), and higher interest rates.

So, within this picture are actual event sequences and latent scenarios, which are possible doorways into alternative futures. But just because they weren't activated doesn't mean that their potential didn't exist. And all or some of this could be disrupted by some random event such as Putin choking to death on a nut at a banquet or dying of a heart attack—sometimes known as a "Black Swan event" (Taleb 2007) or improbable but a high-impact event. But in scenario work, we should neither ignore these totally but maybe look at one, for example, what if Putin got cancer. Thanks to Google, there are rumors about that. He does seem to have put on weight because of cancer drugs (see Talab). The eruption of a volcano in Iceland causing an immense dust storm that stopped European flights for days was such an event in 2010.

Besides any specific insights, another very important output is the learning from a piece of work like this. For instance, when I showed my picture to friends over dinner, they said: "Wow! that looks complex" which I had thought already. As an experienced scenario picture drawer, it is undeniable that we have a knotty problem with many stakeholders. So this horrible conflict could easily be unresolved after a year.

So, my learning was that this was a seriously complex problem and that's why when you listen to the media, they seem to go around in circles and yet cover little. What they do cover is either the past or what's happening just now, or rather broad and near-term speculation about the future. But this type of picture creates a fluid map that you can hone in on. Maybe draw new connections or find specifics to deep dive into like Putin's history or NATO's history.

Another useful learning for me was the importance not rushing this as a task-driven thing and to immerse oneself in the process. So, it is best not to rush. In fact, I can say that I was not just taking my time but in a state of cognitive flow (term coined by Mihaly Csikszentmihalyi in 1990). Unusually for me, I hadn't logged the time. I started around mid-afternoon and when "I came too" as it were, after reaching saturation, it was 4.38 p.m.! This was a perfect example of "slow thinking" (Kahneman 2011).

I have suggested (2018) that strategic thinking is best accomplished by a combination of slow, reflective, and more mindful thinking and bursts of faster intuitive thinking while preserving cognitive flow. Well, for me, it was as if time had stood still. The take-away for the reader is that doing scenarios is an enjoyable if at times scary and real, but it is certainly not a management task that you just bash your way through. Although we are out of space here for a cognitive flow curve, you might wish to draw one for a problem that comes up like "My central door locking system has lost its code and I can't get the shopping out of the boot." That is a very low cognitive flow at the start (panic!) to very good as it is sorted out with the garage!

Reader Exercise

For a recent problem-solving experience surrounding uncertainty, draw a cognitive flow-over-time curve. What did this tell you about the experience? How was that affected by any use of analysis techniques of the same or similar kind in this book? When you were confronted with a new uncertainty wave, did that disrupt your cognitive flow and if so, how? If not, how did to manage to smooth that cognitive flow for example, deep breathing to let that all go, a deliberate switch of gear to slower thinking, just visualizing final success?

Next, try this exercise out for a fresh experience of something reasonably similar. How did that go and how effective were you in maintaining the flow? Did that in your view affect the effectiveness of the process and the end result?

Indeed, one of the delights is that when you are done with the futures, you can do some "helicopter thinking" as I used to teach in my executive courses at Cranfield. This means "to see the bigger picture," for example, as follows:

Another storyline yet to run its full course just now is that of the British Prime Minister Boris Johnson's party gate scandal where senior UK government ministers and officials were partying against social contact rules and breaking the law. Then they denied that they understood that they were actually committing an offense. This event as I write could still force him to resign. However, the Ukrainian invasion by Russia has caused the media, some of the public, and the Conservative Party to be distracted so much that the imminent danger has lessened. Boris has come back fighting as we knew he would and even staged a day trip to walk around Kyiv, the Ukrainian capital, looking ultra-serious and shocked but like Winston Churchill, the wartime Prime Minister, except with yellow hair. The Ukraine event chain may have saved him, or at least deferred eventual loss of his job, but party-gate has for sure shortened his half-life.

The condition of the European and global economy is another event chain directly impacted by Russia versus Ukraine too. And it hasn't escaped my attention that China is regarded increasingly as being a clear and future or present danger. Could the Chinese stage an invasion of Taiwan at the same time NATO is tied up with Ukraine? Or has that been put back following the poor showing by Russia in Ukraine? Would they be capable and willing and are they ready too? *So here you have several interdependent games going on.*

What with the United States jolting round in their foreign policy with President Trump and Biden, has its role as the Global Police Force run its course and we're seeing the emergence of several politico-economic blocs vying for power—West, Russia, East? Where does the climate change program sit in all of this with short- and medium-term price hikes or will there be more gas and oil production elsewhere to balance the Russian supply gap?

So, we might be just seeing a lot going on here but, still only part of the bigger picture, which is a *tapestry or patchwork of scenarios*. What is fairly certain though is that there will be no shortage of uncertainty waves to make things more turbulent. Here there is an interplay between the more static, structural, and dynamic factors (see the revised $M = C^2$ equation in Chapter 9).

Summary and Key Concluding Insights

In Chapter 2, we saw that much can be done to make the task of understanding uncertainty easier, especially through visual representation. We might try to shed light on it by asking the right questions plus very well targeted data analysis. The better pathway is to use the uncertainty grid to highlight the "danger zone."

Key Concluding Insights

- Uncertainty is a term used often to categorize issues that appear simply too hard or worrying to think about and all that doesn't have to be the case, especially if we break that all down into its drivers and operationalize them by defining the key assumptions and prioritizing them with the uncertainty grid.
- Look out for one of these assumptions or at least key ones breaking down into micro and "subatomic" assumptions.
- Uncertainty is dynamic and will change over time so we should see this as being curved and draw it that way accordingly.
- Another way is to use fishbone analysis to diagnose future causes of an outcome as opposed to its traditional use either for a present or past problem.
- Even more powerful is to deploy root cause systems analysis to understand the interdependences between uncertain variables and assumptions.
- Sometimes there are more than just one game going on, amplifying uncertainty.
- Finally, scenario storylines can also be generated from the event tree or event chains as different causal clusters either are spawned from each other or more simply, collide with each other. This highlights extracting Key Insights generally—a process I call "KIA for Key Insights Analysis"—essential for Top levels in business.

CHAPTER 3

Scenario Building Tools, Concepts, and Process

In Chapter 3, we enter into the heart of this book. The chapter is structured as follows:

- The scenario process
- Scenario storytelling—the process with the War in the Pacific case study
- Defining the playing field—the scope and focus
- Using the strategic onion model for generating common assumptions
- Drivers for change—Systems models for discontinuities
- The business value system
- Injecting dynamics with the uncertainty tunnel
- The strategic option grid
- Cognitive and emotional bias
- Risky shift
- Key concluding insights

In this chapter, we will focus on the analytical work of forming the scenario process rather than on the detailed mechanics process-wise, which is covered in Chapter 4.

The Scenario Process

Figure 3.1 captures the classic example of a scenario process as illustrated by Shell (Grundy 1993). Looking at it now, it is hard to see omissions without overcluttering the process. I guess candidates for inclusion might be: stakeholder analysis, role playing, and game theory. Game theory

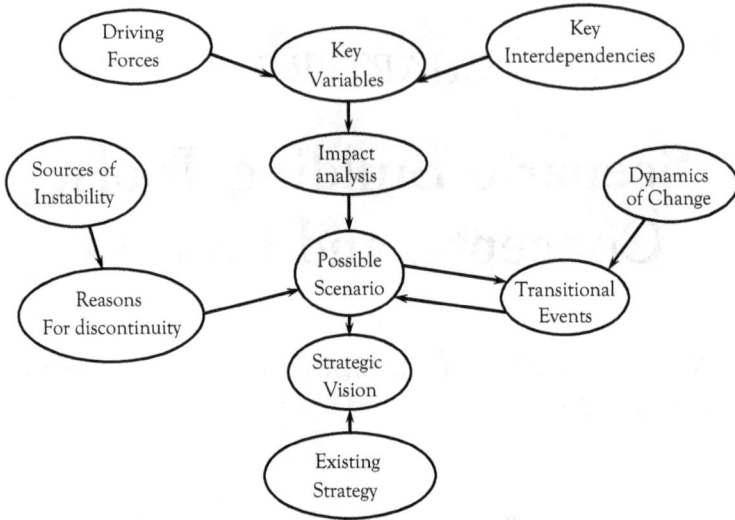

Figure 3.1 The Shell scenario process

helps formulate strategies relative to what others might do and also what the rules of the game are and how they might change. Originally highly mathematical and structured, game theory is less useful here for fuzzy issues and more wicked uncertainties in broad terms. But it is also essential to factor in, at the macro level, the industry, the organizational, and the stakeholder levels (Von Neumann and Morgenstern 1944).

Figure 3.1 starts off with defining the key variables, which comes from systems thinking (Senge 1990) or an event tree analysis structure to get a working model. Variables could be market growth, the rate of global warming, increases in GNP per capita, and so on.

To the left and the right of the key variables are the key driving forces that are causal factors underlying these variables and also the key interdependences between the variables as will be flushed out in a systems model or an event tree. Driving forces behind GNP per capita might include:

- Fiscal stimuli
- Monetary growth
- Business confidence
- Consumer's real disposable income and confidence
- A lower exchange rate stimulating exports

In other words, looking at the shopping list and the Shell process, one can see the influence of economic thinking; no surprise as Shell would have its economists. This does look rather like an econometric model with more softer elements for context, richness, and depth. But it is actually behavioral analysis.

The key variables then result in an impact analysis. But this analysis is done very much at the level of what's currently in the pipeline, without disturbances that might push us off into a new trajectory as depicted in my second "arrow of time" in Figure 2.2.

While the impact analysis does help shape any scenarios, the main thrusts come from sources of instability—yes, you guessed it—driven off the uncertainty grid (see Figure 2.4 and some detailed thinking about the reasons for instability).

Of course, traditional tools like PEST, growth drivers, and Porter's competitive forces can also suggest possible shifts, provided they are dynamic pictures, of course.

But the elixir that so often shapes the scenario storytelling often comes from *the transitional events*. These are the catalysts that push shifts over the hill to start to gather momentum—sometimes called "tipping points."

Reader Exercise—Tipping Points in Your Career/Life

Looking back on your career or even your personal life, what examples can you think of where your trajectory was thrown suddenly into a new direction? For example, you were headhunted, there was a big argument with someone which started the end of a relationship, a major accident, you caught COVID, you were arrested, or got lost in a rain forest?

What were the chains of events that converged or even conspired to crystallize that maneuver? By being more reflective and mindful of past event chains helps you gain more foresight about possible futures.

Driving the transitional events can also be the "dynamics of change." These are things like the speed of change driven both from factors within and from outside the core system that you are studying. For instance, in the Russia versus Ukraine example in Chapters 1 and 2, we have as a major influence the European gas market, which is highly dependent on Russian gas. And why is that the case? Well, one might argue that is because the EU has not moved fast enough to substitute clean energy sources for oil and gas despite the clear signals that global warming calls for far more rapid substitution plus better efficacy, for example, insulation.

Also, the withdrawal of U.S. and international forces from Afghanistan in late 2021 sent a very clear signal to Russia that the United States and NATO would not field ground forces or air power against Russia in the case of an invasion. These are all driving forces that make transitional events accidents waiting to happen.

A very helpful model of industry change is that of *Clock Speed* (Fine 1998), a book written well ahead of its time. Charles Fine suggested that there was a wide variation between the speed of development and evolution of industries. For instance, the car industry has a relatively slow clock speed historically, although there is rapid acceleration now due to electric cars. Fine suggests the software industry is at the other extreme as are digital businesses too. In Chapter 9, we consider how clock speed reduces reaction time to events like a kind of jet stream.

In his book, he begins with the analogy of the fruit fly. Fruit flies typically live about 8 to 15 days. So they are excellent vehicles for studying evolution as in just a year they might go through 30 lives! As Thomas Hobbes, the Philosopher, once said: "Life is nasty, brutish and short"!

At the other end of the industrial spectrum, there are still industries relatively sheltered from rapid change, especially through technological and social change with slow clock speeds, such as funerals. I have studied this market for 25 years as it is uniquely slow and relatively protected and fertile for innovation.

Years ago, I worked with the board of a major player in the funerals industry to explore new opportunities. All credit to them for choosing to enter the preneed market, which helped open that market up in the UK based on our work together. We also identified sales being managed over the Internet as a possible business model and the possible redundancy of much of their retail network as a possible threat, but new entrants moved in first to challenge the traditional players.

So, what we saw here was a bit of time travel and with my role playing an Alien who wanted to close their network down in our workshops.

Their clock speed didn't accelerate as much as it might have. Maybe that was too hard a thing to contemplate at that time given their position at the heart of the traditional paradigm of the industry.

In the UK supermarket industry, the clock speed of the discounters seems much faster than some traditional companies. Later on, I will say that you can time travel a bit into the future sometimes by looking at companies with more advanced business models. Equally sometimes you can time travel backward. We shop in London at Lidl for our core shop, which is cheap and efficient, but then have to shop for extras at one of the majors. Service there is much worse than Tesco was 25 years ago when I consulted on their service strategy. I time traveling backward there.

Recently, I finished shopping to be met by a big till queue. So, I started my stopwatch.

After three minutes, there was little progress So, I amused myself with some Qi Gong exercises. After six minutes, I decided to do a head stand (I do these at odd places like the atrium of ASDA's central office in Leeds). *I was vertical for a minute without even attracting any attention!* I came down reenergized and after paying I gave a senior member of staff another yellow card for bad service. She said:

> Ten minutes? That's not long—we are "busy." That isn't very long in the bigger scheme of things.

They were not busy at all. She had obviously not heard of "time-based competitive advantage." This store personified an attitude of "Why compete at all if we have a hold of a local near monopoly?"

Having time traveled back a few decades as I left to return to the present, I felt giddy. It reminded me of the Blackadder video of the "Back and Forth," where the TV hero time travels back to Dinosaur times.

Blackadder B&F See Full YouTube Video

My take-away from this is that the "present" that we started with or current position is actually a blur of positions so that we can observe both future and past partially within the present.

Another example of how clock speed can be a variable comes from the pharmaceutical industry, which I know very well and whose clock speed is slowed by a jungle of regulations. Then COVID-19 came along and allegedly AstraZeneca synthesized a successful vaccination formula over a weekend in early 2020. The regulatory process was fast-tracked and by late 2020, vaccination began and was rolled out through 2021, which enabled us to avoid further lockdowns in the UK in late 2021.

I know that I have found the idea of clock speed very useful not only in developing scenarios but also in my strategy facilitation too.

Coming back to the Shell scenario process in Figure 3.1, we see to the left the need to pinpoint the reasons for discontinuity and sources of instability. So, in the case of COVID-19, there is the globalization of the planet, which has been boosted by cheap travel such that any disease like this would spread even quicker. The Spanish flu epidemic was far less obviously threatening in comparison. Also, lifestyles were even more anchored in "going out," with the hospitality industry being the beneficiary of this trend. In addition, many governments were in denial as in the UK, resulting in lags to recognize and respond to the threat. Finally, while there had been threats in the past from severe acute respiratory syndrome (SARS) and bird flu, these had made institutions complacent and the perceived low probability of a major and global pandemic had made it hard to get appropriate investment in contingent countermeasures. In just two words, many countries were "self-insured" and lack of preparedness was a source of instability.

The scenarios finally emerge and crystallize, and invariably there are more plausible scenarios than can be fully developed into storylines. When they have been told and reflected on, for example, how plausible are these and internally consistent? Are these favorable or less favorable and what's their "so what"? More specifically, how do these impact the current strategy? Not shown in the Shell case process, also ask: what are the strategic options now in that new context(s)?

Then as per Shell, do we need a new strategic vision? (*For me, that is usually best attempted after having gone through a systematic development of the options including the evaluation of their attractiveness so that we do have a supported and well thought through strategic vision rather than arriving at it in one swift leap*, which would be akin to a Western where the cowboy "shoots from the hip.")

In conclusion, the Shell process does take you through the major stages in a logical way and does generate a challenging and structured, yet creative, process.

Scenario Storytelling—the Process With the War in the Pacific

The book *The Great War in the Pacific* came to my attention on the Discovery Channel. Drawing on documentary material, the program told the story of how a British military journalist Hector Bywater (1925) pieced together the dynamics of military rivalry on the Pacific between Japan and the United States. It accurately foretold the surprise attack on a new U.S. base in the Pacific, the great military battle (midway), and the final defeat of Japan though:

- Meticulous data collection on the balance of forces
- Assessments of the psychologies, the ambitions, and the agendas of the rival powers and the interplay per time
- Storytelling based on fictional events and battle tactics to try to paint a realist picture of a battle environments and its tactics

I commend the book as a classic example of true scenario storytelling. Make the drivers, trends, and strategies come to life with specific people, actions, events, and consequences and knock-on effects.

I researched storytelling and found increasing interest in its possible influence on neurological processing. For example, with neural coupling, the storyteller induces similar neuro patterns in his/her brain as the listener. It seemed to be a most effective way of communication of complex, patterned data. This promises to be a fertile area for research and practice development.

https://neuroleadership.com/your-brain-at-work/the-neuroscience-of-storytelling/.

Defining the Playing Field—the Scope and Focus

In this shorter section, I cover the reach of a scenario exercise. By "scope," I mean:

- The physical boundaries that mark its extent, and thus space
- The beginning and ending and the duration of the storyline
- The economic models and systems
- The range and nature of the issues
- The range of people and their decisions and actions and behaviors

This pretty well covers 95 to 98 percent of the preparatory issues.

An example would be that of a current study of some organizational futures in a high-technology company. The scope is both the EU and the United States geographically, the next three years and the last years previously. The issues are behaviors around diversity, the behaviors that may or may not emerge and solidify as a result of organizational interventions in the future through to what if any economic impact those interventions might have. The "people" are the general population with selected focus on the project managers and consultants involved. "Focus" is on even more specific areas where an even more detail is worth deep diving into, for example:

- Stakeholder agendas broken down by group
- The impact a strategy for diversity has on recruitment and retention as well as engagement

Once the playing field has been tentatively set, we start to travel through the process in Figure 3.1, taking us into the strategic onion model for understanding shifts, which are predominantly trends.

Using the Strategic Onion Model for Generating Common Assumptions

The strategic onion model (Grundy 2012) in Figure 3.2 came out of my consulting work over the years. It consists of four main layers, the largest of which is at a macro level—the PEST factors, which stand

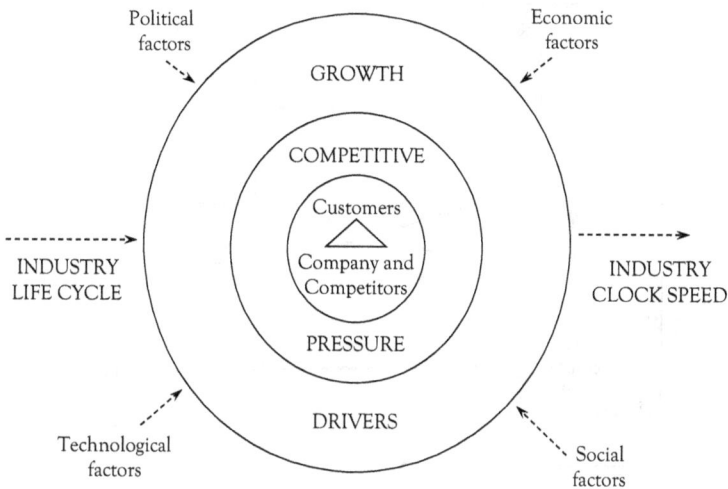

Figure 3.2 The "strategic onion"

for political (and regulatory), economic, social (and demographic), and technological factors that are at work in the external environment. It also has the industry life cycle, growth drivers, and Porter's competitive forces (Porter 1980). These can be rated positive or negative and interdependences identified.

Reader Exercise—PEST

Using PEST analysis for a market that you are in, determine the following:

- What are the most important factors and why?

Rate these as positive and negative:

- What key intercedences exist?
- Overall, how volatile is this market due to the PEST factors alone?
- What ideas for a new scenario spring from this?

See Figure 3.3.

For more recent students of PEST, you may have been fed the longer PESTEL model with the L meaning "legislative." For me, adding that as

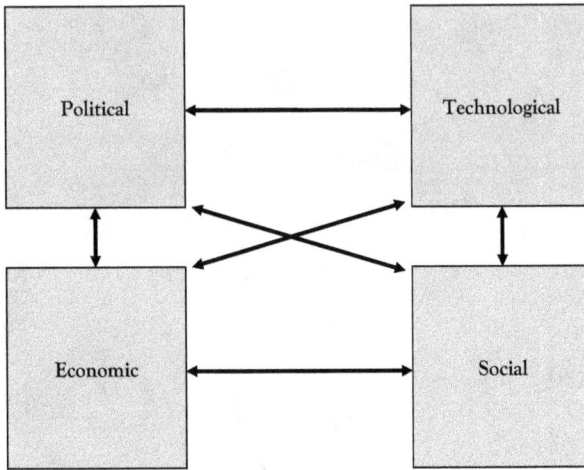

Figure 3.3 PEST analysis

Note: PEST factors may also be considered in evaluating growth drivers, particularly to test sustainability of growth.

an extra subsystem doesn't add enough to compensate for the resulting loss of simplicity. Likewise, although I am a staunch advocate of green and eco-management, it can be subsumed under "social" for economy.

Many businesses school programs and books on strategy typically jump from the PEST to the competitive forces analysis of Prof. Michael Porter (1980). But I feel, and strongly, that it would make a very big omission. For me, of great importance is the relative growth of a market and thus of its underlying growth drivers and brakes. In Figure 3.4, we see the growth drivers depicted as vectors whose arrow levels are drawn proportionate to the relative strength × the relative importance of that force. The same approach is taken to the growth brakes.

So, what are these initially mysterious things?

I define "growth driver" as:

An external force in the market that is driving the volume or the price (or both) up over time.

A "growth brake" is an external force in the market that is slowing growth in volume or price down or even causing either or both to shrink.

The idea here is that drawing a growth drivers and brakes picture for the past, present, or future, or two or three of these, gives you a better

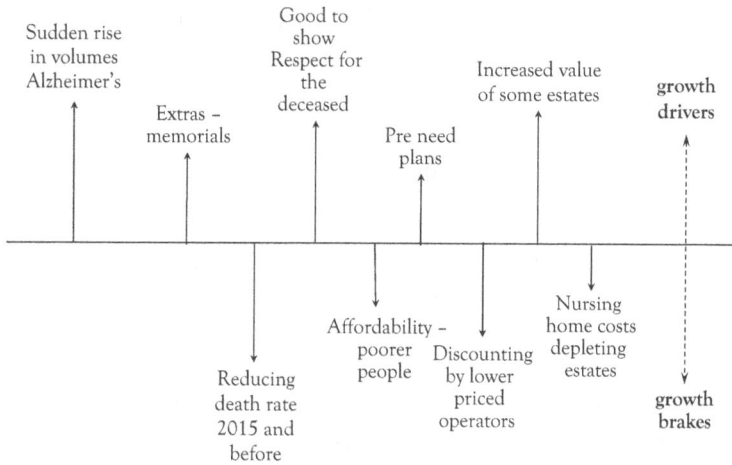

Figure 3.4 Growth drivers: funeral market

feel of the market growth trends (Grundy 2012). Obviously, it also helps to brave some degree of evidential basis such as actual statistics as a time series, or at least to have people surface the underlying reasons for their assumptions. However imperfect the growth drivers maybe, they are a key part of the environmental picture besides the PEST factors. Some PEST factors may have a favorable or unfavorable impact on the growth drivers.

Reader Exercise—Growth Drivers

For the same market that you did the PEST analysis for:

- What are the factors driving external market growth?
- What are the factors putting a brake on market growth, reducing it, or making it negative?
- How strong and important are these?
- By weighting strength and importance together, draw a vector picture.
- How are these likely to change and does this suggest a new scenario?

After growth drivers, we see the competitive forces (Porter 1980), which have been justifiably done to death in strategy books (Grundy 2014). Porter wanted to get a quick handle on the longer-term fundamental attractiveness of an industry and brilliantly distilled these competitive forces into a set of five. These are stated here with brevity rather than the well-known picture for sake of space:

- Entry barriers (high is good to protect it)
- Substitutes (low is good)
- Competitive rivalry (low is good)
- Buyer power (low is good)
- Supplier power (low is good)

These can be again scored for attractiveness (favorable versus unfavorable) times their relative importance, which yields a static model. This is a useful model, but we could do with something more dynamic to flush out the trends. This could be another vector-style model like the growth drivers (see Figure 3.4), which depicts the UK funeral market.

Or you could represent the drivers as shifts perhaps using an FT model (Grundy 2002a), which was originally a change management model. For instance, as of 2022, we could have the following shifts of the funeral market in the UK as:

From–To (FT) Analysis of the UK Funeral Market

	From 2022	To 2027
Entry barriers	Medium/High	Medium
Substitutes	Low/Medium	Medium
Competitive rivalry	Low	Medium
Buyer power	Very low	Lower/Medium
Supplier power	Low	Low/Medium

This from–to analysis represents quite a significant shift in an industry with a low but accelerating clock speed. I found my assumed shifts on the rise of the preneed market—don't wait until you are dead to organize your funeral; the rise of Internet shopping for services; the intent of new, different entrants; shifting social behaviors and values; and the impact of investigations by the Competition and Markets Authority in December 2020 (a must read and quite gripping too for any would-be scenario storyteller within the industry!)

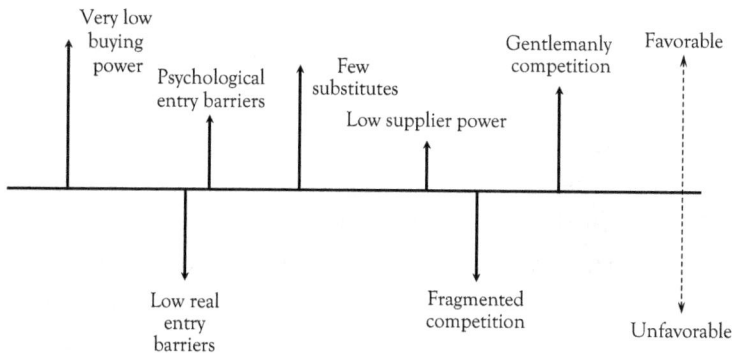

Figure 3.5 Funerals—competitive force field analysis

Such forces can be evaluated for different time phases—past, present, or future—or even the future sliced into phases either using a vector model (see Figure 3.4 for funerals showing that it is still attractive from a competitive force perspective), or using a curve of its competitive forces over time, or both. Such analyses can be used before the scenario story-telling, or following on from that, or both.

Reader Exercise—Competitive Forces Analysis

- Using a similar process to the growth drivers, do a vector analysis to suggest how externally attractive that market is using the five competitive forces alone.
- How vulnerable to change is that analysis, and is a new scenario suggested by those forces on its own or also suggested by the previous growth drivers and/or PEST analyses you have done?

Following the strategic onion model, it won't be a surprise that the growth drivers influence the attractiveness of a market as suggested by the five competitive forces.

Finally, at the core of the onion model, there is the underlying relative competitive advantage of any chosen company in question. This isn't needed as such for a purer scenario analysis up to and until any analysis of the impact the competitive forces might have on the strategy and future strategic options. Doing further deep dives here into this core might take us into competitor profiling, which positions a company against one or more peers. Or it may take you even into the land of resource-based theory (RBT) to isolate any unique and valuable strategic assets, competences, or cultural values and behaviors (Grundy 2012). (I will stop there as otherwise I will go off the track and into the core terrain of strategy.)

To complete the model, I have overlaid the industry life cycle, which also shapes industry attractiveness and the industry mindset (shared industry beliefs, assumptions, and expectations—the force which I believe Porter missed) (Grundy 2012, 2014, 2018). The stages of the industry cycle could be:

- Emergence
- Growth
- Business model development
- Maturity
- Innovation, disruption, adaptation
- Decline-protective strategy

Industries also vary according to how clear, well protected, and permeable their boundaries are and also a concept neglected in mainstream strategy of "*strategic mobility.*"

I will define "strategic mobility" as being "maneuvering in markets and across markets to seize opportunities and avoiding threats, and being able to migrate across boundaries yet still being true to one's distinctive capabilities." Strategic mobility figures much in military thinking, especially with much greater mechanization, IT, and intelligence systems since the world wars. Yet, strangely it hardly seems to figure in business strategy even though it seems to be self-evidently important.

For me, strategic mobility combines four things—flexibility, agility, speed, and intelligence—as an integrated package. "Flexibility" applies to mind set, commitment levels to the strategy, and how you do things. "Agility" is the ability to make rapid adjustments in the face of circumstances. "Speed" is not just a matter of operational routines but about how fast can things be reset, rethought, and realigned. "Intelligence" is picking up weak (and stronger) signals including the scenario and study them, which we are stressing on in this book.

Since 2018 I have now added the idea of clock speed (Fine 1998) to capture more dynamic movement. Finally, Figure 3.6 stretches our vision even more by depicting the shifts from one constellation of an industry to another to stretch our thinking and be more mindful of change. Indeed, Figure 3.6 links to the idea originally proposed by Igor Ansoff, the alleged founder of corporate planning of "weak signals" (Ansoff 1975) like the early cases of COVID-19 in Wuhan, China, which was the early warning of a pandemic. In environmental scanning, a supporting process and a skill of scenario development, weak signals can either be marked as transitional events but even if not as precursors of these events or of a general shift.

"Strategic mobility" seems to offer a lot more than the more traditional idea of diversification as it isn't just about spreading risks. It is much more subtle than that. In the animal world, its personification is the Honey Badger who is not only a supreme escapologist but can vary its diet from its favorite food honey to frozen bacon, however well protected it is, using its breaking and entering skills to raid fridges! (see case study in Grundy 2018). We should learn from the animal world.

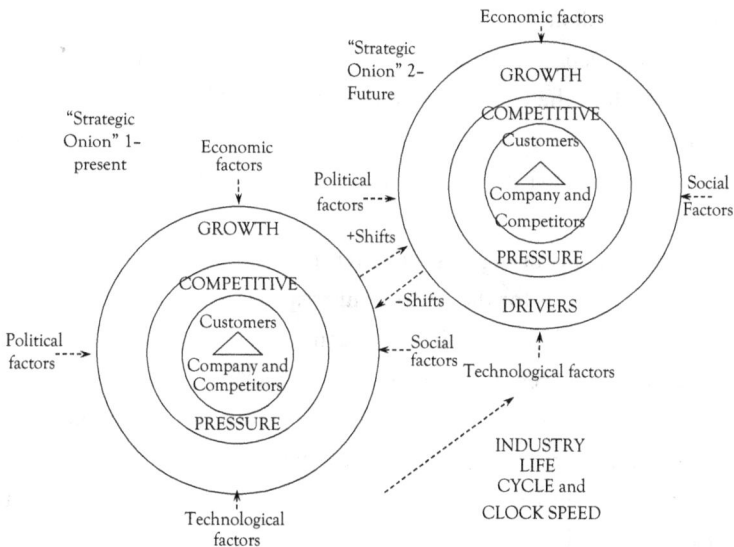

Figure 3.6 The shifting "strategic onion"

If there seems quite a lot going on by now here, that is probably true. But as in a toolbox you don't try to use every tool all at once and you look for useful combinations and sequences. With a bit of time and practice, they will try to talk to each other! If you are feeling you are getting lost, then just go back to the process in Figure 3.1.

The sister to strategic mobility in this book is strategic momentum in the $E = MC^2$ section in Chapter 9.

Drivers for Change—Systems Models for Discontinuities

Besides the continuities, we also need to sweep up the discontinuities. The arrow of time in Figure 2.2 visually represented them graphically. The uncertainty grid in Figure 2.3 is also extremely helpful for "cutting to the chase" and doing some rapid focusing on the most volatile assumptions—those that are not just very important but also very uncertain; maybe then do a mix and match of the most threatening, particularly where very disruptive change is being faced.

Where the shape of the future depends on many interdependent factors, then it may be a good thing before touching the uncertainty grid to do some mapping and exploration of the future system and its drivers first. Take a look at the picture in Figure 3.7 that I drew for the Strategic Planning Department of the National Iranian Oil Company on the island of Kish in the Gulf. They were understandably not so sure how to "predict" the future price of oil. While not offering a perfect panacea, this figure can be used to get a sense of directional shifts for future prices along with some storytelling.

We will be illustrating this tool later in Chapter 8, which is a worked example of scenarios for the MBA industry.

Notice that while this picture is complex, it helps considerably to break it down between demand and supply. Each one of these factors can then be segmented for example, by markets (demand) or by resource and technology. Then there's always the breakdown by stakeholders to factor in. I also skimmed BP's long-range projections report for the market to check if nothing big was missed.

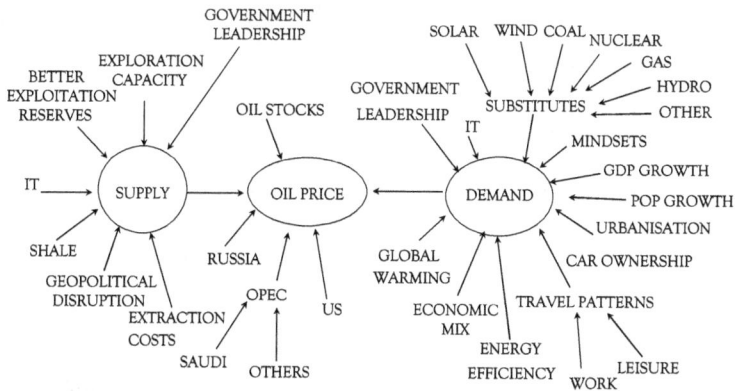

Figure 3.7 Systemic model—for scenario storytelling: the global oil industry

If one were to have rerun this for the oil market post the apparent downscaling of COVID-19 restrictions in early 2022, the skyrocketing oil and gas prices, which ensued, would have been a "no brainer" to project. Demand for oil is price inelastic, which means it isn't very sensitive to price (it is a necessity). Especially after such a long lull with lockdown, the oil production and distribution systems globally would resemble a steam train setting off and jolting its carriages, manifesting itself as a price spike. This is a reasonably simple use of this model.

Each systemic model needs to be carefully tailored to its application. For instance, the systems pictures for future organizational strategy, a digitization program, or a regulatory threat would all be very different. It is far more an art than science.

On occasion, one can also vary the style and the end product by using "rich pictures." This is a piece of artwork, which represents the system, rather than using bubbles and arrows. Such pictures can be used to capture the feelings around the future rather than just the cognition. These are especially useful for change scenarios (Checkland 1981).

When drawing systems pictures, it can be a great idea to think about what alternative perspectives can be used to make sense of a complex and dynamic system. For instance, Graham Allison (2012) used four main perspectives to describe what was going on when Russia was putting tactical nukes into Cuba:

- Political
- Defense strategy
- Military technology
- Game theory

The rational agent model (RAM) versus the organizational behavior model, and the organizational politics model, were all applied in a gripping account of the crisis that nearly brought about a nuclear war. This article can be downloaded and should be read alongside my thinking (a must read and later in this book useful on predicting President Putin).

I was eight at the time the threat was on and was totally scared even in Bolton of a possible Third World War and oblivion....

The Business Value System

One specific systems model is my "business value system" (Grundy 2002b) as a way of picturing either an industry or company business model for past, present, and future: here our interest is mainly the future. The earliest example of a business value system is how it depicts the various ways that the UK Premier League, after its launch on Sky satellite TV network, revolutionized the game. This was led by Manchester United FC, which ruthlessly exploited its brand, generating huge new income streams not just from TV advertising but from sponsorship and from merchandise. Revenues and profits have expanded enormously over the last 30 years, transforming its value creation, inviting the question: "What next?"

It does have a raw simplicity of showing how not just a business but an industry can be remodeled into the future creatively—for the football industry, this adds sponsorship and media coverage as income streams to core activities like game takings and merchandising as a wider and richer system.

Besides future market attractiveness and competitive advantage a business also has a "future economic value," which is the value of its cash streams (DCF/NPV) as an adjusted annuity based on these two variables at a future point in time called the "terminal value." This can be really important and up to 70 percent of the total business value—the "so what?" of that is to do some in-depth scenario work to support assumptions about future value and cost drivers (Grundy 2002a).

The arrows in the business value system aren't just lines to express some relationship but actually (see Figure 3.8) represent flows of economic value added—cash flows. This economic grounding comes from my research into EVA (economic value added), which looks at the best estimate of the net present values of a business strategy, or of a strategic decision (Grundy 1998, 2002b).

In the business value system, these arrows are things that generate extra cash flows or savings either directly or indirectly, so they can be subject to some estimation, ranging from the hard to the softer.

I can attest to the utility of this in my own business where things like writing books seldom directly pay the mortgage, but giving a complimentary copy might land a strategic consulting work. (The value of interdependences like the value of the players is the value of the total set (in the latter case, being the team).)

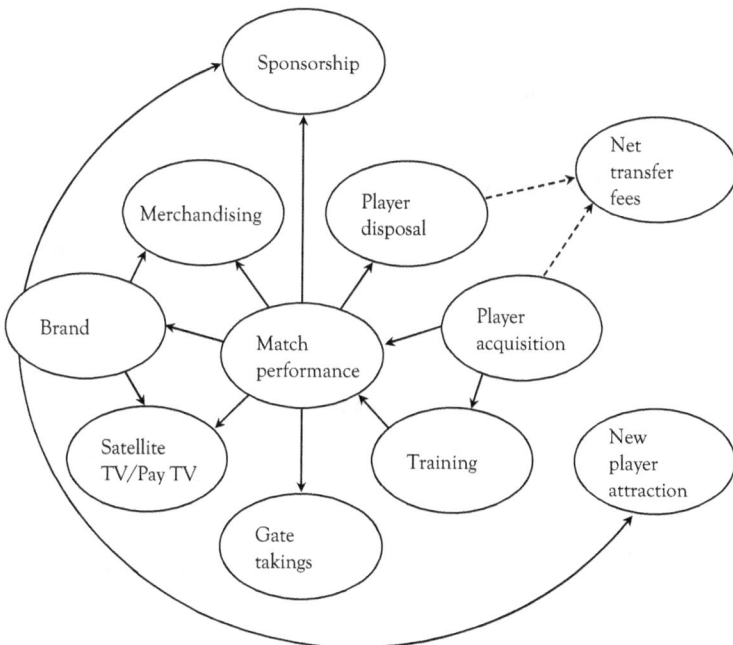

Figure 3.8 *The business value system—UK Premier Football Clubs*

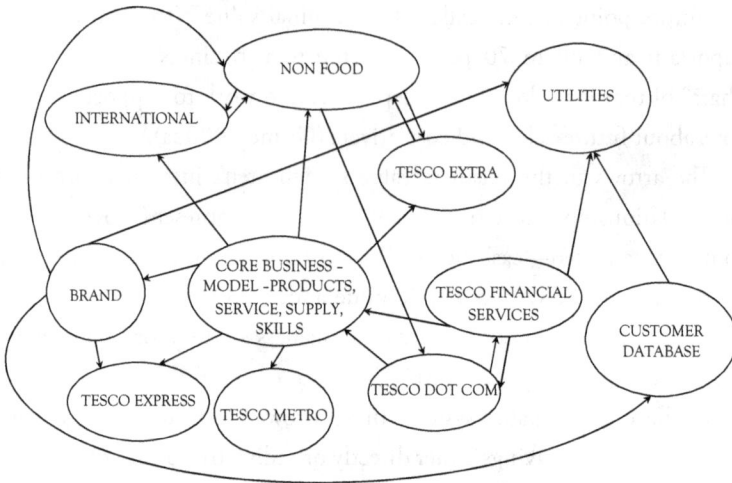

Figure 3.9 Business value system—TESCO's decade of 2000–2010

This now sets the business value system in a scenario context and will be particularly interesting for all readers contemplating actually using these processes in a real and uncertain environment for strategy development. As the case of any really outstanding football "team," Tesco's strategic success from 1996 to 2006 was very much born out of "the set" or of the entire system—Tesco Express, Metro, Non-Food and Direct (Tesco .com)—all of which had the scenario process applied to, with resulting sales of at least £15 billion per annum extra.

Reader Exercise—The Business Value System

Use the business value system for mapping key value-adding activities (that generate cash streams) for one of your businesses or for a sector of your industry:

- What does that highlight about the interdependencies— could that be an immature model, out of date, provide opportunities for further development, or change and how attractive might these interdependencies be?
- In particular, what would the possible effect be of deleting one, or adding a new one, for example, in terms of enhancing value added, changing its difficulty or resilience?

- How would that position itself in relation to any new scenario externally?
- Might that of itself suggest a new, possible scenario and what might its impact be?

Managing Uncertainty Strategically—a Case of Scorpions at Large

Returning to "one and the second big things I forgot," I was told a story by my wife Carolina after returning from a trip to the Colombian hills to visit family on a remote "farm" with no electricity or Internet:

"Oh Tony, while we were inside the farm and engrossed in chatting, a baby scorpion scuttled out and then ran away—near miss."

My brother-in-law Camilo later on started kicking objects around the room. I asked, "Why are you doing that?" "Well," he said, "they are usually around in pairs so we have to still investigate to surface the mate." That explains too, why, whenever they go into a room generally, they kick things around a bit.

She added, "We try to kill them not just because of the danger but also because if you are stung for example by the mate, the antidote is to smear the juices from the dead body over the bite!"

So, there's a countermeasure for many uncertainties.

- Moral 1: "Ask what's the one and the second big thing we have forgotten?"—Scorpion 1 and Scorpion 2.
- Moral 2: "For even very unlikely uncertainties, you can still anticipate these things."
- Moral 3: "On every threat there is a potential opportunity," for example, commercializing Scorpion Bite Crème.

Injecting Dynamics With the Uncertainty Tunnel

The uncertainty tunnel (see Figure 3.10) was inspired by a visit to a physics lab at Cambridge University years ago (open day) where we were told that a way of conceptualizing energy particles is to think that they are shaped like tubes of pasta. I reframed that model into a pasta tube. It was more like a narrowing and then widening the tunnel. When we move through time in a similar way, we go from a space of stability through an "uncertainty tube" where the tube narrows down and spits you out as it widens out into a new state of the world (see Figure 3.10) hopefully into a more stable space. Figure 3.11 represents multiple tunnels.

On the way, one's trajectory is influenced by the "precursors," possibly one or more transitional events led up to it all. Within the tunnel, further events, or actions, might increase the pressure for change-"amplifiers." Other events and actions might then calm the extent of change, so these are "stabilizers."

In the 2022 version of the tool (new), the velocity of the change might then be boosted by the "accelerators" that quicken the process such as disruptive new entrants or quickening industry clock speed. Or they might be slowed down by the "retarders," such as the rejection of regulatory boundaries or other protective actions by traditional incumbents. Finally, once emerging or spat out of the tube, there are first, second, and third order consequences (or even more than three?)

I had a car crash that inspired this tool. Actually a lorry backed into me when I was returning from a meeting with our Strategy Group at Cranfield School of Management, my business school home for 14 years.

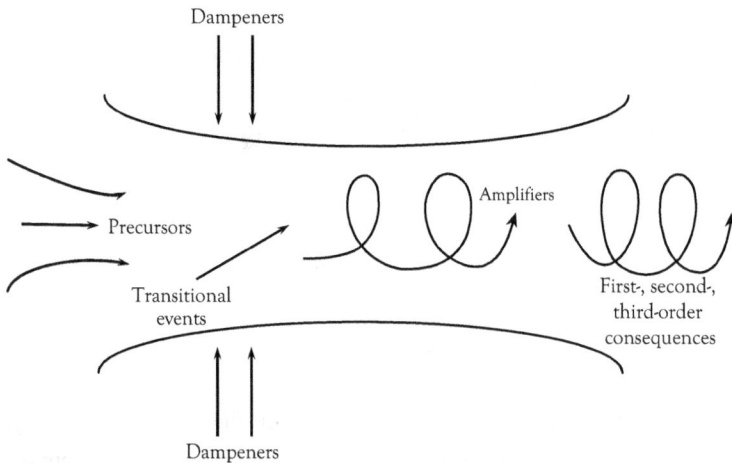

Figure 3.10 The uncertainty tunnel

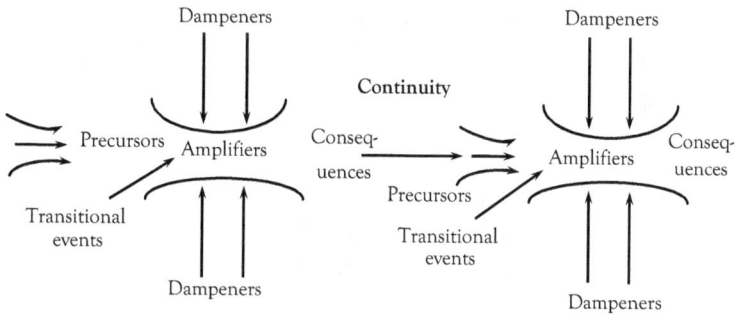

Figure 3.11 Multiple uncertainty tunnels

If one had been looking down onto this particular "MEST" universe (Mass–Energy–Space–Time), one would have seen the following:

- *Precursors* (signified P1, P2 etc.): I left the meeting too quickly (not very interesting) and forgot my "I am a devil" tea mug. So I went back to get it, losing 75 seconds. As a result, I arrived at the junction in the village later than I would have otherwise ("P1"), thus not escaping the lorry that my car was just now about to get overly intimate with on a physical level. A lorry was doing maneuvers to do a U-turn and began to turn, reversing toward me slowly, getting closer and closer. The driver was also in a dream ("P2")—a night out with the lads? Also, as my Mazda Xedos car was low and a gray color (ideal for being low priority on police car speed traps; this made me almost invisible anyway) ("P3"). The final precursors were ("P4") that I was more relaxed and in a state of trust ("P5"—silly me!)
- *Amplifiers*: After the impact at 3 mph, instead of stopping, the lorry carried on squashing the nice smooth front of my Mazda. This set off the alarm in a bad way and traumatized me (a knock-on consequence). Worse, I panicked and opened the bonnet and turned the alarm off manually, which was a wrong decision. The siren went up in volume around 1,500 percent and could be heard, I estimated, for a few miles part of the way to Bedford.

- *Dampeners*: I can't think of any! Other than the AA breakdown guys turned the alarm off to get rid of the car and took me home 40 miles.
- *Accelerators/retarders*: Actually, it was a pretty slow crash!
- *The knock-on consequences*: It took seven weeks to repair the car, so I was using buses and taxies. But much worse was I suffered mild trauma and felt a bit off for a few weeks.

Note: "MEST" (not to be confused with PEST) is a scientology concept. To be clear, I am not a scientologist but more of an Existentialist, a yoga-holic, and an Arsenal fan.

A reflection on this experience was that I wish I had been more mindful at the time. There were weak signals that the guy in the lorry was on a blind collision course. Why didn't I story tell that possible future at that time? Secondly, it highlights nicely and at a visible level the ingredients of the uncertainty tunnel beautifully. Thirdly, it is clearly a great way of visualizing the impacts of precursors, transitional events, and the knock-on consequences, and the role of assumptions and interdependencies.

Fourthly, it demonstrates the impact of time sensitivities and decision sensitivities in determining causal chains; for example, if I had left the meeting when I wanted to, or if I had left my mug, which only cost a pound, I would have been okay. This all reminds me of the *Sliding Doors* film where getting on or not getting on a tube sends the actor slice into two lives and two states of the world. *Time sensitivities to an event happening are often critical in uncertainty.*

We also showed Figure 3.11 which is a more complex set of possibilities where the trajectory takes us not just through one uncertainty tunnel but through two or more. Lockdown 1 and Lockdown 2 were examples of the uncertainty tunnels in the UK in 2020 and 2021. Arguably, a third was the overheating economy and inflation in late 2020 and early 2021. Even a fourth would be the Russia versus Ukraine war. A fifth tunnel might be added to this lengthy channel, with possibly a continued rise of gas and oil prices and consumer and business confidence, resulting in a significant recession in late 2022–2023(?).

As was put to me by a friend Mandy in Selsdon: "It has the ingredients of the Apocalypse: first the pestilence, then the war, what's the next one, oh that's famine. *I can see the queues for food in the shops, now.*"

Reader Exercise: The Uncertainty Tunnel

Think of a possible shift(s) in your industry, business, organization, job, or life:

- What might the precursors be?
- Do we have any weak signals yet?
- What are the amplifiers and dampers?
- What are the accelerators and the retarders?
- And their first, second, and third order consequences?

For a worked example of a grid see Figure 3.12 illustrating the same option in two different scenarios.

The uncertainty tunnel offers a range of applications especially to the emotional where there can be much turbulence: for instance think about what happens when you are disturbed and anxiety sets off—monitor how the cognitive and emotional dynamics are mobilized

Options / Criteria	Option 1 "out"	Option 2 "in"	Option 3	Option 4
Strategic Attractiveness	★★☆	★		
Financial Attractiveness*	★☆	★		
Implementation Difficulty	★★★	★		
Uncertainty and Risk	★★	★		
Acceptability (to Stakeholders)	★★☆	★		

Figure 3.12 The strategic option grid—same option in No Brexit versus With Brexit scenarios

Score: 3 = very attractive, 2 = medium attractive, 1 = low attractiveness.

through the uncertainty tunnel e.g. the event triggers , worry routines amplifiers , putting it all into perspective (dampeners)… via an Anxiety Tunnel ….

At this point, I will mention an area of theory that comes from science. It was discovered years ago that small events could set of chains of consequences that gave rise to spirals of turbulence, which could become dramatic. This was named chaos theory, popularized by Gleick (1997). Captured best through the "butterfly effect," it was conceived of as if a butterfly were to flap its wings in one part of the world and set off a domino of escalating energy, that could cause a storm or a hurricane elsewhere. Such theory has a mathematical underpinning (Levy 1994).

Scientists built this theory on empirical data. For example, if you run a second weather forecast based on some assumptions by changing them totally microscopically, it has surprisingly divergent results from the original.

This does support very much the idea that we need to watch for pre-cursors of scenario vis-a-vis the uncertainty tunnel. However, in my view, chaos theory doesn't imply that we abandon all attempts at forecasting or planning, and of scenario storytelling. Unless we are predicting broad shifts like H. Wells (1985), even interacting macro uncertainties will eventually screw up foreseeability. And minor events, even microscopic, may curiously bring that closer. But unless we are in a meltdown, there is still a big advantage in getting under the skin of uncertainty as in this book, pushing the visibility horizon further away. Even after chaos and the impact of entropy (the trend toward disorder in the natural world) in humankind, there are forces for creating order again.

With the weather, we are observing gases and fluids and clouds. But the human and the business worlds have many structures, so let's not get carried away by chaotic tornados.

Evaluating Strategies With the "Strategic Option" Grid

Now we come to Figure 3.13 for testing the impact on existing strategy and generation of any new strategic options with the "strategic options grid" as follows.

Options Criteria	Option 1	Option 2	Option 3	Option 4
Strategic Attractiveness				
Financial Attractiveness*				
Implementation Difficulty				
Uncertainty and Risk				
Acceptability (to Stakeholders)				

Figure 3.13 The strategic option grid

Score: 3 = very attractive, 2 = medium attractive, 1 = low attractiveness.
* Benefits less costs, - net cash flows relative to investment

The strategic option grid, which is a shortened account of the full process for brevity; for more see Grundy 2018 or as a business journal paper, Grundy 2004:

Once we have derived a really interesting set of options (and also preferably once we have done further work to optimize them), and maybe add some new ones, we are then set to do our evaluation using the strategic option grid.

The strategic option grid can be used for a whole range of applications at the corporate, business, functional, project, team, and individual level, and it can be used for market development, product/service development, and new technology development. Apart from the really big corporate strategic decisions, it really comes into its own with acquisitions, divestments, alliances, diversification, and turnarounds. Then there are also organizational structuring options, all strategic projects, cost breakthroughs, right through to career strategies.

The grid can also be used as part of gaming (game theory): how attractive/unattractive are various options for different stakeholders and what is their intent you infer from decisions, behavior, and follow through?

To use the strategic option grid, you will need to:

- Explore what options might be available;
- Then as a second stage look at options for "how" a strategic option might be done, and the timing options;
- For each option, a "cunning plan" is developed.

then you evaluate the scores, based on what is behind these criteria
(Note that high implementation difficulty and "uncertainty and risk"
these are scores of 1, and not 3 ticks as where these are high that is bad.)

- After that, it may be time to check out any facts—especially
  the cells on the grids, which the option grid evaluation looks
  most sensitive to.
- Finally, we may need to revisit the cunning plan and finally
  ask the question "what's the one big thing that you have
  missed?" (as I asked in the Tesco.com case earlier).

We define the criteria as follows:

- *Strategic attractiveness*: This is the external market
  attractiveness and the relative competitive position. "Market
  attractiveness" is based on things like the growth drivers,
  Porter's five forces, and perhaps PEST analysis.
- *Financial attractiveness*: These are the long- and short-term
  returns from the option (or possibly its economic profit).
- *Implementation difficulty*: This is the sum of difficulty over
  time to achieve the strategic goals.
- *Uncertainty and risk*: These are the extent of the volatility of
  the assumptions underlying a specific strategic option.
- *Stakeholder acceptability*: This is the extent to which
  stakeholders' favor, disfavor, or are neutral regarding that
  option.

The strategic option grid can be done for the very same option, splitting the scores for two very different states of the world. The strategic
option grid can cope with divergent realities, thus again being able to
handle external and dynamic uncertainty.

"Strategic attractiveness" (for an externally facing strategy) should
be checked out with the outer three layers of the strategic onion (see
Figure 3.2). "Financial attractiveness" means essentially those factors
which (in combination) will deliver a return on investment, or cash flow
based, "shareholder value creation" will add incremental economic value.

Uncertainty and risk are arrived at by using the uncertainty–importance grid.

For stakeholder acceptability, see stakeholder analysis (Chapter 7):

The strategic option grid scores may not tell us the best possible thinking about each option. Frequently, there is further scope to outline the options to make them better—to make them "cunning" (highly innovative) or even (with further refinement) the "stunning" plan.

To test the resilience strategy or an option against different possible states of the world (or "scenarios"), the *same* option is scored across the different columns—each one reflecting a different alternative future.

Reader Exercise—The Strategic Option Grid

For one strategic option, evaluate its attractiveness using the strategic option grid against:

- A state of the world One;
- A state of the world Two;
- Maybe Three, too;
- What's the "so what?" of the different scores?

The strategic option grid is especially helpful for understanding and resolving dilemmas as it allows you to trade off the criteria that you are using to do the evaluation, especially where you can't easily have it all or even both ways. Especially important here is the trade-off between strategic and financial attractiveness vis-a-vis uncertainty and risk, just setting the other two criteria aside for a while.

Cognitive and Emotional Bias

Cognitive bias is a very important mediator of our perceptions of uncertainty. Decisions made under uncertainty can be influenced by our expectations and beliefs and assumptions drawn from past experiences. Cognitive bias became a lot more prominent in mainstream thinking since the work of Kahneman (2011) who suggested that very quick and intuitive thinking can lead to misjudgments and errors.

While the application of the techniques in this book is not insulated from the potential effects of bias because they typically slow thinking down and can be challenged a lot more visually, the effects of bias should be mitigated. Nevertheless, we will maintain vigilance in the book and flag the risks from time to time.

I like to couple cognitive bias with emotional bias as they can amplify each other under stress. So it is best to have clear and calm reflection so that emotions don't disturb the mirror of the water. Feelings do influence cognition. Anxiety and fear shake the perceptions of uncertainty. So the latter is amplified or even anesthetized. For more on cognitive bias, see Grundy (2018).

Overall, one way of mitigating cognitive bias is to try to see a phenomenon from multiple perspectives. Dragonflies have an array of eyes pointing in many directions so that they can picture the environments of their prey and their enemies with great clarity and with incredible fine-grain detail. That can be reassuring when you are confronted with an instantly concerning habitat with considerable complexity and uncertainty, rather like the books on Harry Potter. This has stood the dragonfly in good stead, which as a species are 275 million years old.

But that's not easy. Indeed Kahneman (2011) warns us about seeing what we want to see with his acronym "What you see is all there is," or WYSIATI. To really understand that point, there's a brilliant film *Focus* about a con-couple acted by Will Smith and Margot Robbie who bring off the most amazing con by laying a trail of bait that causes a compulsive gambler to bet the wrong way. Attention is magnetic, selective, and generates snap judgments—with limited rationality. So, one has to be very mindful and dragon-eyed to avoid mistaking reality. *You are a very part of your own uncertainty generation* just as some people seem to be attractive to disasters. In addition to cognitive bias, there are many other influences on strategic decision making, some of which are mentioned in the following.

Coping With "Risky Shift"

When doing my first degree, I was fascinated with Social Psychology and particularly the influence of social interaction. In 1968, Stonehouse found that some groups when formed made riskier decisions than third constituent individuals would have made. This was called "risky shift." So, we see that a potential group bias toward uncertainty and risk that is tolerated by a group can be greater than that individual would be able to deal with. The way this works can be likened to what happens on a family visit to a theme park. Family members are contemplating on daunting rides like Air, the Black Hole, or Nemesis in the UK's Alton Towers. One might be emboldened by the daring of the leading person, impelling him or her to jump on the ride despite their better judgment to give it a miss.

There are those who are individually turned on by risk and are attracted to it; for instance, very young people and teenagers, or those with less cumulative experience of phenomenon; *indeed it is true to say the much of uncertainty is in the eye of the beholder.*

Groupthink, risky shift, and cognitive and emotional bias together pose considerable challenges. Witness the UK Government's procrastination over instigating special measures to slow COVID-19 in February and March 2020. So, there are many layers in the biases that can limit the effectiveness of decision making under uncertainty, especially of the more complex and wicked kinds illustrated in this book to be mindful of, namely:

- Personal agendas
- Political agendas
- Cognitive bias
- Emotional bias
- Territorial anxiety
- Personality dysfunctions
- Groupthink
- Risky shift
- Institutional inertia
- Industry mind set (Grundy 2018)
- Industry clock speed

These dilute agility and resilience.

Of course, strategic thinking and strategic mindfulness (Grundy 2012, 2014, 2018) do a lot to dissolve the uncertainties and are necessary but may be insufficient.

And finally, I mention my myth of the two-headed snake with each at opposite ends of its body.

The Scenario Snake

When talking to a UCL MBA student, Dino Mariutti, about scenarios for electric motor bikes, I described their evolution two ways:

> Imagine a two-headed snake with one head in the present and one in the future. The body is bendy and nonlinear. You can journey up and down the snake from the head in the present or backward from the future, or alternate between both. The snake can bite you both in the present and in the future with either head and can shape itself differently to picture different trajectories.

To experiment with this model, try this out in a Netflix suspense series like Stranger Things or Original Angel.

Key Concluding Insights

- It is important to have a clear and structured scenario process, which will enable the more fluid and creative aspects of the exercise to be grounded on.
- The Shell process is a very good start from which you can then tailor it to the company's appetite for analysis and reflection and to a specific issue.
- A useful starting point is to do a quick and dirty analysis of the issues using the strategic onion model, applied dynamically, with some thinking around changing clock speeds and shifts over it.
- Dynamically looking backward and/or forward maybe with an from–to (FT) analysis can help identify the drivers of uncertainty.
- Early on, there is a need to set boundaries for the work; for example, geographic, market space, and time horizons.

- The PEST, growth drivers, and competitive forces models as snapshots and dynamically as curves over time can help with both the assumptions on trends and also in highlighting possible discontinuities.
- To draw a background contextual map, invariably a systemic picture can help generate the critical assumptions, particularly those that are most important and uncertain as a prelude to scenario development and storytelling.
- Where the industry setup might be challenged or there is some new field of opportunity beckoning as with Internet supermarket shopping or the Sky-based Premier League, then it may be useful to hone in on the business value system model.
- Transitional events, possibly generated out of one or more assumptions about the future that are particularly uncertain and important, can act as the start of the storytelling framed using the uncertainty tunnel.
- Or you might decide to start your mental time traveling with some future and different world and work backward from that to the present again using the uncertainty tunnel.
- When constructing scenarios, pause time to think what the most limiting constraint is or may be (see Tesco.com case).
- And also ask, "What is the one big thing we have missed?" and "the second big thing we have missed?" both for the scenario(s) and for the strategy (see Tesco.com case).
- With any business value system that is hypothesized, given its complexity and novelty, how workable will it be and who will be best placed to exploit this effectively?
- Is it overcomplex or actually underdeveloped, and how sustainable will it be and what clock speed can we expect?
- Remember that the value and reliability of the process will depend too on the background economic and psychological analysis and thus your skills and the richness of any data.
- When looping back to sense-check any pre-existing strategy at the end of the process in Figure 3.1, or to embark on

new strategy to exploit or deal with any new scenarios, it
is important not to see this as a quick bolt on, but a new,
linked piece of work often after some time for digestion and
reflection.

- You are a cause of your own uncertainty mediated by bias—
  mindfulness and dragon-eyed vision can mitigate bias.

CHAPTER 4

Step-by-Step Scenario Tools and Processes

In this chapter we look at:

- Introduction
- Scenario storytelling
- Learning from history
- Slicing the future up into different "futures"
- People and skills
- Facilitation and workshops
- Key concluding insights

Introduction

So far, we have introduced the idea of thinking about future uncertainty through a structured process and visualization through pictures in order to make an imaginative journey. That journey has taken us through things like the arrow of time, the uncertainty grid, the systemic model, and others. But in addition, we need to attend to the softer process elements.

The most important ingredient of scenario is storytelling, which is rightly at the heart of scenario development.

Scenario Storytelling—the Process With the War in the Pacific Case Study

Scenario storytelling ought to be a straightforward process as it actually requires little direct use of tools. They have set the scene but aren't really needed for an enactment of events, a drama, if you like. It involves a sequence of events, actions, or decisions over a period of time with some causal sequence to them. They can be constructed working forward from now, or from some future time, or backward from some event into the future.

Within the narrative, there is likely to be some pivotal or transitional events that might take the scenario trajectory off in a new direction, or possibly in two alternative directions. So, for example, at the time of writing, early March 2022, the Metropolitan Police are investigating possible infringements of COVID restrictions in 2000–2001 by 50 members of Downing Street, including ones by the Prime Minister. The results are now to be made public over the coming weeks, and if they show extensive infringements, especially by the Prime Minister, and also reveal, as some have said, unquestionable lying by him to Parliament, he will be under pressure to resign. In that backdrop what might happen is this:

Prime Minister Boris Johnson says, as he has before, that he regrets what happened but denies that he lied as his view at the time he was quizzed in late 2021 was that these were innocent half "let's chill" social activities where most of the chat was around government issues so these were productive working sessions.

Although he is then savaged by the Leader of the Opposition, Kier Starmer, because there is perceived to be still no better alternative (especially as the Chancellor of the Exchequer is found guilty too). A credible alternative to Boris (rumored to be called "Big Dog" in inner circles) is lacking. Boris has recently come over well in the media during the Ukraine conflict, and memories of his most obvious and rather obvious attempts to duck and dive are fading.

Boris then wins a vote of no confidence (actually happened in early June 2022), but after a positive turnaround budget in 2022 after Boris slips on more banana skills, he gets deposed and Rishi Sunak, who has shrugged off minor social misdemeanors, gets elected in a hung parliament in 2024.

An alternative storyline is that Boris survives a no confidence motion and he continues in office, and Labour gains a landslide in the next election in May 2024, which is just 26 months away now.

These are raw storylines, but they are fairly rich based on cause and effect and have actions and transitional events. For example, the Met

Police (and the Civil Service reports), leadership contests, and election narratives appear internally consistent. They are not attempts to forecast *the future*, in the sense of being *accurate*, but ways of sensing an array of possibilities over a time horizon.

Here lies a paradox of scenarios—while they don't intend to forecast the future as they are held in that purity, paradoxically they can come close as in my little case study of the War in the Pacific.

Many years ago, I recorded a video on Discovery Channel called "The War in the Pacific." Using old footage and interviews with military historians, it told the story of the events that led up to the Japanese attack on Pearl Harbor and the way the war unfolded after that. It reveals how the attack and the war were anticipated very closely indeed by a British journalist, Hector Bywater, who wrote a novel about the future war in great detail and with considerable accuracy, including casualties.

The book was originally published in 1925 and is still available on Amazon. It is a story, a novel, with characters, events, and chains of events over 300 pages that are so engrossing and realistic you have to pinch yourself to realize it was fiction at the time. Bywater clearly had no problem lifting off from the structured thinking he evidently did on the sources of discontinuity, the dynamics of change, and the transitional events that he implicitly used for storytelling. He was not just a structured thinker but a natural mental time traveler.

In the words of a U.S. victim of that attack (in the novel):

All around us the sea spouted and boiled. In only a few seconds I heard a gigantic crash as if a Wedgewood tree had fallen. Another ear-splitting crash and everything came to an end for me. When I recovered my senses from our boat, we could see the Japanese mopping up the rest of our flotilla, shortly before our flagship went down.

Bywater founded that story on an analysis of the Japanese psyche, which not only had some Imperialist expansionary elements but was also defensive as the Japanese felt vulnerable to the threat of losing access to strategic materials such as oil, rubber, coal, and iron from the Far East. U.S. naval forces were stationed in the Philippines and on other islands.

That said, more impressive was his interest in painting a picture of the future with storylines.

The documentary goes on to examine how these very clever scenarios were arrived at. First of all, Bywater studied intimately the dynamics of a potential arms race and geopolitical rivalry between the Japanese and the Americans that goes back to the early 1920s, when the Japanese occupied some small islands that were closer to the western seaboard of the United States than the U.S. islands of the Philippines, thus posing a perceived threat to the United States, especially when the Japanese chose to fortify the islands.

The Japanese had become a lot more expansionist and, at one stage, went to war with China, alerting the United States to the possible eastern danger. For their part, the Japanese were worried that the United States would cut off their supplies to strategic resources, especially oil and rubber for military and industrial uses, from Indonesia. So, there were natural precursors for rivalry and conflict that Bywater was only too aware of.

Also, he modeled the potential dynamics of the balance of military power in the Pacific and even came close to anticipating the formula that was agreed upon between the Japanese, the Americans, and the British over the ratios of the capital ships that each was allowed to have so that no side could easily predominate over the other—an effective stalemate.

Bywater also saw that by forging an apparent stalemate in the balance of forces between the United States and the Japanese, it was itself a precarious equilibrium as it made both sides, especially the Japanese, more nervous and maybe willing to entertain a pre-emptive strike.

This was further emphasized by another hypothesis that Bywater was drawn to make that the United States would provide a staging post to support the Philippines in case of a Japanese attack and build a naval base somewhere between the West Coast and those islands. These two things together then created the possibility of a *transitional event*, which is something new that happens, destabilizing one system and leading to another. In effect, we move from one world to another. (This is the very thing that scenario storytelling helps us to imagine.)

The precursors were there in terms of Imperialistic expansion, Japanese fear, and a plausible looking plan for a pre-emptive strike.

The consequences were the following:

- The devastating destruction of U.S. forces at what was to be called Pearl Harbor;
- The Japanese advance through the Pacific;
- The waging of a very large battle between the capital ships of both navies, which the United States were too narrowly win (which became the battle of Midway);
- The massive production of armaments by U.S. industry giving firepower that eventually overcame the ferocity of the Japanese fighters;
- Eventually the implosion of the Japanese forces as the occupied islands were taken one by one by the United States in bloody battles.

The remarkable thing, however, was that the story was told by way of a long, comprehensive, and coherent novel with ship names, the names and characters of the commanders, details of the fire power mustered, the battle scenes, the chain of events in the fighting, the losses and casualties, and the strategies and tactics deployed. While deliberately not attempting to forecast the future, paradoxically, by sensing it and telling it as a story, Bywater managed to come remarkably close to actually doing that. I actually call this "the scenario paradox": the less that you try to do a forecast, the more likely that you will!

The other and crucial thing that Bywater succeeded in doing was to get inside the heads of the major players in the conflict: we call this the "out-of-body experience." Of course, through his interactions with the military and the politicians, for example, during their negotiations of who was allowed to have how many carriers and so on, he would have gotten a really keen insight into not just what they thought, but also how they thought too.

In turn, it enabled him to model their thoughts, anxieties, ambitions, and their behaviors and actions over the four years of the war. This also extended to modeling the shift in attitude throughout the U.S. population away from isolationism as a result of a devastating attack on their soil, and the reaction of the U.S. economy to militarize.

Without calling it these things, Hector Bywater brought together systemic thinking, behavioral modeling, game theory, dynamic causal sequencing, and, of course, storytelling in his scenarios.

So, as I have suggested, many managers find storytelling hard. As the Director of Strategy of a Global Banking Group once said to me after a day of developing scenarios:

> We do struggle with the scenario storytelling. I think maybe part of that is *because we do so many PowerPoint presentations that we can only think in bullet points.*

So why is that so terribly difficult? I think that this could happen because of the following:

- A prevailing linear thinking style
- As in the bank case, too much focus on analytical thinking, less on synthesis
- Hard to let go of the idea "we are forecasting"
- Fear of "getting it wrong" or just looking silly
- Inability to detach, stand back
- Freezing up when it's time to jump from analysis to making a very specific chain(s) of events
- Not looking at it dynamically
- Being too dry in the stakeholder dimension—haven't tried to be in the agendas and the mindset of key stakeholders
- Lack of input from those who are very intimate with the group
- Possibly the team mix and cognitive skills and style, and balance

Or a number of these.

Turning this around to the positive, we are looking for teams of talented linear and nonlinear thinkers that can synthesize, creatively imagine, and even invent more, are unafraid to make "mistakes," and are open to learning within and from outside the team. *So, storytelling depends on emotional maturity and control, curiosity, and receptiveness, all attitudinal and thus cultural.*

Accepting that storytelling can come with difficulty, think of times you have done it well, for example, with young children at bedtime. Surely you can translate that into a business context. Also, try to practice it every day to anticipate outcomes from transitional events in your life, for instance, going on a holiday or a long journey.

What about when you are watching a crime mystery or an action film or series as an area of practice? My wife (who is a clinical psychologist) loves telling stories of serial murder series, especially trying to do profiling as part of the storytelling, which helps one to story tell what they might do next ("profiling" is a process developed by the FBI at its famed center at Quantico). If we can get so good at it in fictional worlds where there are clues but they are well hidden, that can transfer to business. In real life, the "weak signals" that there's discontinuous change coming are often anything but weak.

I was talking about this book and storytelling with my wife (Dr. Carolina Yepes) and friends at a dinner party. She is a leader in the field of EMDR (eye movement desensitization reprocessing), a therapeutic methodology that uses a combination of storytelling and rapid eye movements to help release deep traumas and blockages and accelerate psychological healing.

She said:

> When I listen to what Tony says about the processes in his book, there are many parallels between how he uses storytelling and what we do in EMDR. There we start with the past and use storytelling to surface past patterns. We do the same for the present—these all bring release. *But most importantly we then tell stories about how the client might behave and experience things in the future, and this helps reconfigure the neural patterns so that we can actually create our own future(s).*

In the same way, managers can increase their readiness for an uncertain event with agility through visualizing and modeling the future just as my lion in the street story (told later in this chapter).

There are differences, obviously, as EMDR works with individuals while scenario storytelling happens with groups, but there are very similar surfacing, role-playing, picturing, and enactment processes going on. She added, "What we both are doing is priming the psyche and, in our case, the body too, for a smoother trajectory into the future and the experience it brings, and (added by Tony), actually changing that future."

Reader Exercise

For an area of uncertainty that you are very aware of, think of one outcome that is positive and one that is negative:

- What chain of events, actions, and decisions could bring about that positive outcome?
- What chain of events, actions, and decisions could bring about that negative outcome?

When telling the story, also try to insert "who did what, when, and why."

Slicing the Future Into Different "Futures"

When we look at uncertainty, we often talk about *the future* as if it were a singularity. Not only may that take us down different roads depending on decisions or events, but they can also go through phases that are useful to distinguish between. For instance, in the case of the War in the Pacific that take us through:

- Prewar arms race
- Pearl Harbor and Japanese islands invasion
- Mobilization of the U.S. military industrial complex
- The Battle of Midway that was so devastating for the Japanese
- Relentless counterattack by the United States taking island by island
- The atomic bombs being dropped on Japan

Each of these phases, or "slices of the future," will have its own subset of assumptions and at least one uncertainty tunnel to navigate. Each will have a role in the storytelling.

So how might that work in a real situation? Years ago, I had been working to facilitate the strategic thinking of a leading Scottish insurance company's Independent Financial Advisers (IFA) division, which seemed to go down well. Indeed, its MD was something of a fan and told me, "Thanks for your input, Tony. I am just recovering from a session with 'M and Jos'—disguised strategy consultants. Please, can anyone help me? *How can I avoid strategy consultants?!*"

That was inspiring for me as I hit on the idea of writing a book on how to avoid strategy consultants, which was published as *Be Your Own Strategy Consultant* (Grundy 2002a).

So, it wasn't a shock when I got a call from Jeannie, their Strategic Planning Director, one day:

> Hi Tony, I am so pleased to catch you. We just have a big issue to deal with. As you may know, we have a new regulator who is being asked by the government to do a lot of tightening up and we are a wee bit concerned that things could land awkwardly as this new guy seems to want to make a name for himself and isn't so familiar on what makes it tick. What we were thinking was: could you possibly try to get inside this guy's head for a couple of days?

So, I spent two days immersing myself in the issues, the drivers of change, the concerns of the government, the customer agendas, and especially building up a rich picture of the new regulator's agenda. A key part of that was to profile him, not just his career moves and reputation but also his education, affiliations, and the extent of his personal agenda. Then I role played for myself what he might well do and laid out the phases over which this would unfold, especially the changes.

I presented my output and (using the uncertainty tunnel) described what the different slices of the future would be, especially:

- Future 1—the regulator's investigation
- Future 2—the first-order consequences: the changes announced, reactions by the IFA companies
- Future 3—the second-order consequences: their impact on the existing market
- Future 4—the third-order consequences: adaptations of the old strategies and new ones too (with, again, gaming)

This not only prepared the company for the regulator's announcements on change but also saved the digestion period and enabled its management to be a lot more on the front foot.

Postscript: I read about the changes a few months later with great interest and was pleasantly surprised to find that the hit rate was around 85 percent.

In conclusion, unless the scenario process has quite discrete and short time horizons, some slicing up into futures is almost certainly on the cards.

As an add-on to time slicing, one of the common and big uncertainties is when things will start and go on both in terms of events and durations. Scenarios have a range of earliest and latest start time and finish times.

Time Sensitivity of Events

This was highlighted for me in a wonderful MBA project that two Singaporeans, Jimmy and Sampson, undertook in 2020 on the impact of COVID. The format for this project is represented as a schematic in Figure 4.1. The result was a bit like a project Gannt chart except with external shifts and then imagine their knock-on effects in flexing scenarios. One then just had to mentally slide an event or a phase of

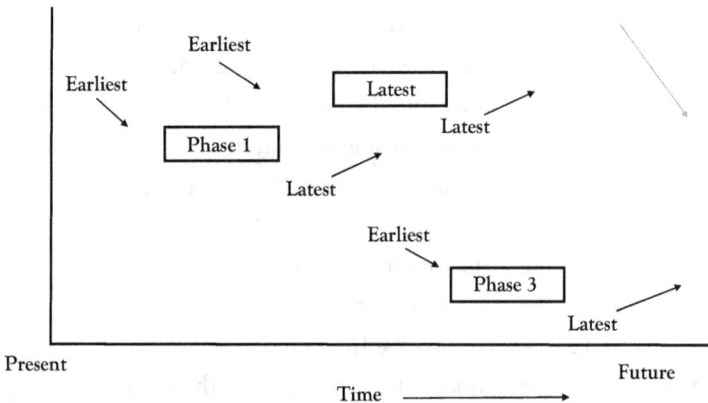

Figure 4.1 The time sensitivity of events Jimmy and Sampson Low, MBA, 2020

development backward or forward as if these were time controls in the BBC series *Dr. Who* TARDIS time and space machine!

An obvious application of this project would be to bring forward in time the point at which an electric vehicle's lifetime cost is less than that of a petrol or diesel car.

People and Skills

Having some tools and a tailored process for scenario development are very important, and strong facilitation is necessary at least initially. But equally important is the deployment of people with appropriate skills. I once had the opportunity to observe this firsthand. A water company wanted to explore the future, and the Director of Management Development set up two sessions. One was with more senior and experienced managers to evolve some alternative futures in an era of greater competition. For the second session, a second cohort was formed with a group of younger managers who it was thought would be more likely to be creative.

While the older managers had no problem talking around the existing industry structure, the younger group had a clear edge in terms of their imagination and creativity. Of course, a mixture of older and younger managers with a facilitator being very active in surfacing the less senior people's ideas and opinions might have been a more optimal mix. This case study might tentatively suggest a premium on lateral thinking over linear thinking in scenario development and storytelling.

A very useful source for digging deeper into the ideal mix of cognitive and emotional styles is Tetlock and Garner (2015). Their concerns were with the slightly wider topic of what makes some people better at forecasting than others. In their fascinating and well-argued book *Superforecasting*, they list:

- Analytical ability
- A deep drive to understand ("inquisitive")
- Intelligence

- Numeracy
- Probabilistic thinking

I would add to that strategic thinking is the basic capability to see the bigger picture and think about the future, options, and trade-offs. Having trained 1,500 senior managers to do that, I am acutely aware that this is sadly lacking at that level. For the purpose of doing scenarios, strategic thinking is a basic competence. It is like passing the ball and not losing it as in football. That helps to avoid losing but not in actually scoring the goals. Indeed, strategy and scenarios go together as processes that, in combination, I often suggest to corporates running a combined workshop or an "SAS" event or "Strategy and Scenarios."

Also, Kahneman (2011) distinguishes "fast" and "slow" thinking as two styles, the former being more prone to bias, thus increasing uncertainty, and the latter being more balanced and providing multiperspective views, requiring gestation. I argue, based on my deep study of six CEOs (2014), that strategic mindfulness and slower thinking can be of great value in framing the issues, especially through processes and tools like those in this book. This entails juggling the two forms of thinking, agility from individuals, optimization of group dynamics, checking for hints of groupthink, and challenging facilitation.

"Strategic mindfulness" is a state that entails (Buddhist style) inner peace, constant alertness for "weak signals," and 360-degree awareness of environmental shifts (Grundy 2014).

Returning to Tetlock and Garner's (2015) skills list, some are relatively self-evident, like analytical skills and intelligence. Numeracy is extremely useful as there are often quantifiable data elements to making projections—for example, in the case of my time series of the spread of COVID-19 in Chapter 1 with the numbers in the on line material. I have training in finance and also in economics, in addition to statistics. So that really helps me keep track of trends and some of the key driving causes of change.

If you are flaky on that, then I would suggest you spend some time absorbing the fundamentals. As economists are notoriously prone to never agreeing with each other, you can't just pick up and run with conventional wisdom, for example, on the likely rate of growth of income in the economy. Also, things like the growth driver picture we saw in Chapter 2 are helpful, for instance, in understanding growth trends and predicting them.

Tetlock and Garner list probabilistic analysis as being crucial, too. When doing a concrete forecast, it is essential as we see as follows. In operations management, the approach of calculating expected values is really helpful for assessing a central forecast out of a range of possibilities. Following the invasion of the Ukraine in 2022, the stock market fell 6 percent in the first 15 days. Let's suppose that in a year's time there were:

- A 20 percent chance of a ceasefire and resolution, then prices go up by 8 percent;
- A 20 percent chance of Putin being deposed and a price up by 10 percent;
- A 50 percent chance of Cold War number prices down by another 6 percent;
- A wider conflict with NATO repelling the invasion of Finland and nuclear weapons mobilized, resulting in political panic with a 10 percent chance and stock market prices down another 20 percent a year on, we have:
  - Expected price shift = $(20\% \times 8\%) + (20\% \times 10\%) +$
    $(50\% \times -6\%) + (10\% \times -20\%)$
    $$= 1.6\% + 2\% - 3\% - 2\%$$
    $$= -1.4\%$$

Notice how sensitive this trend is to outliers like a coup bringing Putin down on the upside and the invasion of another country under a nuclear umbrella causing NATO to launch an offensive, pushing the Russians back. And, if we were to think the unthinkable, there is a possibility we have not considered—an all-out war with very limited exchange of tactical nuclear weapons, with a probability of 10 percent with the stock market down 60 percent and an expected impact of –6 percent! Have I got your attention? And was that disconcerting? Would you have stopped in your array of possible projections with a fall of 1.4 percent without my leading you there by the nose?

So probabilistic assessments of futures here are essential, but they mustn't drive out the more qualitative thinking that underpins the forecasting. For instance, you still need to ask, "What is the one big thing we forgot?" Such as a semideliberate nuclear accident before a Russian withdrawal, with Russia blaming Ukraine and the NATO as a precursor to dropping a battlefield nuke on the countryside as provocation. *Probably as in a football game where there are shots that hit the post that won't happen, but it could.…*

Another limitation of using probabilities or weightings of importance is that few senior and top managers are comfortable with that calculation. When researching strategic investment decisions for my PhD, the (then) Strategic Planning Director of Rolls Royce Aeroengines said, "Hmm, probabilities, even when they have engineering backgrounds, some of our top people tend to lose interest rapidly when you introduce any probabilistic assessments."

I never fully got to the bottom of that then, but looking back, this probably had a lot to do with the notion that "managing" is all about control, being accountable, and avoiding being or seeming to be wrong. That's the main meal. The more strategic stuff may be the dessert, but you can't screw up the main dish even at the cost of ignoring the best estimates of key events that will drive outcomes. So, my own take is that even where the board might struggle with such mathematical estimations, we can nudge them through using "high," "medium," and "low" assessments of probability and the same for importance using the uncertainty grid.

For me, in addition to these competencies, the critical skill is modeling the world. Our brains need to create working structures to interpret reality—nonsocially and socially (Berger and Luckman 1966)—which are models. A gristly illustration of that is carried by the often-told story of a Lion in the Street.

A Story of a Lion in the Street

Picture me going out of my house into the street, which is wonderfully green with trees and two roads separated by a wide green stretch of grass and showcase gardens. London's Docklands are in the distance. It is so peaceful (apart from our family's music) that a police car calling in at a house is a Big Event.

So, what if I notice a lion under the conifer tree? Should I be inquisitive and see what it is up to? Or call someone, but who?

How has it gotten there? Could it have escaped, or did someone let it out? Is it well fed, ravenous, angry, or depressed? Is it actually a lion or a giant fake croissant in the shape of a lion? (Google: "Mystery Tree Beast turned out to be a Croissant," BBC News, April 15, 2021.)

What's the likely speed and acceleration of the lion, and what is my reaction time? What are our relative speeds, should I need to run for it, and how long before I get caught?

Has it actually seen me, and if not, smelled me?

How might I defend myself from it, and could that rebound on me from animal protection bodies if I hurt it or will there be serious legal trouble?

How long would it take for tranquilizer darts to arrive, and, in the meantime, can we corral them in No. 37's ("007") immaculate front lounge, luring them in with a batch of raw beef burgers through the door?

Can I succeed in capturing this for social media, and will this make TV news?

There are so many facets to model and when we get to play with combinations, there are a huge number of possibilities, providing much fertile scenario material. *Models can have a multitude of variables, some of which are interdependent, and their importance needs to be weighted, all under conditions of uncertainty.* That's why we need pictures on paper, laptops, or in our heads to be able to peer into the future.

In sum, a structured and creative modeling is at the heart of our work in understanding uncertainty and managing it. This calls for a truly agile mind.

Returning to Tetlock and Garner, other emotionally based competences that are important are the following:

- "Humbleness"—not being arrogant, sweeping, and over-confident
- Open-mindedness—avoiding overly anchored belief systems
- Caution—not dismissing potential uncertainties

- Reflection—digesting your work to date, looking at new angles, new lines of equity, posing new questions
- Nondeterminism—being wary about making strong views of what will be about to come and deductively assembling data that will produce that result ("confirmatory bias")
- Pragmatism—not striving for purity, obsession with micro detail and completeness, and keeping a track of time

In addition, they also stressed on the need to:

- Identify things that would change your mind;
- Seek out information that would prove you wrong;
- Be like a detective and absorb data (I have often role played the U.S. Detective Colombo famous for his dithering but occasionally devastating "lines of inquiry");
- Listen to people's language to discern what variables they are implicitly relying on to understand what's going on and what might be going on in the future.

In a later case study in Chapter 8 on scenarios for the MBA market, I did change my mind on how saturated the UK market was for MBAs at one point when I looked at the statistics differently. So I concluded that the market was half as saturated as in my earlier (crude) thinking. That extends to proactively trying to disprove your theories and conjectures.

I do like the notion of being like a detective, uncovering new lines of enquiry: in the MBA case study, there were a very large number of surprising discoveries that the mind was bulging! Also, like a detective, it is critical to display (as in the old U.S. crime series with Lieutenant Colombo) tenacity and doggedness. In addition, any good detective has to be highly sensitive to critically important clues that may be partially visible. I call that "strategic mindfulness" in the strategy/scenarios context (Grundy 2014) where there is great receptiveness to weak signals (back to Tatlock and Garner's "openness" again).

Indeed. I was recently talking to an MBA student about how and when it was good to do a "deep-dive" beneath the surface and likened this to our fishpond, where the fish were all eaten by a nasty pelican and the surface is very green and overgrown. "Now what might I learn from diving into the pond?" I asked. (Actually, someone did that at a teenager's party that was happening in our garden. One of them stepped off into it mistakenly believing that it was a mini garden and would serve as a quickie toilet. It was a big mistake. The pond was two feet deep and very slimy.) A deep dive is going beneath the surface.

Returning to my augment, whether you are doing an MBA research project or a market scenario, the same applies: a pond can see alluringly tranquil and going beneath it can reveal some deep surprises. I now call this "pond theory" or "beware what lies beneath"—a simple concept but one most relevant to "managing uncertainty strategically."

Listening to language: In qualitative research, this is sometimes called "content analysis," where you count up the number of times a word or a group of words (a "category") occurs. For example, a group of words that are combined allows the words to be unstressed, whether this is on video, in conventional media, or in social media.

The extent to which this models the systems in the **social and economic behavioral environment** can help with prediction. Indeed, that very collection of five words in bold above could be a "category."

They also emphasize that the vision required for future scenario work is not like conventional two-eyed sight but is more like that of a dragonfly, as we saw in Chapter 3.

Finally, Tetlock and Garner talk about grit—the sheer determination to conduct a thorough inquiry rather than close it off in a hurry or let it fade away as it sometimes can feel tiring, difficult, and frustrating. Patience and persistence always yield their rewards.

Facilitation and Workshops

Just as with strategic thinking, scenarios are not just about tools but very much about process too. Apart from deploying a suitable blend of people, it is also important to have suitable facilitators. They could be picked in-house, but that may not always be affordable as an in-situ resource, and they may not have the necessary independence of thinking and be able to operate politics-free, or at least in a low-politics way.

It is all about trade-offs.

It can be hard to take off, navigate, and land a scenario exercise with depth in just a day. That's quite a cognitive challenge. Moreover, it can be quite an emotional upheaval, too. For example, I did a scenario exercise for small and medium-sized high-street supermarkets for Tesco Metro, when they only had 12 in the UK. I rang their Business Head years ago to check out the day after the workshop to get a sense of how he felt after a future-based testing of the market trajectory and its implications. His response was:

> It felt as if all the chairs in the room (assumptions) were thrown up in the air and when they all landed the room looked very different. But I tell you today I feel really shattered and I don't know why. Normally when I come up to Head Office in Cheshunt, northeast of London from the southeast, but that day I stayed over, yet I felt much more tired—odd.

This exercise had been accomplished in just a day. With hindsight, while that worked (just) cognitively, emotionally that was probably too short—don't skimp!

On the other hand, you don't need to go to the other extreme of having a stream of one-day workshops spread over a period. Apart from likely dropouts and the stop–start experience, this can take the immediacy and urgency of the experience down a notch. Some scenario books seem to overelaborate the workshop process. Sometimes there is a subtle feel of a package of a maybe overelaborate consultancy process being on the cards.

For me, once the scope and boundaries of a process and some key objectives have been defined, the next stage is to define in a suitably linked series a set of key research questions that will drive the workshop. After the transformation of these questions into time amounts for exercise setup, group work, feedback, and critique, you can estimate if the workshop can be finished in one day, an evening, and a day, or two days without an evening. Do leave some time to reflect, digest, and begin to plan next work at the end.

Other things to plan for include:

- Selection of tools to help with the exercises—the groups of key questions
- Any further data or preparation (capture this in prework)

- Provision of recording output—flip charts and maybe someone to type them in real time with any additional narrative; trust me, if you leave it over a weekend, by Monday, you will sometimes be wondering: "why did she/he say that?"

Facilitation has a variety of functions:

- Time management
- Project management
- Assigning to groups
- Setting expectations, surfacing concerns about the topic, the process, group dynamics, and what the implications might be, for example for change
- Setting ground rules, for example avoiding "P" behaviors (we want to avoid being personal, political, picky, procrastinating, being overly pessimistic, having preconceptions, and so on)
- Listening to groups, spotting early tensions, and signs of conflict
- Suggesting areas for just-in-time search for in fill data for example, by googling
- Making "building comments," for example, on whether the lines of enquiry emerging have promise and maybe suggesting further ones, especially if a group were to be getting stuck
- Explaining the tools and also how best to be free of preconceptions
- Constructive and critical commentary on feedback
- Very important: summarizing subgroup and group output, and drawing out any implications

It is always useful to break a medium and larger-sized group, say 8 to 15, into two or three subgroups. Otherwise, individuals get lost. Maybe try not to go over 10 in a group. An option is if the medium is strategic coaching, not a workshop, you might get somewhere with a one-to-one or one-to two or three, although the output may not be that rich, rounded, and reliable. This can be a useful way of preparing for a workshop, although be wary of annoying people: don't just blurt out, "on my/our scenarios, we had this coming out." as that will dilute ownership.

A final plea is to arrange a suitable and comfortable space for the event. Ideally, plan the workshop off-site to minimize distractions. Have generous coffees, teas, cakes, and bacon and vegan rolls. Do have widows with natural light flowing in. The Prudential, the insurance company, booked a hotel basement to use to develop scenarios over three days. The scenarios were around the future of the market involving role playing a number of customers in the future where these characters were very animated.

While the experience was very insightful, due to having no natural light, day one was hard, day two was very hard, and the most important day three was extremely tough and very tiring. Be good to yourselves!

If you are short of vision, give people who want it a sherry. Just doing anything outside of normal habits or rules can lead to the necessary relaxation. I use humor and other surprises a lot—like announcing this is an "end of the world workshop" and we have to create plausible and self-consistent scenarios before. I once did that at Microsoft and at 3 p.m., the participants were flagging. So I ran over to the window crying, "Look! It's coming!" and there were voices: "What's coming, what?" So, I said "the asteroid." To which they all asked, "Where, where?" Then I said, "No, silly, you just need to imagine one." That "thought experiment" finally did the trick!

In conclusion, workshops are really useful for time traveling with a group of informed managers to sense the future, but they will flounder without solid preparation, planning, and very skilled, credible, and balanced facilitation. We will return to this topic in more depth in Chapter 9.

Key Concluding Insights

- Storytelling can be remarkably accurate, even though its intent is more to explore plausible future scenarios than to make specific predictions as in the War in the Pacific.
- Storytelling works best if there is chronological development, with one event leading to another and specific times and actors there to color it.
- Future slicing can add more plausibility to the time dimension.

- Workshop design is crucial and needs to have structure, timing, background work, key tools, key strategic questions, and facilities congenial to creativity with low distractions.
- Facilitation is a must and needs to be behaviorally and politically from a business and strategically savvy person who is naturally creative as well as good at distilling insights and landing the process and its output.

CHAPTER 5

Managing Organizational Change Scenarios

Introduction

Soon after I began to play with scenario methods in my consulting, it became apparent that not only external environment but also the internal environment could be volatile. Whereas the cycles of external change could happen every five to ten years, they could occur once in six to twelve months internally. Organizational change strategies often seemed to be more emergent than their sister competitive strategies.

I turned that idea into a reality by storytelling.

For instance, during my time at KPMG, I was seconded to be Divisional FD of a genetic technology division of a diversified multinational. The secondment was for six months. There was a lot going on including dealing with the indigestion problems of postacquisition of a business and attempts to buy more without very solid criteria. When they had found a successor to me, I remember two things—a night out in London to see Swan Lake, a tranquil contrast to my time there, and also a neo-interrogation by the Group FD and his deputy where I was asked: "Tony, do you have any concerns to tell us before you go?"

I replied, "Well, I do have anxieties about the management of the UK business." There was a very intense silence in response. Inwardly I had put timescales for that change at three to six months. Within two months, there was a major management change. *The lesson here is that organizational change when foreseen can come at you much quicker than thought.*

My deduction is that the thought of a severely negative event and of its real occurrence introduces an emotional paralysis, which is so pervasive that it introduces a severe cognitive paralysis. In addition to the impaired cognitive functioning, there is often typically a lead time to personally and organizationally recognize this as an issue and a problem before that can be turned into any kind of decision. This can take weeks or even over a month or two depending on the routines that are relied upon and agility. Even then, this led in turn to an action paralysis. In marketing theory this is called "AIDA" or:

- Awareness
- Interest
- Desire
- Action

all with time lags.

In this chapter, we look specifically at how uncertainty can cause and be generated by organizational change. This chapter is structured as follows:

- The change process
- Predicting adverse organizational events and fishbone analysis
- Root cause systems
- Organizational visioning and wishbone analysis
- Organizational shifts and FT analysis
- Organizational scenarios: Cases and uncertainty tunnels
- Key concluding insights

This is a mixture of analysis of the issues around a change situation and its context, and its dynamics.

The Change Process and Organizational Trajectories

While there is plenty of uncertainty in the environment (Chapters 1 to 4), *there is even more uncertainty in internal change.*

Around 35 years ago, change theory burst through to popularity with change gurus like Tom Peters and Rosa Beth Moss Kanter packing conference venues with managers eager to find the direction to plough the frontiers of change theory. Much of this work was highly prescriptive and suggestive of "if you do X well then you will get Y" (where Y meant "superior performance").

Change process models were typically staged, generic, and linear. For instance, Kotter's famous eight-stage model suggested that a major change goes through:

- Create urgency
- Build coalition
- Form strategic vision
- Enlist volunteers
- Enable and remove barriers
- Short-term wins
- Accelerate and sustain
- Institute(ionize) change

Reading that now, I think it needs to be summed up as "ESTD," a nice, catchy, and memorable acronym for "Easier Said than Done."

If I were an alien management consultant from outer space, I might have the following comments:

- So many stages? These humans have complex behaviors.
- The order seems rather random.
- Are we sure it is so linear?
- The process seems to be framed as something we *do* and with a high degree of control (in the original each step begins with a verb)—is that so?
- Is there anything important that is missing, for example, diagnosis and monitoring and control?

We can speculate about how a simpler process could look, for example:

- Diagnosis (enablers and constraints)
- Strategic vision
- Coalition building
- Small wins
- Accelerate and sustain

Simpler and better? Maybe. But still this revised and reordered process feels rather deterministic, directive, and linear, yet this is the standard model espoused by most business schools. In strategy terms, this is very much a deliberate strategy (see Figure 5.1, based on Henry Mintzberg) mode where there is the hope that we get from where we are now to where we want to be through some kind of a plan. It is not really in the model of emergence where the strategy tends to emerge over time as a pattern in a series of decisions or actions. But in reality, the alleged "pattern" is much less ordered than we see here in that figure *and even more so when we are talking about change*. And disorder means more uncertainty.

"Emergent strategy" is often far more common than the more rational forms of external strategy really allow for. But if you have spent some years in a corporate organization, you will almost certainly recognize that the predominant mode of strategy is more likely to be emergent rather than deliberate. That also means that it is likely to be very uncertain and may be inclined to drift according to the model in Figure 5.2 on the strategy mix.

Because of lack of clarity and agility surrounding organizational change, we have even more uncertainty, but strategic thinking mitigates uncertainty.

This also means that going through a strategic vision phase in a change strategy process may be too top down and ungrounded to really fuel a major change. It also highlights that change strategy might need to be relatively open and agile. It could even be a "contingent strategy" to be able to deal with heightened uncertainty than previously thought.

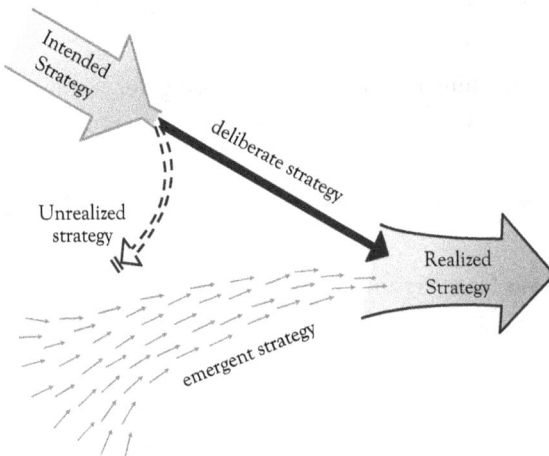

Figure 5.1 Some forms of strategy

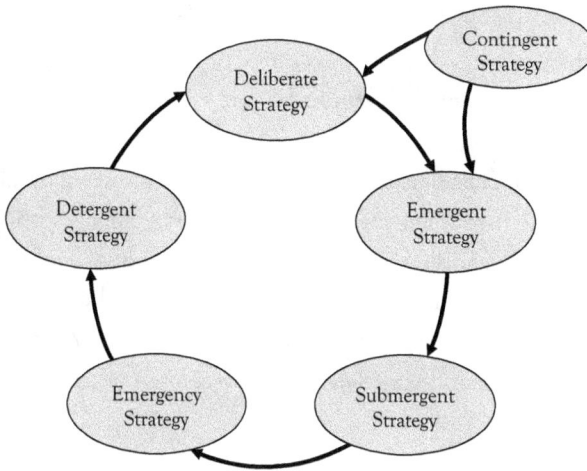

Figure 5.2 The Strategy mix

(A "contingent strategy" is one that needs to line up many factors before the strategy will crystallize in concrete action (Grundy 2014, 2018).)

Contingent strategies make a lot of sense—that you intend to pursue a course of action if and only if all the key alignment factors are lined up. This tackles uncertainty directly. *But that's tough when people within the organization are expecting clarity of direction and certitude.* The solution lies in very well-positioned communication and expectations set by the leadership.

But many managements models like Kotter's model are not really dynamic with the exception possibly of "accelerate or sustain" phase and invariably they are orientated around control, as opposed to observing organizational dynamics and picking just the right moment to stage an intervention. Speaking in 2022 and not in 1993 (see my book *Implementing Strategic Change*, Grundy 1993), I would now emphasize things like "readiness for change" and the sensing of the potential organizational trajectories than some set-piece deliberate change strategy.

In contrast to prescriptive change management strategies propagated by management gurus, Figure 5.3 was created for the Futures MBA project course at UCL School of Management. It depicts fluctuations in the rate of external change in several waves that result in lagged change internally. Such a dynamic would cause acute organizational stress and the internal curves, which depict slower reaction by the organization, might also suggest mounting strain. Unless the organization is extremely resilient, a vicious cycle might be triggered.

Another variable that might come into play is the effectiveness of internal change, which may fizzle off over time as the organization loses energy. The impact of interventions wears off, attention diluted, and energy is lost.

In conclusion, just like much uncertainty is encountered by a business in its external environment in a trajectory, internal changes bring much more uncertainty and volatility. Dynamic curves and storytelling can be just as valuable in that context as formulaic processes. Also, while external and internal change are subsystems impacted by uncertainty, they are very interdependent within themselves and between each other.

Reader Exercise

Using the picture of external and internal change we saw in Figure 5.3, what does that look like for your organization over the last 18 months to two years? What does this reveal about the stress the organization has had to deal with and how well that has been managed?

Predicting Adverse Organizational Events and Fishbone Analysis

We have already encountered fishbone analysis as a way of performing a cause-and-effect diagnosis in Chapter 2 (Figure 2.3). Fishbone analysis was typically used for diagnosing something that had gone wrong in the

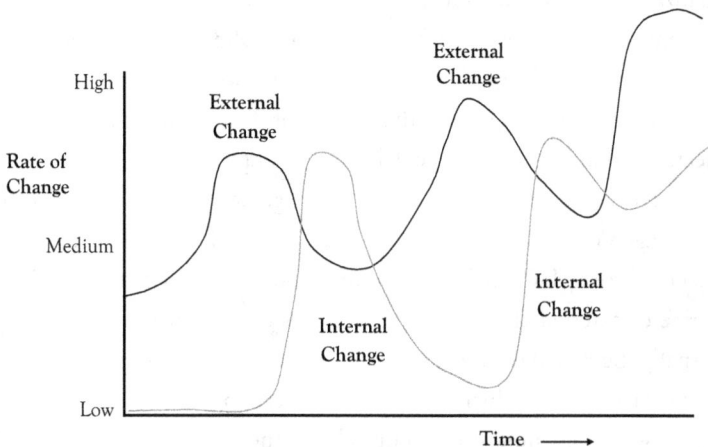

Figure 5.3 Rate of change curves

past. But equally it can be used for something that might go wrong in the future. So, one would be anticipating a future adverse event.

Remarkably, I had been a user of fishbone analysis for nearly 10 years before I realized that! Sometimes the best things are nonobvious. Here a future fishbone as a fictitious example is shown in Figure 5.4.

Here we see the future fishbone showing a number of future causes that might together trigger a major downsizing from root causes of organizational stresses might bring more weaknesses than amplified by the arrival of a new CEO and a major strategic review. Then in Figure 5.5 we see that fishbone flipped over to represent the knock-on effects, which looks like a simplified uncertainty tunnel.

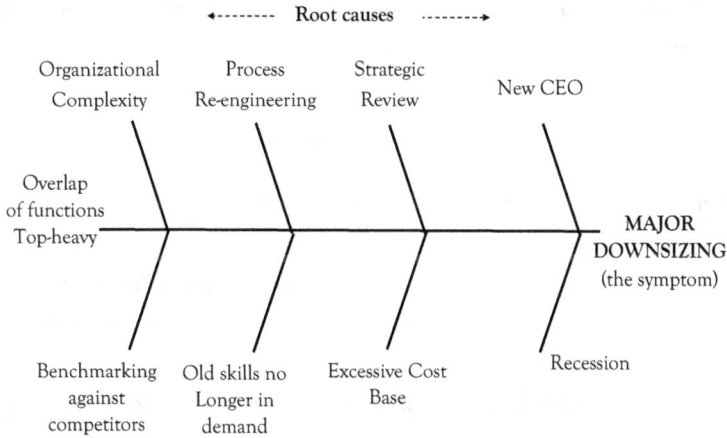

Figure 5.4 Future fishbone analysis—major downsizing

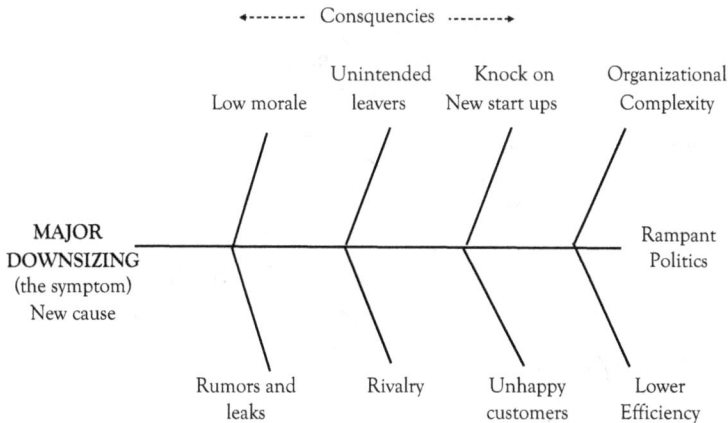

Figure 5.5 Reversed fishbone analysis—major downsizing

These two back-to-back techniques can be used either on a scrap of paper or in your head, but be warned that doing just the latter is a strain cognitively unless there are no more than five or six root causes on each picture. So, in conclusion, fishbone analysis of some future event can help one pre-sense the way in which that event might be brought about, hence mitigating uncertainty.

Reader Exercise

For some event in the future that would be adverse, what would the future root causes be, what early warning signals would you need to watch for, and what might you do now to avoid it or dampen it?

Where you have done a future reverse fishbone analysis, what might the impact be and how bad can it get?

Root Cause Systems Analysis

After using fishbone analysis for many years, I realized that many of the root causes were interdependent and I decided to see what I learned by drawing systems pictures of these causes. The result was "root cause systems analysis" (see Figure 5.6), which reframes the earlier future fishbone analysis (see Grundy 2003a).

Figure 5.7 is a vehicle for exploring the degree of stretch of a change that we will explore very soon.

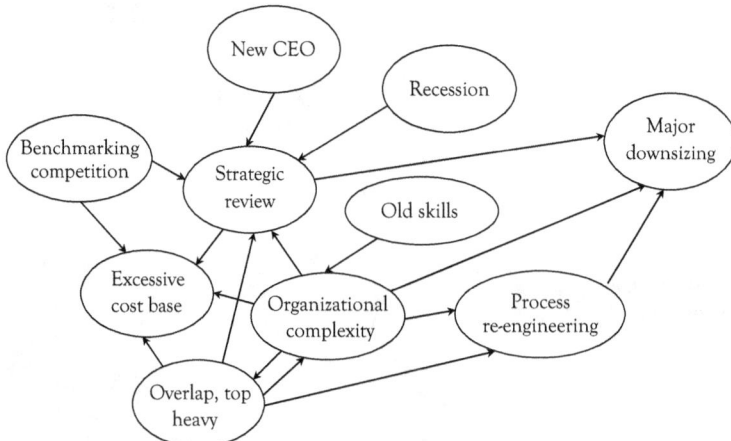

Figure 5.6 Root cause systems of future major restructuring

1 2 3 4 5

FROM TACTICAL		TO STRATEGIC
Short term focus*	1 to 3	Med/longer
Incremental*	2 to 4	Bigger picture
Internal only*	3 to 5	Internal and External
Cost focus*	3 to 5	Value focus
Getting things done*	2 to 4	Thinking/learning

Figure 5.7 Using From–To (FT) analysis—for change vision example

Just look at how a root cause systems analysis brings the future fish-bone analysis to life. The new CEO is the trigger of the strategic review along with the recession. The benchmarking against the competition is pivotal in a strategic repositioning entailing downsizing. Organizational complexity is another important knot within the fishbone network, with influences from "overlapping and top-heavy management," "old outdated skills," and also resulting in the need for business process engineering.

The picture was drawn quite quickly on a piece of paper in about three minutes as I already had a good sense of the overall structure and I only had to adjust and iterate a bit. Had the fishbone been more complex, I would have used little Post-its to play around with the design framework, The PowerPoint slide took about 30 minutes, so the process is pretty quick.

The picture's value comes mainly from its interpretation and its "so what?" How plausible is the event chain? What are the possible and maybe the likely trajectories in this future world? When might it come to pass? What scenario story lines can we talk about it and what are the critical issues?

I was just finishing that root causes systems analysis and my wife Carolina came in. After looking at it she said:

I was in a sharing meeting at work yesterday with other therapists and people were anxious about future change. I felt like saying, "Why don't you do one of Tony's Pictures of the Future and maybe it will all be less scary!"

She is a clinical psychologist. So she knows how being able to frame complex, threatening issues can mitigate potentially trauma here encountered in the context of a regular organizational meeting where discussions go around and around!

Reader Exercise

Construct a root cause systems picture for a problem that you think is foreseeable for the future (after doing a quick fishbone first). What does it tell you about that future? For example, its plausibility and what precursors and transitional events may be about to happen soon?

So, root cause systems can again help you and quickly to visualize the interactions of root causes, thus deepening the insights coming just out of a future fishbone.

Organizational Visioning and Wishbone Analysis

Not all uncertainty and change are around problems or things that have gone wrong, but they can be opportunities or even pictures of the ideal or organizational visions. Some three years into using fishbone analysis, I was working with insurance giant Aviva and a group of managers said to me that they wanted a breakdown of the positive causes of an ideal end result and wanted to turn the fishbone on its side, like a Christmas Tree. So we did and that vision was the fairy at the top and the baubles, which were the steps on the way. The resulting analysis was very useful and powerful and I logged that.

Initially, I thought of calling it "Christmas tree analysis," but if I did, it would have connotations of being once a year analysis. Then I had a better idea of calling it a "wishbone" analysis, which was not only just perfect as it was very "visionary" and it also rhymed. I decided to abandon a vertical tree shape for a reversed fishbone shape (like Figure 5.5). That way I could capitalize on the familiarity of the fishbone shape. The wishbone thus takes the user on a time travel journey that goes left to right and forward, not backward.

It became central to my mini strategy process (Grundy 2002a) for solving any strategic problem, the steps for which are as follows:

- Diagnosis: what are the problem's key symptoms and why is it a problem? (fishbone analysis)
- Vision: what do we really want and what are all the alignment factors sufficient to get there? (wishbone analysis)
- Evaluation: how attractive and difficult are these to do?
- Buy in: who are the stakeholders and what are their positions on these changes and how can we influence them (stakeholder analysis)? (see Chapter 6)

In this role, the wishbone analysis can help greatly in formulating strategy where the present is the starting point, but equally it can play a role when starting off with the future (see Figure 5.8) as a sequence going the other way-from present to future-this is displayed on Figure 5.9.

In a wishbone analysis this includes some things that Dyson has little control or influence over. It is really important that you don't just do a shopping list of things to do. *These are the necessary and sufficient conditions of the vision being realized.* This also means that you need to ask that golden question, "What is the one big thing we missed? to stress test its uncertainty?"

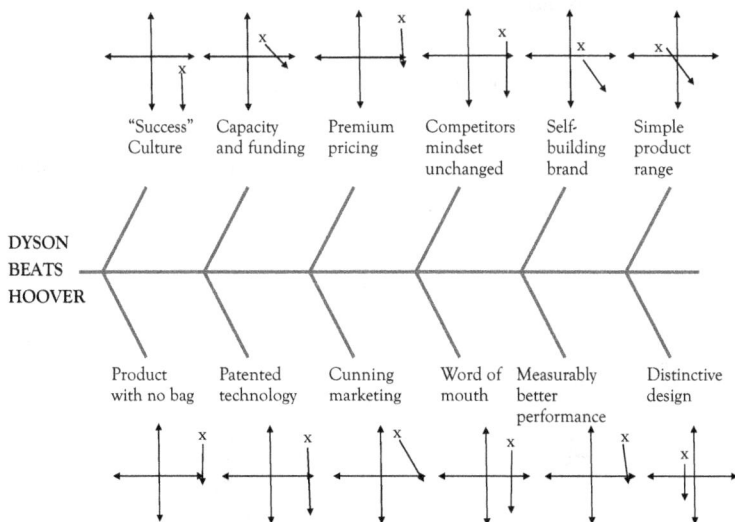

Figure 5.8 Wishbone analysis—with uncertainty grid overlay

Organizational Vision	Wishbone Analysis and Uncertainty Grids	From-To Analysis	Difficulty-Over-Time Curve(s)	Overall Uncertainty Evaluation

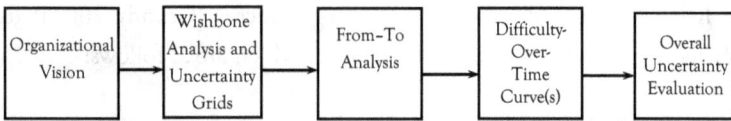

Figure 5.9 Process for evaluating the uncertainty of an organizational change

You may also wish to test the resilience of the wishbone to see what interdependences might kick in. Using two closely interrelated tools like wishbone analysis and multiple uncertainty grids for its alignment factors can do a great job for surfacing and evaluating the critical uncertainties underpinning a bold vision for organizational change.

Finally, these alignment factors can be tested with the uncertainty grid, which we are now so familiar. By now we are beginning to blur the domains of strategy and scenarios a bit, but that is not a bad thing given the epidemic of uncertainty affecting businesses since January 2020!

So, we have now shown you relatively quickly the hoof tools for exploring uncertain January 2020 and positive for potential organizational change.

Reader Exercise

For one area of opportunity, use wishbone analysis to define the necessary and sufficient factors that would need to align to deliver the expected result. Which factors are very important and very uncertain and why? To what extent is that within your sphere of influence? How resilient is the vision and its supporting strategy? How uncertain does it seem and why?

Not mentioned yet is strategic vision in relation to scenarios. Strategic visions are often far too broad, vague, and nonspecific and need to be tested for viability. To be resilient, they therefore really need to be tested against more than one state of the world. That means scenarios.

Organizational Shifts and FT Analysis

While there is considerable body of literature for organizational change, the frameworks tend to be either simplistic and prescriptive or are rather heavily theoretical, making it unsuitable at a practitioner level. I was fortunate to have been a member of the then Strategy Group at Cranfield School of Management where much work was being done into organizational paradigms way back ("how do we do things around here"). Ingredients here include systems, power structures, controls, rituals, routines, symbols, and stories too, a combination of "hard" and "soft" ingredients.

I for sure found it useful to gain a more theoretically complete diagnosis of the existing culture, but when dealing with deliberate or emergent culture shift, its diagnosis function didn't seem very realistic to me and my clients to cope with the uncertainties of change management. So, my preference was to have all that stuff in the back of my head as things to consider, and to then invest time and attention in constructing tailored, specific, and simple frameworks to capture cultural shifts and their dynamics. For sure, culture and broader organizational change was very uncertain indeed. (Around these earlier days, I was fortunate to work with people like BP, HP, the Prudential, Tesco, and, well you guessed it, the Metropolitan Police (time to go back soon?) so the model was well tested out.)

Ask managers the following questions:

- What shifts are you trying to make now breaking down the change? Expressed as descriptive from–to (FT) analysis (see earlier)?
- Where are you now (score out of e.g., a 5 or a 10)?
- Where do you want to be?
- What's the gap and how can we bridge that?
- What are the key uncertainties? (the "uncertainty grid")?

Organizational scenarios can then be brought in through storytelling: for instance, how the change went smoothly, or was derailed, or simply died a slow and quiet death see Figure 5.10.

Actually, I did tell stories about the future to the Chief People Officer of a new bank in the UK around 2015 about the possible dilution of its customer-obsessed culture to the effect that "Your greatest uncertainty is that this will corrode as you grow and there is turnover of staff and you end up just like the rest." In late 2022, the bank messed up two payments and sent me a vague letter of apology when I needed an explanation. It took five calls to get their investigator to ring me up.

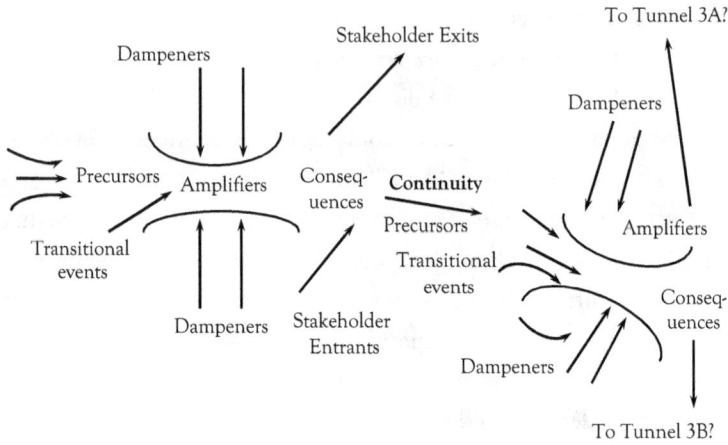

Figure 5.10 Multiple uncertainty tunnels—for organizational change

It was truly an awful experience and most revealing, sufficient for me to diagnose the culture drift. It just goes to show how prescient organizational storytelling can help you become. Eventually I was satisfied they had learnt a lesson.

In conclusion, even when dealing with major organizational changes, there are still ways of getting to grips with softer uncertainties that otherwise promise to be "wicked."

To loop back to our theme of uncertainty though the added value from–to analysis over and above its strategic planning role is that it helps to surface more of the underlying uncertainty through separating out the uncertainty of:

• Where we are now? (broken down by separate dimensions);
• The feasibility of achieving the total vision;
• Likely resilience of the organizational breakthroughs to accomplish these shifts.

Thus, it is better to perform a much more robust test of resilience than relying on a kind of Nietzschean "will to power" of Boldly posing a vision and just hoping for the best! (Nietzsche, the philosopher's work, of 1902).

In summary, another two dimensions of uncertainty of organizational change can be identified, which deal with the current position and the gap between that position and goals and across different organizational interventions, too. Each of these frames the dynamics of uncertainty in a change context and thus thinking about the degree of assumed stretch in relation to the impact on uncertainty is a very healthy thing to do.

An astute reader might have spotted here that a good sequence of thinking steps could be:

- The wishbone analysis with the uncertainty grids broken down
- A from–to analysis, see figure 5.7, to surface the gap and to reality check against the assumed breakthrough interventions (for example, a top team building event, strategic planning process, senior management development process, new 360-degrees performance management process)
- Possibly too, the difficulty-over-time curves for the change breakthroughs individually or consolidated, or both
- Finally, the overall uncertainty evaluation (no specific tools)

See again Figure 5.8 earlier.

Organizational Scenarios—Cases and Uncertainty Tunnels

In this section, I now look at a couple of organizational case studies and how organizational change can go through not just one but two or several uncertainty tunnels, thus moving us back to dynamic analysis. I have revisited the uncertainty tunnel, which we saw in Figure 3.10, on generic scenarios as one set less linear and more turbulent environment. This depicts the use of two uncertainty tunnels with the second one splitting the organization into a new direction. After that, there is either a return to the original direction (scenario tunnel 3A) or a twist even further down the way (scenario tunnel 3B—detailed tunnels not shown due to space constraints). An example of the first part of this is the organizational changes by John Lewis Partnership, a major UK retailer, between 2019 and 2022 shifting the business toward online. In some ways, it led to a tension of organizational models. So we have a version somewhere between 3A and 3B-see Figure 5.10.

Note that I added a new feature—stakeholder entrants and exits—so that the power base of the organization is shifting either in an adaptive of no adaptive way, or a mixture of both.

Such pictures are, of course, rather abstract without some storytelling, but are useful to frame the thinking, of course. So how can we make one up? Well, at the time of writing (June 2022), a change pending is the transition within the British royalty, more specifically a change in the monarchy. Despite her resilience, HRM the Queen is 96 in 2022. According to Google's actuarial tables, her chances of making 101 in five years' time are about 4 percent. So, her passage with us is very likely to be over sadly in those five years skewed toward 2024 to 2026.

There are already plans for the wife of Prince Charles, Camilla, to have the special status of Princess Consort. But what else? The world knows that the next generation has had somewhat mixed experiences in adulthood and that at times the Queen has been displeased with certain chains of events. There has been media commentary to the effect that there seems to be a top-heavy structure of the monarchy, which is expensive. *This story has not been changed to reflect the sad events of September 8, 2022—it was written late spring 2022.*

I am not going to draw my pictures for the story of royalty ahead such as the curves of external change and internal change (are certain features anachronisms?), but I feel certain that the "family" may be listening much more to the outside world.

I have a personal little story to suggest that behind the façade, there is a lot of humanness part based on experience. When Prince Charles was about to get married the second time, he needed to do it in a registry wedding, not in a cathedral. My then (second) wife spotted that the couple were to be married in such a wedding in Windsor. She said reading her mail, "OMG, the registrar for Charles and Camilla is going to be the one we had in High Wycombe." So I wrote to Prince Charles to say that they were going to be in good hands:

We are delighted to tell you that far from moving downmarket to us commoners you are in for a wonderful experience. When Clair married us in 2002, she was incredibly flexible—even allowing us to have a cardboard cut-out of Sven Erickson, then England football manager, as an extra witness.

My letter finished with two postscripts:

PS: Maybe you can get a similar cardboard cut-out of the Queen who I don't think wants to come for some strange reason.

PS: If you do have need of a strategy adviser (which I do for a living), I guess I could do a special rate for royals.

In early 2023, I did spot Prince Harry might need some advice after his book critical of the family was published. For sure not endearing him to his father King Charles. Now that's an opportunity to story tell—the future of the monarchy!

Weeks went past and the couple were married. Then out of the blue, I got an unusually posh envelope with HMR, which I mistook for HMRC tax, from Prince Charles' Assistant.

Clearly Prince Charles had been highly amused by the letter and clarified that the Queen had been there in St. George's Chapel.

Well, if I were to be his strategy consultant, what story might I tell?

In 2022, after Russia reached a stalemate in Ukraine and refused to retreat after a ceasefire, an uneasy peace broke out. The COVID hangover lingered and dragged the economy down along with unprecedented high inflation rate. Dissent resumed in politics, but Prime Minister Boris Johnson clung onto power. Yet from several directions there came voiced abhorrence to the decline in British values. At the same time, economic scarcity and general unhappiness came to bite more and more (Uncertainty Tunnel 1).

Sadly, the Queen finally passes away in 2022 of old age, and the country was deeply moved. *There is a very deep sense of great loss shared by nearly all, in fact an emotional and cultural shock unparalleled since D-Day in the Second World War, causing the entire nation to rethink its identity and core values* (Uncertainty Tunnel 2). This impacts the country's attitudes to privilege and inequality and its colonial heritage. There are two days of public holidays (Day 1 to mourn and Day 2 to look afresh). Charles rolls out his plan that was agreed with the Queen before her death for:

- Downsizing the core of the family;
- Modernizing some of its routines and rituals;

- Clarification of its roles and added value;
  (The behind the scenes work for this change was done by
  a bunch of business school facilitators, Gerry Johnson (my
  former PhD supervisor) and Kevan Scholes, who I also
  know, and even myself (?), all using the culture web, scenario
  storytelling, and change interventions (it isn't really a job for a
  big consultancy firm!—too impersonal));
- Greater focus on efficiency and value for money;
- An adventurous PR strategy going forward.

This forms Uncertainty Tunnel 3; during which the roles of the key players in the royal family, namely the princes and their wives, are adjusted and the actual implementation process takes place throughout Buckingham Palace.

In a subscenario (a possible subplot within this story's context), there are couple of years of ridding government of the shadiness that surrounded Party-Gate during COVID and the apparent corruption surrounding many government contracts associated with COVID (Uncertainty Tunnel 4).

Another subscenario might be that either the royal family headed by King Charles is seen as being more relevant, grounded, and more central to UK culture, or this might be seen as weakly led with much behind the scenes bickering. Partly that might depend upon the balance of opinion with the over forties being very pro-Charles and Co. and the under-thirties not quite seeing the point of it much at all. That would all need checking out with some opinion leaders and maybe some empirical research (calling for more data).

How's that for a start? Some useful insights? Should I send it to Prince Charles? Will he actually reply? What are the scenarios for how he might respond and how is the timing of sending it likely to impact its trajectory (stakeholder scenario)?

In conclusion, we can see now why organizational change can be even more volatile than market or environmental uncertainty. There can be a disproportionate reaction to any change within or outside the system. The effect can differ too much depending on the timing of events. For example, if the above shift were to happen, say in 2022, 2023 or 2024, what with a next General Election? Also, there will be parallel stories, for example, on the economy, the pandemic, Ukraine and Russia, and other global political issues, and energy and climate change maybe having a further shaping influence.

But is that all just too much to think about? I don't think so. To give in would be like turning your windscreen wipers and headlights off in a snowstorm.

On Thursday, September 8, 2022, when I heard the saddest news that the Queen had passed away, I had no deep sense of surprise as I had time traveled to the future so cognitively that I felt great preparedness. I did not feel disorientated and that clarity dampened the feeling of shock, yet there was still a deep sense of shared sadness. I felt okay to move on at both levels. I feel that I responded with less disruption and more acceptance and eagerness to move through the change. Without doubt, I was more resilient without being uncaring. Scenarios can for sure prepare yourself for emotional as well as cognitive futures. I guess it depends on the degree of immediate loss and its meaning in running emotional scenarios—when our dog Max was put down recently even though I thought I was prepared I wasn't—but one thing missing was seriously putting an actual date on that in my story telling—a lesson.

I would like to bring back the idea of organizational scenarios now to businesses in the next case study.

A Scenario Breakthrough—a Story From a Client

Some time ago, I was coaching a young but Senior Director of a large IFA Division of a larger insurance company. We will call him Jeff, as he isn't responding to LinkedIn messages! He was a big convert to the scenario approach as a vehicle for strategic thinking. Indeed, when working with him and his team, on one occasion, they wanted to do some organizational futures, which I emphasized in this book. It was a tall order as we could only find 60 minutes for the particular challenge. So, I split the process up into five steps with a number of minutes for each one (prespecified).

They worked well as a strategic team and used their time wisely and didn't go off in unproductive directions. At the end, they did an incisive presentation of the thought process that culminated in a picture of the future organizational shape married to business success factors and aligned with the configuration of the stakeholders aid their agendas. *The exercise was planned for 60 minutes with five stages and the number of minutes set for each*. It was brilliantly incisive and after the applause and my feedback, I asked Jeff what he took away from that and he replied:

> Well, that's about to happen—that's one thing. But the other thing is how incredible to work through a process like that in just an hour.

Jeff was also one of those rare managers who found it easy and natural to do storytelling. But there was one particular story he told me that will stick in my memory forever:

> Last November, we had a Senior Management Team meeting in which we were discussing how we were doing. I had grown increasingly concerned that after a bumper year that we might have a dip early in the next year as we drifted into a little complacency.
>
> So, at the meeting I said to them:
>
> Guys, would you mind me thinking aloud...
>
> In the last couple of weeks, I keep having a repeating dream. In it we ended the first eleven months with some fantastic results. At the end of year sales conference and mass party, we will all get seriously drunk and we will still feel hung over in early January. In the New Year, things will go slow and that will be aggravated by a big freeze and deep snow so that our client visits are much lower as the cars are stuck on drives. By the time we get the January results, we will be all panic-stricken so that February and March are very high stress months.
>
> And as I was talking, their heads were bobbing up and down like the little dogs you see in cars.
>
> So, I asked them "What's the 'so what' of that?"
>
> What do you mean? they asked.
>
> Well, it's going to happen, isn't it?

Yes. They all said.

So, what are we going to do about it, then?

A classic ending! Always draw out the implications of a scenario story.

Reader Exercises

- For your organization, what assumptions underpin its success over the next three years and where are these positioned on the uncertainty grid?
- What scenarios can you foresee as a result of those most important and uncertain and fleshed out with the uncertainty tunnel?

Key Insights

This chapter was once again rich with many insights:

- Organizational change is particularly uncertain as the strategy mix for change is often emergent and ambiguous and there is no set best change process.
- An integrated process as given in Figure 5.7 can be really helpful.
- Storytelling is a really rich way of deep diving into some dynamic possibilities.
- This is made harder when there is some event that is particularly sensitive to think about like the Queen's passing away. Nevertheless, pushing through that discomfort barrier can be very helpful.
- Such stories may well break into subscenarios.
- Scenario storytelling is an essential ingredient in strategic visioning.
- Once again, we see the various recipes for guiding foresight and becoming more farsighted do help us make strides in managing uncertainty.

- With an effective process, a good team, and a suitable facilitator, much value and insights can be derived surprisingly quickly.
- One of the key points of storytelling is using it to actually decide what you need to do differently.

CHAPTER 6

Decision—Specific Uncertainties and Scenarios

Introduction

So, by now we have looked at why uncertainty is such a problem and how it can be dissolved by looking at the challenges of the Ukraine invasion, COVID-19 (via online), and getting a taste of scenarios with the Shell process (in Chapter 1). We then considered concepts for conceiving of the journey through time with the arrow of time in Chapter 2. In that same chapter, we considered what tools could help us to get out of the uncertainty fog such as the uncertainty grid. We then went much deeper into the nature and the root causes of uncertainty with examples and reader exercises. We then went through a stage-by-stage a process very similar to the Shell model.

Chapter 3 then caused us to rethink the other tools and processes such as storytelling with the case of the War in the Pacific. To help uncover further the infrastructure, we need to create scenarios. We got further help in this chapter from some of the more usual strategy tools like PEST, growth drivers, and the competitive forces unified in the strategic onion frameworks, and also some less obvious like the systems picture and from–to analysis.

The dynamic aspects were dealt with by deploying variables over time curves, like uncertainty-over-time. The time dimension also took us into how fast positioning could be changed over time with the idea of "strategic mobility" and also by bringing in the concept of "industry clock speed" for assessing the evolutionary speed of that industry too.

Chapter 5 took us through the special challenges of dealing with the uncertainties surrounding the vexed problem of organizational change with tools like future fishbone analysis, from–to analysis, wishbone analysis for visioning sequenced as a mini process. We then had an initial shot at some most interesting storytelling of future change in the British monarchy 2002–2007.

The next sections take us through a number of other difficult areas of strategic management that are typically characterized by high levels of uncertainty such as:

- Uncertainty and economic value creation/destruction
- Acquisitions
- Alliances
- International strategies
- Marketing strategies
- Innovation and technology
- Key insights

The format we will follow will be:

- Most common tools applicable
- Particularly sensitive assumptions and uncertainties
- Application

Generally, I will do a short introduction to each one to highlight, from the nature of the topic, what the impact might be on uncertainty. A common theme will be the importance of behavioral influences, so you have to be something of a psychologist to surface many of the key uncertainty drivers (or at least, psychologically aware).

Uncertainty and Economic Value Creation/Destruction

"Economic value" is a term used to mean "the management of a corporate, business or project's net cash flow over time to secure a positive return over the Cost of Capital, given the strategic and other assumptions which are reasonable given Uncertainty" (see also Grundy 2002b).

So, this means a number of important things:

- We are not using profit as a measure but adjusted to get as close as possible to seeing the subject of our analysis as cash based (so we add back any depreciation as that's not cash).
- Money has a time value—cash in the future has a net present value lower later than now.
- Capital isn't free; it has a cost, like rent—how to calculate that is complex and outside our scope (see Grundy 2002b for more). That cost does carry a charge for uncertainty and risk (like a kind of insurance premium) and that has to do with the variance of the sector a business is in relative to the volatility of the stock market. It does not factor in business or project-based risk as that will be tested for when playing with the assumptions and modeling the effect.
- The assumptions are crucial in determining EVA, especially the strategic ones (Grundy 2002b).

The Most Common Tools Applicable

The strategic onion model, growth drivers, competitive forces, business value system, the strategic option grid, the uncertainty grid, the value-over-time curve, scenario storytelling, particularly for assessing the value of the ongoing cash streams after the end of the forecasting period (often 10 years but variable).

Particularly Sensitive Assumptions and Uncertainties

- Sales growth rate
- Operating profit (with depreciation added back) margin
- The rate of incremental working capital investment
- Fixed assets investment

- The corporate tax rates
- The cost of capital (debt and risk capital)
- The competitive advantage over time curve

These variables are drawn from EVA (economic value added) theory and will need embellishing for the specific situation and context.

In addition to the aforementioned assumptions, which are generic, they are also specific to the business like regulatory and competitive change and so on. They are heavily weighted toward the quantitative and need embedding in strategic assumptions and thinking and the value drivers.

Application

Modeling, gaming (of other players for example new entrants versus incumbents, bidders for licenses etc.)

Final note: Often managers get sucked into the numbers and playing with the numbers for example, what would the effect of tweaking one or more variables by + or – 10 percent be on net present value (EVA metric). A far better approach is to use the uncertainty grid to tease out the most volatile variables and hopefully to do some scenario storytelling, and then and only then to:

- Test for +or – percent according to that perceived volatility (15 percent or 20 percent?); and
- To do tolerance testing: how bad could a variable get before the net present value is wiped out?

A more specific application is to EVA is protective value. When investment cash flows are not incremental as compared with now, but if you don't do it, they will decline. While there is a logic for that by exception if all investment is of that nature, you have a problem. When people allude to intangibles, they often mean that. Where you are protecting against a very unlikely event, the value can be assessed just like an insurance premium.

Reader Exercise

For a business case you are about to propose or to review or for a reasonably recent one that might have some uncertainties:

- What are the really key external and internal assumptions that underpin the uncertainty (try to set the parameters as specifically as possible)?
- Which are most important and uncertain and with those that are "most"; what is the impact of a major variance from expectations? What is the "so what" for the strategy for this? For adapting it for greater agility, maybe adopt a "contingent" strategy?

Acquisitions

Acquisitions are a particularly tricky area and which are often very uncertain due to a number of factors. For instance, we have imperfect information, especially in the form of asymmetric information: the seller typically knows a lot more about the nature of the beast than the buyer; and that is after "due diligence" too! (Grundy 2003b).

I often explain this to people with the analogy of searching for a partner or "possible wife designates" midlife (effectively the "second hand market"). I listed 13 criteria on the back of a Tesco Couscous packet including things like:

- Professional
- Attractive
- Bright
- Not low on energy

and so on.

During the Future 1 of the relationship (the first nine months when I was high on that natural substance oxytocin), I believed that they were all met, but the cracks in the relationship were beginning to show. Yet my commitment level was maintained sufficient to carry me along to the actual wedding, which was fun, as you know, with the cardboard cut-out story I told earlier. But looking back at the end, only four criteria were fulfilled and very partially and went down over time.

As I have said, I did remarry (brave me), but this time around I did 12 criteria, which were much clearer and specific. Each criterion was supported by five subcriteria (that's 60 in all!) and I have secured a very happy result! On her part, my present (and permanent) wife had five totally non-negotiable things she needed and also did little behavioral experiments to test me out—very cunning! She is a clinical psychologist and was taking great care in her choice, which is very sensible indeed! She even set up little "tests" to see if what she saw was what she was really getting! *All these measures reduced uncertainty, again emphasizing that we often have much control over uncertainty.*

The analogy with the situation of acquisitions is very strong indeed as much of the drivers of uncertainty are down to three things:

1. Lack or complete and accurate data
2. How people may behave when events come up
3. Emotional commitment levels

So, many of the drivers of uncertainty are emotional. In the case of acquisitions, there is much emotion too as it is very much about the escalation of commitment through the "due diligence" process. After that, there is rapid onset of the syndrome of "I can't face thinking and admitting that I got this wrong." The scenario tools are brilliant in getting hold of such wicked uncertainties and led me to my present wife.

More generally for acquisitions, game theory proves useful when you are sizing up either the vendor or the possible buyers and their relative bargaining power and how that might shift over time. There is also competitor positioning, intent, and agendas to buy the target and all as a game.

Most Common Tools Applicable

These are the strategic onion, competitive forces, the business value system, the strategic option grid, the uncertainty grid, the value-over-time curve, and the difficulty-over-time curve.

In addition, anyone seriously engaged in acquisitions should seriously read up on acquisitions. When I wrote *Mergers and Acquisitions* in 2002, there were only a few examples to show, but there is an embarrassment of riches now. Otherwise, it's like playing with fire without a fire extinguisher if you have never done one before.

Particularly Sensitive Assumptions and Uncertainties

There are many critical assumptions, including the following:

- The continued level of commitment and from whom both before and after the acquisition
- The assumed economic value that will be generated
- The capability of the target is strong
- The acquisition capability of the acquirer is also strong in the preacquisition evaluation, in negotiating a deal, and postacquisition
- The shape of the actual, "difficulty-over-time" curve is near to what was expected
- There are no really big disturbances to the macro environment (e.g., political, economic, and social)
- Equally the competitive structure and behaviors are quite steady
- Key staff in either organization don't leave

An example of a contemporary possible acquisition appeared in the press on March 26, 2022. It was reported that Boots Chemists was up for sale (again). Both Boots and Alliance Unichem, which is part of Boots, were both clients. So, they were are of natural interest to me. The price floated was *£7 billion*, which struck me as an extremely "full" price. Without deep diving into this business's details, Boots has an enviable high-street presence that has been very protected for over 30 or maybe even 50 years! In its last financial year, the *Mail* reported profits of Boots of just £131 million, which is an impressive price earnings ratio (share price divided by earnings per share).

I looked at this through the lens of the uncertainty grid. The key assumptions I make to get remotely near such a valuation are:

- There won't be strong incursion from online—medium important and very uncertain.
- Base profits are not to distorted by lucrative COVID tests and other COVID-related products—medium importance and medium uncertainty. Boots' market share won't be eroded through Lidl and or Aldi entering the market (that's not happened, which surprises me).
- Customer service in Boots is sufficient to protect them against players with lower prices or better service or both—lower/medium importance, high uncertainty.
- There are other possible areas of sales growth e.g. through ASDA's latest owners taking it over and putting the Boots brand into the store. That seems theoretical too. ASDA pharmacy is not that big an operation and I would be very shocked to find that such extra sales at the margin would be worth shelling out say £0.5 billion to £1 billion!

Verdict: if offered £8 billion, take it and run!

A good reality test would be to see if a realistic scenario storyline could possibly be constructed to deliver that valuation.

Applications

These include valuation modeling, scenario storytelling, preacquisition workshop, integration workshops.

Reader Exercise

For an acquisition that your company has made, what were the explicit and implicit assumptions that were made? Where did these assumptions sit at the time on the uncertainty grid and looking back now, where should these assumptions have really been, and what are the "so whats?" of this?

Alliances

While an acquisition is a full-blown "we are getting married" proposition, an alliance is much more open. It resembles a long-term relationship. In terms of my "strategy mix" typology, there is likely to be more of an emergent element than an acquisition. Also, the contingent strategy could well have more of a role. Ceteris paribus, *this suggests that it will be more uncertain and riskier than an acquisition*, provided that the acquisition criteria (the do's, the don'ts, and the might do's) are developed and applied well. Also, it works well if the alliance's strategy has been deeply thought through.

Also, while acquisitions are heavily subject to behavioral uncertainties, alliances are perhaps even more so, as they rely that much more on common understanding, trust, and complementarity, and less on structural control. *So, the uncertainties are likely to be that much more behavioral.* This all means in turn that stakeholder agendas and analysis are even more important.

Most Common Tools Applicable

These would include: the strategic onion, Porter's five competitive forces (especially for the strategic option grid, understanding the relative balance of power and influence and how that may change over time), stakeholder analysis (see Chapter 7, the difficulty and value-over-time curves, the uncertainty grid and scenario storytelling.

In addition, the uncertainty tunnel might well come in on a just-in-time basis as the alliance moves into a new and emerging state of development with, for instance new top management changes (if it is a separate organization, its CEO and Directors may well serve less time than a more "settled" organization, resulting in internal discontinuity). Also, external change can be greater, especially if the organization's markets, technologies, and products are still formative as in many alliances.

The conventional mindset for judging acquisitions against alliances' relative levels of uncertainty is often that acquisitions are fraught with higher risk and uncertainty. Personally, I feel that this is more to do with the generally higher degree of commitment once a company has been bought. But that for me is more of a psychological state. But if we regard uncertainty as more to do with the probability of getting a bad result, alliances are less strong candidates. Also, with acquisitions the due diligence process is likely to be much stronger and the control in postacquisition much firmer.

Particularly Sensitive Assumptions and Uncertainties

These include:

- The inherent market attractiveness of the alliance's markets is high and sustainable.
- The capability of the alliance's management team is strong.
- The relative commitment of the partners to the venture is sustained.
- There will be no significant falling out in the team or between partners.
- The strategic and financial positions of the various partners aren't likely to deteriorate such that they might wish to pull out.
- If there are new partners coming in or other changes, then this can be managed smoothly.

Reader Exercise

Just as we have done for business cases generally and for acquisitions, what does the uncertainty grid tell us about the impact of uncertainty on the decision.

Applications

Strategic workshops with scenario development (external or internal), or both: business and financial modeling (this can be just or nearly as important here as for an acquisition).

International Strategies

For a discussion on international alliances, see Online Appendix 4.

Marketing Strategy

Also, for marketing strategies, these are frequently uncertain as they are dependent on the assumed behaviors of:

- Customers
- Markets
- Competitors
- Company staff

And these factors interact with each other in complex ways. For instance, customers' buying patterns will be shaped in part by what is available old and new in the market. Also shifts in what customers want to and need to buy will in the aggregate shape market demand and growth.

New competition may help grow the market or might cause much greater price competition, thus deflating demand as per volume times price. The market may autonomously be inclined to grow, but this might be impaired by the insular behavior of staff who "can't be asked to provide half decent customer service." The behavior of staff within companies is often a root cause of market growth brakes.

Figure 6.1 depicts the interaction of the market behaviors within a more key behavior that generates uncertainty. To use it, simply list the key behaviors that are most important in each box and then look at the interdependencies between them. This is a good preparation too for doing a growth driver picture that we saw in Figure 3. 4. I have called this memorably "MBA analysis" after "market behavior analysis."

Reader Exercise

Try out the MBA analysis out from Figure 6.1 for one of your markets, especially one which is rather uncertain. Make sure that you think deeply enough about the interdependences between each box. Allow enough

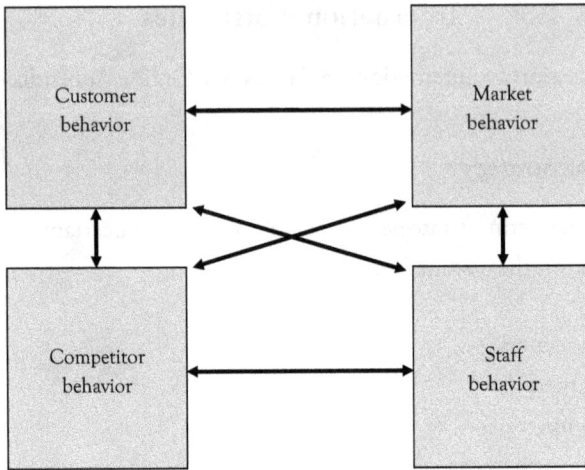

Figure 6.1 Market Behavior Analysis (MBA)

time for that as there are four boxes and ten interdependencies as the arrows go both ways. So that's 14 things to consider. What does this tell you about the interrelationships you see?

Most Common Tools Applicable

These are:

The strategic onion model, growth drivers, Porter's five forces, "MBA" analysis, strategic option grid, uncertainty grid, uncertainty tunnels, and finally we really mustn't forget the wishbone analysis for looking at all the alignment factors that are needed.

Particularly Sensitive Assumptions and Uncertainties

Perhaps the hardest thing to get one's head around is how customers might respond to changes in the behavioral environment, particularly to economic shifts, for example, in prices. For instance, at the fag end of 2022 will customers in the UK be severely curtailing their spending on discretionary spending like meals out, holidays, clothing, or will they be running savings down to part pay for these? Will that then turn into an even more cut back later as reality sinks in! To get a better sense of how consumers (whether these are end customers or business customers) will behave differently or not, try to have the "out-of-body experience" of being them as it were.

Reader Exercise

For a past, present, or future marketing strategy, what does the uncertainty grid tell you about its vulnerability?

Applications

For creating Marketing strategy, brand strategy, product development strategy, customer service strategy

Innovation and Technology Strategy

Innovation and technology strategy can be particularly uncertain as these depend on both market uncertainty (see the last section and also the supply side ("will it work and how will it work?")) and also the costs of an innovation or a new technology. Finally, it is unlikely that if you are onto something really good, no one else has spotted that. And even if they haven't yet, how quickly will they discover it and imitate it? That takes one into the dynamics of uncertainty.

Most Common Tools Applicable

Here we might invoke:

The strategic onion model, growth drivers, Porter's five forces, strategic option grid, uncertainty grid, the difficulty-over-time curve, the uncertainty tunnels, and finally wishbone analysis for looking at all the alignment factors that are needed. Scenario storytelling is up there at the top here, too.

In addition, it is often possible to get some early view of the future through looking to other industries or countries who are already some ways down the road in taking up innovative ideas and exploiting them commercially. By identifying and understanding some early adopters, it can be possible to peer into the future.

Particularly Sensitive Assumptions and Uncertainties

These include:

- The timing to take it to market is not too soon and not too late.
- The proposition isn't just prima facie plausible but also is grounded in concrete actual added value to the customer.
- We are targeting the right people in the market.
- The overall strategy is based on a genuinely "cunning plan."
- Which is not imitable at all, or at least without considerable difficulty.
- The economics including investment, revenues, margins and costs make sense.
- The life cycle is not too short, nor is the product in need of very frequent and expensive imitation.
- We are not likely to lose the brains behind this to a competitor who may offer something that people won't find irresistible.
- There is "no one big thing we forgot."

Another example of change for technology happened on March 16, 2022. Dyson, another old client, announced a new headquarters (HQ) in Singapore. This had been mooted for some time. So it wasn't a big surprise. Dyson's main HQ has been traditionally in Malmsbury, South West England, close to its founder James Dyson's home. It is true that many young engineers were not grabbed by the very rural environment around there. On top of that, for digital revolution, a better area (see international strategy above) like Singapore might have been far more conducive for enabling easier recruitment and retention of top technology skills. There are, however, some assumptions that need probing here such as:

- The time difference won't be too great to get in the way (medium important—down with greater homeworking?—and very uncertain).

- Senior management moved out there won't mind not having gardens, the local education, the lifestyle, the heat, being so far from the UK. So, they won't want to come back after just two years—very important and very uncertain.
- The one off and ongoing extra costs won't greatly dilute any benefits—very important and very uncertain.

Verdict: I would like to know a lot more for example; do they have an organizational strategy for this relocation and how resilient is that? Maybe I need to call them (again)?

Reader Exercise

For a past, present, or future innovation and/or technology strategy innovation, what does the uncertainty grid tell you about its vulnerability?

Applications

Innovation workshops, business cases.

Key Concluding Insights

- While there is a different set assumption for each decision, for specific area, the tools are often quite similar.
- The uncertainty grid has to be central though and immensely useful not just for taking a snapshot but for tracking over time so that learning is heightened.
- The positions of assumptions on the grid are very likely to be informed by other tools like the strategic onion so that the value and cost drivers of the business case are shaped by the wider economic and competitive environment.
- When doing sensitivity analysis, let this be driven by the positionings of assumptions on the uncertainty grid and true stress and resilience tests not as arbitrary + or − 10 percent tests, for example.
- Uncertainty around acquisitions can be very helpfully targeted using the "three Vs" of acquisitions—the inherent value of the

strategy, the value added/lost in the deal, and value added/lost for integration value.

- For both alliances and acquisitions, there are likely to be a lot of assumptions that are of a behavioral nature that need testing on the uncertainty grid.
- International strategies are relatively uncertain as they have not just the imponderables of strategy but also those of international strategy to deal with, making them disproportionately uncertain. This can be made even worse with acquisitions or alliances as we would now have three levels of uncertainty going on—business, international, and the structure of strategic deals.
- Surprise (or not)!—Marketing strategies generally have a lot of imponderables and uncertainties—this is the land of behavioral factors par excellence.
- Innovation and technology strategies are also very susceptible to uncertainty as we have two levels here—external, market-related, and internal.

CHAPTER 7

Behavioral Scenarios, Stakeholders, and Role Playing

Introduction

This chapter takes a "deep dive" into the world of stakeholders and their agendas, which play a massive role in shaping behaviors as well as decisions and actions, which in turn cause uncertainty.

But before we get into the different angles on stakeholders, let's first be clear what we mean by them. I define a "stakeholder" as being "either a decision maker, or an influencer, or an implementor or a victim of some decision or action." So, they can belong to different segments given that their power and influence may be quite different in not just strength but nature too. For instance, their influence can be positive or negative, and they may also show passive resistance. But whatever its strength or nature, ignore it at your own peril.

I go into stakeholders here in depth as they are a major cause of uncertainty wherever you look in the social world. This chapter is structured as follows:

- A change management case at P&O Ferries
- The out-of-body experience
- A legal case
- Psychological factors (normal and abnormal)

Later I look at how stakeholders and their agendas interplay with one another at BT via an online case study 4 based on my behavioral research and a final case study of scenario role plays with Amerada Petroleum, and other material.

Short Case Study: P&O

P&O, a UK ferry company, made 800 employees redundant in 2022 without proper consultation, which set off multiple explosions of rage. The justification was that the company was trading at a loss. It replaced them with agency staff (drawn from other countries) who were paid £5.50 an hour. Did its CEO actually do any scenarios as to where would eruptions happen next?

It seemed as if the board hadn't done any real stakeholder analysis, which might have included not only the staff and the unions but also:

- Parliament;
- Key government departments with contracts with them and also the agencies for health and safety, the media, and TV and press;
- Local councils who had supported the company;
- The shareholders who would now be tarred with investing in an uncaring company.

Within days, the CEO was cross-examined in front of a very angry House of Commons committee to explain his actions and was forced to admit that the way that the decision was implemented was illegal. I thought: "I will bet that he will only be going out for the evening to the pub or for a meal for the foreseeable future with a bag over his head."

I doubt very much whether their CEO had ever come across game theory and gaming.

To get a handle on stakeholder positioning and dynamics, I suggest the following needs to be done:

- Define the topic such as a decision or project or some aspects of them.
- Define who your stakeholders are, remembering to ask the question "what's the one big stakeholder I missed?"
- Given what you visualize are their agendas, position them according to their perceived attitude and strength of

influence on this issue (not generally) on the stakeholder grid (Figure 7.1).

- If needed, deep dive into the agendas of a particular one stakeholder or group, using the vector picture stakeholder agenda analysis (Figure 7.2).
- And if you really wanted to understand a very specific turn on or turn down, then descend to the stakeholder basement and ask: "what are the root causes of their actions?" (fishbone analysis) (Figure 7.3).

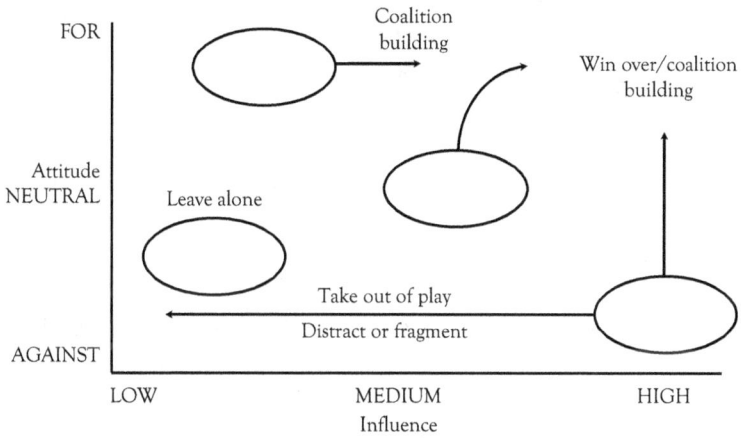

Figure 7.1 Stakeholder analysis
This tool is based on earlier versions by Piercy (1989).

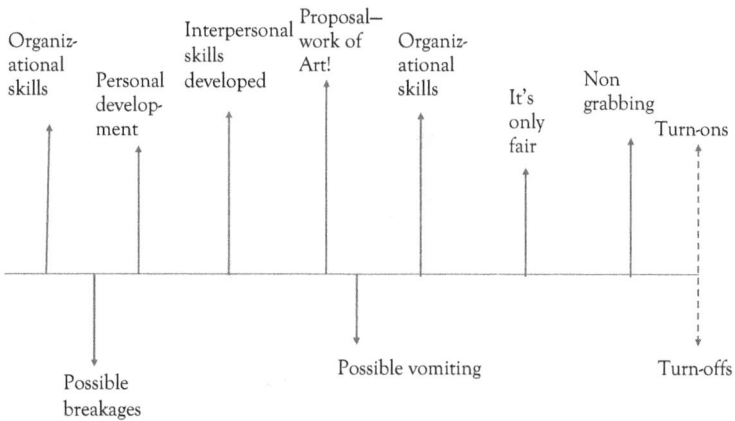

Figure 7.2 Stakeholder agenda analysis—agendas for a Halloween party

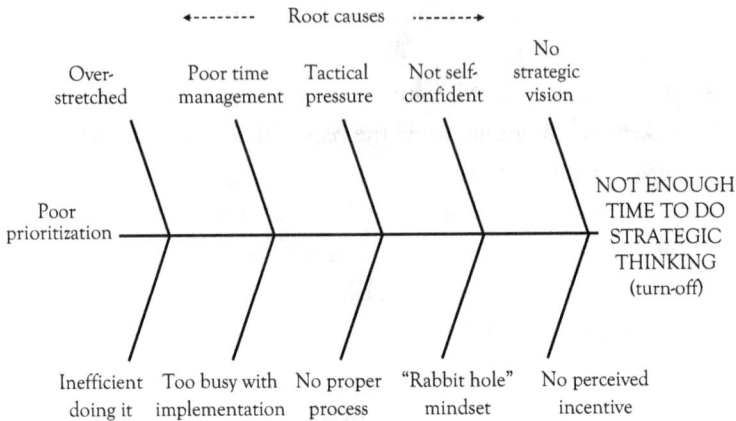

Figure 7.3 Fishbone analysis—diagnosis of a "turn-off"

To do the full stakeholder analysis, it is suggested that you draw the picture (as in Figure 7.1) on a flipchart or white board and write each stakeholder on a Post-it. Move them around so that you have a fair representation of their positions. Then you can play around with the dynamics with "what ifs?" tied to new events or just to explore the potentials. For example, of any cunning influencing plans. That takes you more fully into stakeholder scenario storytelling.

Stakeholder agendas do not only have to mirror corporate agendas but can be those shared in a team or purely personal. The beauty of these tools is that they treat organizational politics as amenable to doing "OBEs" (or "out-of-body experiences"), which is a variable to be factored in, as we see next.

Having introduced stakeholders, we now deal with them as follows:

- Having the full OBE—a tale of stakeholders at British Telecom (BT): Case study;
- Case study of role plays for Amerada Hess: the North Sea gas market;
- Case study of Scottish insurance company: regulatory scenarios;
- Scenarios for scenarios: Imagining the outcomes.

Reader Exercise

For an issue, decision, or project where the outcome is uncertain due to the stakeholders and their influence, determine the following:

- Who are the stakeholders and given their agendas where are they all likely to be on Figure 7.1?
- How might they move around in the future (tell some stakeholder scenario stories)?
- Where there is an important stakeholder who is rather unpredictable, does Figure 7.2 on stakeholder agenda analysis help?
- Does the agenda root cause analysis provide any insight (Figure 7.3)?

Having the Full "Out of Body Experience"

The "out-of-body experience" is an expression from paranormal psychology. For me, it signifies the ability to step outside one's own social construction of reality including perceptions, beliefs, biases and prejudices, desires and agendas, and values and drives and step into those of someone else. The goal is to get somewhere in between 80 and 95 percent accuracy of what these psychological states are and their weightings on a specific topic. That, hopefully, not just positions them but tells you much about how they are likely to react to certain stimuli and what you or others say and do—in the future—and their dynamics. Indeed, that opens the way for influencing them as well as predicting what they will do in the future.

I first began to really use OBE very actively around 25 years ago when I was using stakeholder analysis as a tool as well as stakeholder agenda analysis in my consulting work, especially for strategy and change management.

So, to do it well, you need to already have a good, close knowledge of what someone is like and some familiarity of their preferred cognitive style. This includes having an emotional map of things that they fear the worst and what is fueling their ambitions. Subsequently you might begin to build a model of their future possible intent. Of course, the extent to which this intent is logical and well-articulated, or is far more emergent, are critical things to consider. Do not impose rationality beyond what they are likely to display and the evidence to date.

Besides that, given their central model of their personality, you can also begin to map how that all pans out across different issues for them including any patterns or behavioral themes. In a way, this is akin to the concept of "profiling," which was developed by the FBI to track down serious criminals, particularly serial murderers who have featured in numerous films and the fabulously addictive series, *Criminal Minds*.

In building your stakeholder profile, it is also important to track what they say across a variety of situations (that's the data). It's not just what they say, but how they say it and when. In addition, I also place a lot or emphasis on what they don't say, particularly when you would have expected them to say something. For me, that triggers the instinctive reaction of "filling in the blanks" as I visualize what they were actually thinking.

Another great source of data is nonverbal cues. Estimates of the percent of communication that is down to nonverbal behavior range between 60 and 80 percent, but for sure this is a big give away.

Drawing these all together so that we can give it predictive power, take a look at Figure 7.4. Here we see four key influencing factors for predicting stakeholder intent and behavior. At the bottom, we see the influence of stakeholder agendas, particularly turn-ons and turn-offs. To the left are the fruits of our profiling from interpretations of past behaviors, a mental map of the patterns that shape a stakeholder drive. And to the top, we see

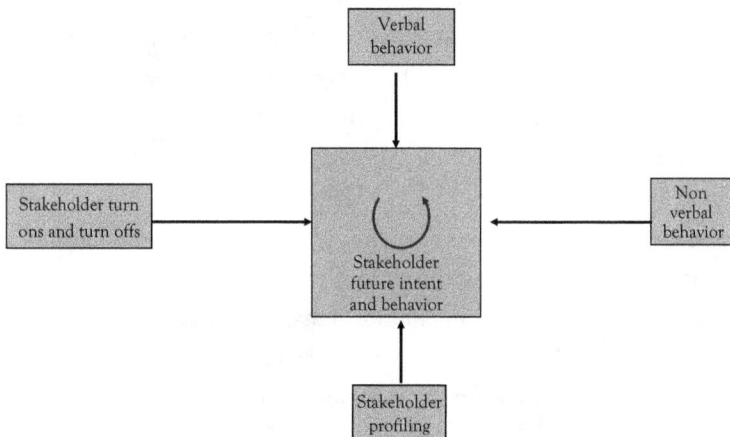

Figure 7.4 Stakeholder spheres of influence

the verbal behaviors around the situation—*not just what is said but also what is not said.* Finally, we have, as mentioned, the nonverbal behaviors. The OBE comes into play through the interpretation of the four spheres of influence for a person on the central box.

Figure 7.4 makes a lot of intuitive sense as it grasps the main ingredients of stakeholder intent and behavior, which play a pivotal role in shaping many zones of acute uncertainty. While this doesn't therefore have to be done in a particularly formal way, it can point the way for inquiry into spheres that we are least sure of. For instance, in spring 2022, it was particularly uncertain as to what the Russian President's intent was as he was in any usual sense not behaving so very "rationally." Looking at Figure 7.4, it became clear to me that I hadn't really profiled him. So, I sought out sources that would help me on that.

There was an informative documentary on TV on Putin's actions and behaviors since he came to power over 20 years ago that I found very helpful not just in terms of his drives but his beliefs. I also watched three documentaries on Hitler versus Stalin, which gave me insights on the psychology of autocratic dictators generally. That helped me quite a lot with my OBE so I could get over the hurdle of being unable to see what his rationality was. He was "rational" based on his assumptions and beliefs, albeit these were underinformed or false, such as the effectiveness of his army and Ukrainian resilience.

Besides some data sources in the public domain and other sources, what came as a surprise was that the invasion should have been an unlikely scenario a few weeks before the invasion to anyone within NATO and the EU, especially given what Putin had been saying over the years.

To help us to comprehend this myopia, see Figure 7.5 on the "pyramid of paralysis."

Here it seems that the thought of a severely negative event (in the above example, an invasion) and of it actually happening introduces an emotional paralysis that was so pervasive so as to introduce a severe cognitive paralysis. In addition to the impaired cognitive functioning, there is often typically a lead time to recognize it at a personal and organizational level as a problem before it can be turned into any kind of decision. This can take weeks or even over a month or two depending on the routines in force and the extent to which these threats can be transcended by agility and even then, lead to paralysis.

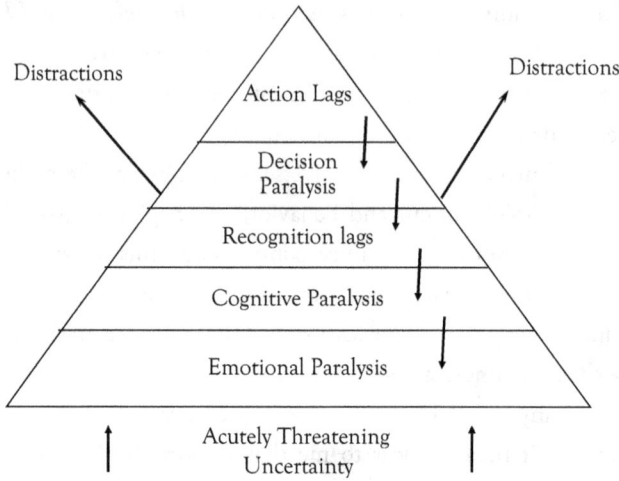

Figure 7.5 The pyramid of paralysis

Individuals, teams, and organizations can very be slow to react to very severe threats even where they are staring at them in the face, making the impact psychologically harder to assimilate and absorb.

Reader Exercise

Pick out an important and preferably reasonably less predictable stakeholder to analyze using the spheres of stakeholder influences as per Figure 7.4. Choose a topic that will give you a sufficient focus for analysis like a pending or possible organizational change (assuming this is a business one) or if a personal one, a holiday which you and they are going to take.

- What does their verbal behavior tell you about their future intent and behavior, not just what they say about it, but when the topic comes up, what are they *not* saying about it?
- What have you noticed in their nonverbal behavior that may give you clues as to where they might be coming from and how they would be behaving in future? Consider their body posture (open or arms and/or legs crossed, facial expressions, eye contact, voice tone and pace; do they tough their nose a lot when this comes up? (According to one TV documentary I watched, both serial killers and politicians share that in

common when they are saying something that they know might not be true or isn't what they really believe.)) Skin complexion can be a clue too—when there's a lot of anxiety or discomfort, has their face or neck reddened? Also look out for signs of sweating coming on caused by quickening heart rate (Prince Andrew allegedly can't sweat, a symptom of post-traumatic stress disorder (PTSD)). I find it amusing to watch politicians to detect sweating; it is easily picked up in camera lights.

- Next, to anchor into their drives, what picture do you build up for them from what is known about their attitude to similar things based on past experiences? What does their profiling tell you based on assumed patterns of behavior such as their past experiences of similar challenges? What do you see as being the needs and drives, for example, their need for control and their appetite for power and their need to have structure? Do they have underlying mental health (or mental disequilibrium) issues? Many powerful decision makers have their fair shares of them. Or do they have physical ones? (Does Putin have cancer?) If say there are one percent of the population is psychotic, then there are likely to be some psychotic managers surely.

- Finally, what are their turn-ons and turn-offs looking at the issue through their lenses (Figure 7.2)? By this now the agendas should drop out quite easily, and that's why it may be good to leave this until the last in our clockwise journey around the spheres of stakeholder influence in Figure 7.4.

There are also a lot of interdependences at work, which need some thought. Use Posts-its to cluster the players and draw lines to denote their areas of highest influence on each other. Indeed, sometimes these patterns can become rather incestuous as group thinking is aligned around a number of contestable assumptions and patterns of thinking. This is called "groupthink" where there is artificial convergence of beliefs without an efficient evidential base. What happens then is in effect is a shared cognitive bias at the group level (Janis 1982).

For instance, the groupthink in the UK government at the start of the pandemic in early 2020 was that "this is containable and we don't need to put our lives on hold to avoid an avalanche of deaths." Wrong! Groupthink can distort our perception of uncertainties massively.

Mental disequilibria in the population can very much steer their cognitive bias either toward or away from certain actions, decisions, or behaviors. This can take many forms. Be alert to the possibility of these mental and emotional states profoundly shaping their behavior(s).

Normal and Abnormal Psychology

Mental disequilibria and dysfunctionality can be at work in far more people than is imagined. If, for instance, one were to believe the often-quoted figure that around one percent of the population are psychotic, then perhaps there is a similar, if not worse, proportion of leaders and managers that are psychotic too.

Similarly, if we also believe that the percentage of sociopaths is also around one percent, then a similar conclusion follows:

Millions of sociopaths live among us—Love fraud

https://lovefraud.com › everyday-sociopaths › millions

In the worst-case scenario, you could end up marrying one who is both—if that is possible! A one percent times a one percent chance is 1 in 10,000, which is significant. And they don't tell you, "Darling, I am both!"

But before dismissing these statistics as scaremongering, just sit quietly for three minutes and do a list of people, family, friends, and colleagues who may have exhibited mild, moderate, or worse psychotic disorders or episodes, sociopathic tendencies, large mood swings, depression, undigested traumas, compulsive controlling behaviors, addictive behaviors, and very low self-esteem. *These make their behaviors highly uncertain.* This can be useful in anticipating the actions of autocrats and dictators. But by surfacing these in a coherent way via the profiling, this can make their likely behaviors far more predictable.

But you don't need to be a psychopath or a sociopath to be prone to unusual behaviors or ones that break the rules. For instance, where someone cons another. I was victim of a fraud by someone who concealed that from me for around five years. The subsequent trial was all about understanding behaviors, which implicitly dissolved the uncertainty of intent through profiling stakeholder agendas alongside the facts.

In the preparation for the trial, I used scenario storytelling extensively to tell stories of what the judge would say in her summing up in the future. And then I worked backward to develop scenarios and strategies over 18 months of how that was brought about. It was amazing listening to what I had imagined before acted out in the flesh, with the press out in force in the same courts, which one often sees in cases where celebrities like footballers' wives are having a go at each other.

Moving on swiftly back to the world of business, there is generally much "emergent" strategy, and as we saw earlier in the book, in stakeholder agendas that can shape these strategies deeply. Sometimes these stakeholders are holding onto opposing agendas or at least ones that are in tension. For instance, a business might be approaching customer service through a differentiation strategy and operations may have a cost leadership strategy.

In earlier writings, I have called this "strat-o-aphrenia," or a situation where multiple and opposing strategies are pursued at the same or slightly different times. The effect of this is to blur intent and to make future behavior less predictable and thus to increase uncertainty. This makes the task of doing the OBE harder, but that just means you need to think more what the tipping points and the transitional events might be.

Some psychologists also talk about looking at the personality as a system so that a person has a range of alternative selves. So the decision making is partly a function of who has the ball at a crucial time just as in football. In psychology, the equivalent of this in most extreme form is that of dissociative identity disorders where the unity of the self begins to come apart and what the person does is subject to shifts in who has the ball. To understand more on this phenomenon, there are many films on it, for example, *Voices Within: The Lives of Trudi Chase*, *The Three Faces of Eve*, and *Split*.

The effect of encountering someone with dissociative identity disorder is said to be quite unnerving as there can be stability of the personality for a period and then there just seems to be no way of knowing what is to come next. But even in extremis such as this, the pattern in the dynamics can be discerned by careful and mindful observation and subsequent reflection. Eventually some degree of prediction is possible even in this extreme case! This can be done to a degree by observing and interpreting patterns in behaviors and their dynamics.

While in business and organization we are not commonly confronted with such extreme personalities, there can be troublesome and changeable individuals who can be volatile in not entirely dissimilar ways (see Figure 7.6) on the mood over time curve. People don't have to be consistently mad to exhibit instability and thus uncertainty.

The best scenario storytellers more generally richly immerse themselves in "where are they coming from and why?" warts and all, and are very focused in getting into the role plays and story lines rather than just give up saying, "this is all just too difficult." Sectors where I have come across more challenging individuals are retail and insurance and, strangely, in academia. The world of politics is very clearly a fertile habitat for some, like the UK parliament.

In decision theory going way back (Simon 1957), there is talk generally too of "bounded rationality" to suggest that while rationality has limitations so that we don't just respond to limitations by giving up. I have empathy with that, but for me, there are more than two zones of decision making. Yes, there's the bounded rationality, but there is also stakeholder rationality where things are rational from a pay-off perspective at the stakeholder level alone. Finally, there is the irrationality level where there are no clear reasons, or the assumptions are plain false. That is rare.

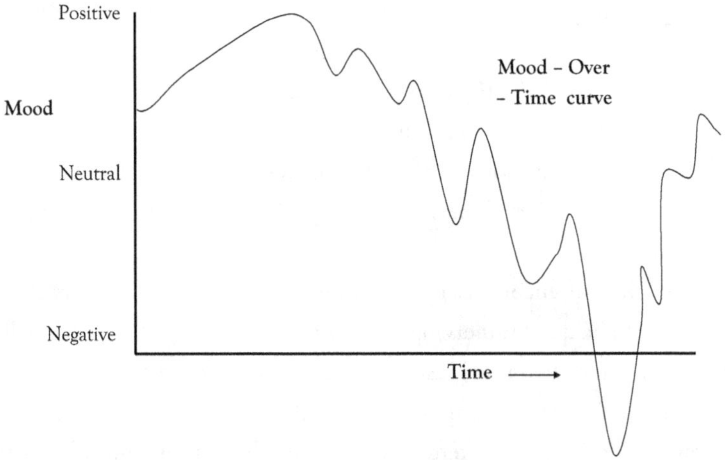

Figure 7.6 Mood-over-time curve

As we saw in the fraud case earlier, trust shapes uncertainty too. Trust is a key way of managing many areas of uncertainty, especially tactical ones, but sometimes, say in a strategic alliance or a marriage. To be able to rely on someone deeply and implicitly, it is unwise not to do "due diligence" however. You can tap into this by using the "OBE." Also, maybe supported by a stakeholder agenda analysis. That invites a weighted vector picture on the issue(s) that you are trusting about. But for sure, you should be drawing up a trust-over-time curve same axis as Figure 7.6 with "trust" written instead of "mood" (Figure 7.7).

I wish I had managed that trust better in the aforementioned legal case, but emotions tangle those situations and make uncertainty appear far less than it really is.

Reader Exercise: The Trust-Over-Time Curve

Going back in time, choose someone from business, family, or from your social life and draw a curve on how you trusted them either as just generally, or as a trust curve specific to an issue.

- Why did that fluctuate both in going up and down?
- To what extent was that as a result of careful physical observation or was that down to overoptimism or misplaced paranoia?
- Are there any approaches suggested in this chapter that might have helped you to gain better objectivity and deeper insights?

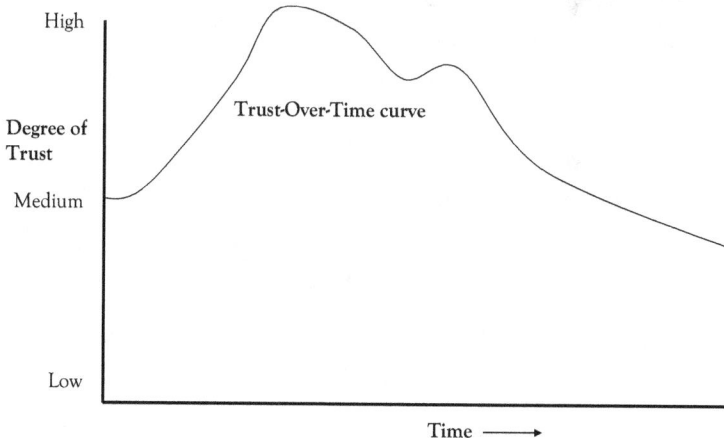

Figure 7.7 Degree of trust

The following conclusions on OBE can be drawn:

- The OBE is central to the exploration of scenarios as stakeholder agendas shape many actions and reactions to events.
- This can be done as a semistructured process drawing from the four spheres of stakeholder influence.
- The rationality of stakeholders may be limited in terms of both business rationality and stakeholder rationality. So don't force fit a rational model when that's not how things are on the ground.
- In more extreme cases, some pattern in the drives and beliefs of a particular stakeholder can be "the tail that wags the dog," which we will see writ large in the case study in the next section.

For those readers wanting more on the drivers of uncertainty in teams, do a deep dive into online case study 4, "BT and Behavioral Uncertainty."

A mood-over-time grid also allows you to track and to forecast the attitude, behavior, and receptiveness of someone whether they are "normal." Usually, they are normal but there are exceptions to positively not normal. See Figure 7.6 for someone who illustrates the latter and is at the mercy of different shades of personality with a bent toward downswings as interactions go on and fresh feelings (negative) typically materialize. This is the profile over a typical 90-minute encounter.

There are several actual mood trackers on the market.

Likely, or even, actual mood-over-time curves have implications for when you say something, it has potentially sensitive impact on someone:

Total Sensitivity = Sensitivity of the Issue Generally × Sensitivity of the Person to that Particular Issue

Case Study of Role Plays for Amerada Hess— the North Sea Gas Market

One example of one of my most interesting scenario building exercises was for Amerada Petroleum's feasibility study to enter the gas supply market in the North Sea that the UK government was de-regulating. I worked closely with its Strategic Planning Department to build a systemic model of the main variables in the market: supply–demand balance, likely new competitive structure, new investment, costs, workings of the market, effects of deregulation, and so on.

It all sounds like posh economics, but it was simpler than that. Although fairly complex, we created a monster map on two flipcharts cello-taped together. This looked at the forces of supply of demand, regulation, competition, long-term contracts, the various entry strategies, and strategic intent of all the players. This was a simpler and a more localized picture than the ones which we saw earlier in Figure 3.6. These factors were then interlinked with arrows indicating their directional causal flows so that their more dynamic properties could be explored.

Another ingredient was to compile some detailed profiles of the strategic position and intent of each one of the potential new entrants and also of the government. This was then produced as a two-page document, a profile at the company level with:

- Current resources and capabilities
- War chest
- Strategic options
- Likely leadership agendas
- Likely strategic intent

We then did a simulation together to pilot the process and to get an advanced view of potential individual moves by the players. Next, we invited some of the senior management to a two-day workshop at the Bull Inn, Gerrard's Cross, Buckinghamshire. These managers were allocated into small teams to try to get inside the heads of the other key players.

Facilitating them was no mean feat as there were five groups dispersed randomly through the hotel at different ends. These were populated by senior managers with me as the focal facilitator and the strategic planners as supporting facilitators. As the planners had rehearsed the scenarios, I really emphasized that the planners should keep that fact and specific insights they had gleaned to themselves so as to avoid contaminating the process. Over a one-day period, I estimated that I did a couple of miles as I needed to check on each one every half hour or so.

After a couple of hours of building up a shared view of the environment and assumptions for how that might shift and the competitor profiling works, we then let them out so that we could then create a dynamic simulation of the scenarios for competing for blocks in the North Sea and then for the competitive environment afterward.

I had briefed them to role play as closely and as dramatically as they possibly could the actual thinking, behaviors, decisions, and actions that they visualized they would do, based on their out-of-body experiences of visualizing the key stakeholders. They did not disappoint me.

We laid out the room with a big chair at the center where each representative would do a role play. I told them to imagine that when they sat on that chair, they were on *Mastermind*, a TV quiz show where someone who had studied a particular topic to death would answer questions. Typically, this could be as mainstream as the Harry Potter books or as obscure as the historical evolution of the myth of vampires in Transylvania!

So first to go on were the oil majors like BP and Shell. Then we had a niche U.S. oil company who came in, sat nervously down in the chair, and fidgeted for a while, mumbling about their strategy, then suddenly jumped up and bolted for the door limping, crying "Mummy, I have hurt my knee!"

The obvious take on that was put in the position of placing a substantial bet on entering this market, they had felt out of their depth and that the risks and the uncertainties really weren't for them.

Then British Gas wandered in. The person playing British Gas sat down on the big black chair and quickly seemed to struggle to maintain a focus of attention.

"So, what are we really all here for?" mumbled Mr. British Gas. "Something to do with North Sea Gas?!" At that time British Gas was a denationalized company but one that had taken with it much of the culture of a nationalized utility.

Mr. British Gas said: "I do find it rather hot and stuffy in here… in fact…. I feel so tired." He was teetering dangerously.

Just around that time British Gas seemed to slump in his chair and begin to emulate the dormouse in *Alice in Wonderland* who could never seem to keep awake. Eventually British Gas seemed almost certainly unconscious and there was a snoring noise! It was not only hilarious but most insightful.

I role played the British government—actually the Chancellor of the Exchequer. I brought my then shiny, nice, red brief case in and came in muttering to myself like the white rabbit in *Alice in Wonderland*:

Oh, deary me! Whatever am I going to do? Public sector borrowing requirement, such as a terrible headache, headache. We are always borrowing. It makes me feel so bad. Who can I raid this year who has lots of cash? What an absolute pickle? I raided the banks last year, so who next?

I know! Oil companies. Petroleum Revenue Tax (PRT). That's the ticket.

Off I went, twirling and singing "PRT, PRT" out of the room with lots of applause!

What was so wonderful about all this theater was that by really entering into the flow of the drama, we managed to simulate behaviors and events, full of insights. It was remarkably close to things that actually happened.

- There were fewer serious players really up for market entry than expected.
- Some potential entrants would drop by the way.
- British Gas, who you would have expected to have been a key player, was really almost out of it as they were far too slow to put a coherent strategy together.
- PRT might well go up—something that the industry had been assuming would never happen.

This was all game theory and gaming at its best!

The scenario event was not only very rich in insights but paved the way for a very successful entry into this new market for Amerada. Some years later, I did spot that they exited the market for a handsome price—something on the order of £117 million. I am not sure that they continued the process into scenarios for retailing gas, which might have been a great follow on. In the world of sci-fi, a character Dr. Who is famed for his journeys through space and time in a ship called the Tardis. The *Dr. Who* series started on November 23, 1963, 59 years ago. Clearly the space–time machine was found to be of considerable use. So why is it that so often more scenario time travel simply doesn't happen? It is bizarre.

I was later invited to lunch in a posh restaurant some months later in London's West End by the Strategic Planning Director. He told me that the government move, which actually materialized to put up Petroleum Revenue Tax had so shocked the other oil companies that they hadn't even begun to lobby against it. Amerada had by contrast had immediately staged a major campaign to modify the fiscal changes so that they didn't put fresh investments, which would bring incremental tax receipts in at risk.

He said he really couldn't understand the difference in behaviors. I asked him: "Well, don't you see? They had not done a scenario exercise like you did. So they would have been in a state of really deep shock and so their reaction time would have been much, much slower."

There are some most interesting lessons:

- You need to do a fair amount of preparation to get the basic data, for example, on environmental trends first.
- The industry system model needs to be drawn.
- Using the uncertainty grid, the most volatile variables have to be pinned down.
- Then the base positions, capabilities, resources, stakeholder agendas, and strategic intent of each of the key players need to be distilled to enable role playing the specific player.
- Key stakeholders may display very bounded rationality indeed and may even act rationally in a business sense to upset a more ordered game play.
- After each subteam has got inside the head of their allotted player, they then have to place their strategic bet in the competitive arena, having truly had their "out-of-body" experience.
- Then you need to synthesize the whole lot by seeing what the likely results will be of all the external factors as well as the interplay between the behaviors and actions of all the key actor by gaming it.

Finally, there needs to be a "wash up" session afterward that distils the more specific insights, records the main storyline, and draws out the implications. It also formally feeds some strategic option grid analysis into the planning process.

Case Study Scottish Insurance Company— Regulatory Scenarios

Our final case study involves that of a Scottish blue chip insurance company where I worked with its Independent Financial Advisers (IFA) division some years ago. They were very keen on strategic thinking and I did a number of workshops throughout the UK for them. I ran one in Manchester and it seems that my scenario analysis wasn't quite as good as it should have been. I always used to construct an uncertainty grid for each major mission that I did down to "My car won't break down" and "I won't have a car accident." I am not quite sure why I drove because that would have added clutter to my uncertainty grid in the danger zone and pushed up uncertainty.

I could only park a couple of hundred yards from my hotel and unfortunately I had not taken the advice of my then wife to take a suitcase. I had some random bags instead. I had to do a couple of trips and in between had a couple of drinks to chill after the long journey, thus pushing some of my "danger zone" assumptions further southeast.

The next day I had breakfast and then tried to get ready, but oh dear, where were my trousers? Nowhere to be found! Could they have fallen out of the bag?

So, I had to position why I was wearing my jeans, which of course I did by making the point "Always ask the question: What's the one big thing you forgot?" to some considerable laughter with cries of "Do you have recollections, Tony?" "What were you really up to?" I will always remember that with the thought of what happened to them. And who is wearing them now?

My client was very much an exception to the rule that insurance companies are usually quite stuffy and I still entrust them with all my pension. I remember meeting their Divisional MD who inspired me in my own strategy development. He saw me passing by his office and called out: "Tony, come in! I have just had a top strategy firm presenting to us all morning. Can I ask you, 'How can I avoid Strategy Consultants?'" He named a top strategy consulting firm.

I replied: "That's awesome! That could be the title of my next book!!"

Indeed, after long and torturous discussions with a publisher, I eventually got it published as *Be Your Own Strategy Consultant* (Grundy 2002a), which has been my best-selling book up until this point.

I think someone heard this as weeks later. I got a call from Janie from their Strategy Group saying that they had a regulatory review coming up and asked if I have the time to do a deep dive into the driving issues and also try to second guess what the potential pathways might be for how the new regulator might behave over the coming few months.

So, I spent a most interesting two days getting not just inside industry issues but particularly what the personal and strategic agendas of the regulator might be and how these might shape increases or changes in the future shape or regulations.

Apart from absorbing the data, my main focus was a stakeholder agenda analysis as well as the profiling. What made the regulator tick and so on. Looking at his education and schooling, he was clearly a highly ambitious and well-connected person who saw this as a stepping-stone to other and bigger things. Therefore, he would want to stir things up quite a bit to encourage sharper competition. Digestion of change would likely be phased to make it more palatable and digestible. So that would call for early lobbying for greater consultation around implementing change. *So, in this case there would be five futures*: (1) industry consultation, (2) policy formulation, (3) announcement and lobbying, (4) finalization and consolidation, implementation of change, and finally (5) development of new strategies by the players.

A few months after my feedback, which was well received, I was most interested in how close I got. When I read the new regulations in the *Financial Times*, I was able to give myself 85 percent for the decision and future processes.. Profiling was hugely important in getting that close and the quality of my out-of-the-body experience was wonderful.

The key insights from the case study are the following:

- Scenario outcomes are often an outcome from or are influenced by often a small number of individuals and maybe even one of them; so understanding and managing behavioral uncertainties is important.

- Profiling can be immensely helpful in getting a great sense of the general drives which shape their actions, behaviors, and decisions.
- To arrive at a scenario may require absorption in data even when it may seem trivial.

Scenarios for Scenarios—Visualizing the Outcomes

It may seem an odd thing, but it is possible to visualize possible scenarios of scenarios. What will happen during the process and what will the output look like too? Also, what feelings will come out and what will the influence of stakeholder agendas and politics? The latter are all important and it is possible that this political tail will wag the strategic dog.

If the implications of the scenarios are not drawn out at some stage, then maybe we are yet to get real and are skirting around the edges of any adjustment or change. Indeed, political scenarios are some of the most valuable scenarios to create of all. In fact, I used them to excellent effect on the issue of future management of my Executive Strategy courses at a very famous business school where I was on faculty. Two senior people wanted to wrest a lot of the control from me as I was too innovative for them and called a meeting with me. I did my uncertainty grid, storylines and role played the three of us—"Joe 90," "Davide 40," and myself. *I spent three hours visualizing, mental role playing, and so on.*

My stories matched the reality in a truly uncanny way. *I had a sense of déjà vu and there was only one thing that was said that I hadn't got before the meeting.* In a two-on-one game that gave me much edge, I was able to allow them to think that they were 100 percent in control. Try the process out especially with stakeholder agenda analysis and the "OBE" on a political issue like this.

Another astute application of storytelling and scenarios can be important processes like strategic planning or decision-making processes of change management processes.

Key Concluding Insights

There are a number of important insights from this chapter:

- Stakeholders are a major drivers of uncertainty and this invites in-depth analysis to pick out the major drivers.
- A three-level approach may be needed to get a clearer picture of stakeholders through (a) positioning them on the high-level grid, (b) through the vectors of the stakeholder agenda analysis, and (c) through fishbone analysis of the causes of one particular agenda analysis.
- This should be accompanied by storytelling of their moves as a pack, or as individuals, or both.
- Throughout this process, it is essential to *become* them via the "out-of-body experience."
- There are very important inputs from verbal behaviors and nonverbal behaviors alike.
- The process of profiling too is important.
- Game theory and role plays bring the stakeholder dimension to life, adding vital behavioral color.
- We are often concerned as to whether we can trust a particular stakeholder. Try the "trust over time curve." What has trust been like to date and where might this go in future?
- Mood-over-time curves are another important variable.
- Sometimes apparently minor and trivial data may be disproportionately important.
- The various case studies demonstrate how essential and valuable is stakeholder analysis in live scenario building.

CHAPTER 8

Application to MBA

Case Study of Scenarios for the MBA Market

Introduction

The purpose of this chapter is to briefly flag the value that these scenario process and tools can add to MBA courses generally and even more importantly to show a worked example of scenario storytelling based on a case study of the MBA market. The latter forms the core of the chapter and is relevant not just to would-be or live MBA project students but also for Directors and Senior Managers eager to learn what the end product is—an elongated Strategic Position Paper, which also has valuable reflections.

But let's first look at the applications and their value of the process to MBA topics and then to MBA projects generally in two shorter sections on the application of managing uncertainty strategically:

- To MBA modules generally; and
- To MBA projects specifically.

Application of Managing Uncertainty Strategically to MBA Modules Generally

We have already done some work on the application of managing uncertainty in Chapter 6. So the suggestions here will partly overlap them.

An obvious area of synergy is that of Strategic Management, which not only purports to deal with position and direction of an organization to external and internal change. These are often associated with uncertainty, but for most case studies the main focus is usually strategic analysis and choice of options within a reasonably narrow range. With this assumption, more often or not, progression happens within the same or similar worldview rather than with a spread of possible worlds.

This suggests the possibility of making provision for alternatives within fluid and flexible storylines as an addition to the usual process, especially for those chasing distinctions in their projects. So, besides the narrower work, there is an extra phase, which stands back and in a strategically mindful way thinks more about the wider range of pathways the world might take, and also tries to push the envelope of visioning that bit more into the future.

Scenario work and strategy should, as I have argued in this book, go hand in hand together. They should be thought of as "the two sisters" or more boldly, SAS.

But so often strategy is self-contained. Strategy theorists often come over as if uncertainty is just tacked on at the end and if so just as a quick and dirty health check. But in the demonstrably turbulent world we are in characterized by multiple/waves of uncertainty, this does seem a far too limited view. There are those that argue that strategy has become dated and has lost its way. Indeed, I would agree that "strategy needs its own strategy."

Finance is a big and relevant area too for many MBA projects as this is where variability of results are dramatic with the impact of uncertain variables so that we can go way beyond just doing rather mechanistic sensitivity analysis. As many conventional strategy books and many lecture programs too do not devote much time and space to uncertainty, then this book can act as a very good antidote indeed as in Chapter 5.

Of course, the same goes for other MBA modules that are in effect "strategy cocktails," such as International Business and M&A, especially given our coverage of change management.

Areas that would invariably benefit from some of the scenario frameworks that are in this book are: Marketing Strategy, especially New Product Development, the Circular Economy, and Corporate Governance where there can be major knock-on effects of mismanagement that can have catastrophic effects, like the oil spills in the Gulf from BP's *Deepwater Horizon* oil platform.

MBA projects are best therefore framed as multidisciplinary and are best if challenged by uncertainty.

Application of Managing Uncertainty Strategically to MBA Projects Specifically

Anyone who has ever done an MBA project will tell you that it is one of the hardest challenges that you might encounter in your management career and a lot of that is down to uncertainty. Here is a little list of some typical uncertainties of MBA projects:

- Its scope
- Its objectives
- The time needed
- Any delays, disruptions, and distractions
- When and how you will find the time to do it
- What literature to read and what bits to actually use (not necessarily the same thing)
- What methodology will you use?
- Getting access to primary data that is rich
- Sampling
- The actual quantity and quality of data you will get
- How to structure and populate the write-up with material
- Will it be reader-friendly so that anyone coming cold to it isn't exhausted or put to sleep by the "I am writing for myself" syndrome
- What writing speed will be accomplished (including revisions)—many students implicitly plan to do around two words a minute; surely, they should be able to do better than that
- How best to analyze and to evaluate and interpret the data and what findings will emerge?
- What the mark will be, and especially from the second marker whose discipline, research philosophy, and mindset can be at variance with the first marker who is usually the supervisor?

- Cognitive and emotional bias from the supervisor and the second markers that can have an influence on the marks
- Whether the student has adequate personal resilience to get through the difficulties which depends in turn on energy levels, commitment, and motivation and the smoothing of anxiety levels

That is not a totally exhaustive list!

But while this is a daunting list of uncertainty drivers, the good news is that there are opportunities for mitigating many of these, if not most. For example, by planning and time management and by taking on board the guidance of the supervisor (sometimes called "mentor").

For MBA projects, there are some specific areas that scenario approaches are particularly relevant too. Where there is a literature chapter and where there is a high degree of uncertainty about the future, then the literature on scenarios should definitely warrant attention as a possible candidate for inclusion. Also, in Chapter 3, Methodology should offer itself up for evaluation (see Figure 8.1) as a means of choosing the sources and the processes of assessing methodology options used by hundreds of my MBA students (an application of the Strategic Option Grid usually scored out of 15 (these criteria can be changed, adjusted, or simply added to)).

Options Criteria	Option 1	Option 2	Option 3	Option 4
Natural fit to Objectives				
Likelihood-quality Data and Insights				
Implementation Difficulty				
Time				
Natural skill				
Total Score				

Figure 8.1 Research options grid—methodology options evaluation

Score the boxes e.g., 3 = very attractive, 2 = medium attractive, 1 = very low attractiveness. Also add up scores at the bottom: criteria can be tailored.

MBA Project—Scenarios for the UK MBA Market

Executive Summary

This project does a deep dive into some of the key trends in the past, present, and future of the UK MBA market. This is a company-specific project and therefore more than an environmental review. Specific issues are the likelihood of saturation, the main shifts, demand and supply wise, and the constraints and opportunities in the market, particularly more radical innovation.

We found this market relatively complex and fluid. This may be increasingly shaped by accelerated changes through technology, innovation, and competition, making the traditional, functional element of the MBA less central and management skills like visioning, strategic thinking, questioning, decision making, influencing, change management, influencing, and incisive communication and leadership more central.

We foresee a greater focus on the differentiation of product and segmentation of needs in the upper middle tier of schools, more individualization of the experience, and focus on the value of MBA.

A number of scenarios were listed as plausible. Possible futures are, for example, (1) market saturation and market reshaping; (2) reinvention and growth through innovation to deepen market penetration nearer to U.S. levels; (3A) economic growth versus (3B) economic and political turbulence; (4) shifts in the international patterns of trade of MBAs (visas, etc.); and (5) a scramble for quality teaching resource.

We deep dived into just one.

- Zero to very low growth, with demand held back for the next three years due to geopolitical and local political and economic uncertainty, medium and longer term with accelerating innovation.

The key results were that the UK market was mature, recent growth is much less, that there is a backlog of potential change but fundamental innovation although overdue may be slow, incremental, and faltering, which will dampen some potential demand. There are possibilities of more radical thinking spurred on by existing and new forms of competition (not explored here), resources, and their configurations becoming potentially more fluid in the longer term.

Note: Most scenarios when dealing with a preexisting business and market work from Past – Present – Future as a logical build up. Sometimes where these are *all new*, we move much quicker to the future. Also, we might not do the work in that strict order depending on circumstances even when told chronologically eventually.

Chapter 1: Definition of Scope and Purpose

Introduction

In this chapter we cover:

- Statement of authorship
- Overall rationale
- Industry and market definition and delineation
- Delivery options
- Market segmentation
- What businesses are/might MBA courses in
- Substitutes
- Stakeholders
- Scope and focus
- Key deliverables
- Main methods
- Conclusion and insights

Statement of Authorship

As I have had and have relationships with business schools, I need to say that this case study is based on my own thoughts and also that the direction of thinking was based in part on two former and very experienced HR Directors who gave me a very corporate perspective.

Overall Rationale

I wanted ideally to explore the whole and global MBA market, but this would have been far too ambitious in both time and space.

Even Europe was still too broad because of the diversity of business culture. The UK MBA market is also well developed although it is not clear whether it is yet saturated. We focused on UK MBAs and UK business schools are, however, big MBA exporters, especially online. So our focus included them as a secondary interest.

The MBA is associated with an accelerated career path to senior management and making board level decisions through (a) typically rational decision making and (b) excellence in executing implementation through multifunctional skills. In theory, the training of skilled MBAs would hopefully improve resource allocation, hence the importance of MBAs for individuals, their organizations, and society. In return for the investment and effort, the MBA would get a premium salary and benefits, thus enabling a premium for the elite training.

In addition. for nearly 100 years, the MBA cult of management excellence created a magnetic pull and very high emotional value (though prestige) for the individual and much enhanced life chances for this elite. This was besides the high margins and high growth for business schools too.

Industry and Market Definition and Delineation

The market structure was very complex:

Delivery Options

- Full time
- Part time
- Online
- The "blended" model mixture
- Individual versus corporate focus and funding
- General versus specialist
- Possible specialization by industry (finance, oil and gas, pharmaceuticals)

The latter specialization lacks cross-industry vision and limited career opportunities. So this is not considered significant unless backed by someone like Google or Apple and focusing on digital.

Market Segmentation

Many online students come from Europe and the Middle East and Africa to the UK. So the MBA is traded internationally. Indian and Chinese students prefer classroom and get visas. Most schools will wish to restrain the proportion from that segment as it upsets a fine cultural balance and presents language issues.

There are also differences in need between traditional corporate careers and ones that lean toward entrepreneurial environments or even startups, which are becoming increasingly important but unevenly catered for.

Some students are part or fully funded by their employers, the latter few pricings of MBAs are at a premium versus other degrees with the expectation of increased salaries that once was substantial but seems to have declined over the decades. However, salaries have held up in the premium sector over the last 10 to 15 years, but there is less salary premium at the commodity fee end.

The apparent margins appear very attractive to parent universities who are key stakeholders who operate with variable "hands on/off influence" on direction. However, the costs are very high through very high student acquisition and end-placement costs. In the United States, MBAs are a loss leader and, in the UK, too and they act as halo for the business school for other things like corporate relationships, selling volume MSc's, and boosting undergraduate numbers too. MBAs are like the modern football game where the top-end gate revenues are insufficient to fully pay wages but are topped up by advertising on TV and sponsorship. This impression was confirmed at a conference of business school academics.

Smaller cheaper courses might consider retrenchment with market shrinkage, but any exits could be dampened as that would undermine Business School credibility.

Within the UK MBA market, there is also a wide pricing range from around £20,000 to £87,000. So there is some scope at the premium end for fresh innovation.

Online: COVID-19 and the rapid increase in use of Zoom and so on has produced a big stimulus for online MBAs and has changed the MBA experience considerably as in UCL's case. Recently completing two-year MBAs have done their course 100 percent online. So this is huge change in the MBA "feel."

Product content, structure, and style of delivery: MBA courses are delivered almost exclusively by universities who have the dominant paradigm of knowledge acquisition with a bias to areas of the "hard" over the "soft" skills, especially through the case study method. The application of knowledge and actual application to current student experience is less predominant. Many MBA projects are constructed around a conventional model of academic research with behavioral, implementation, advisory, and stakeholder skills peripheral. *A possible scenario is that some schools rejig that mix with much greater focus on critical CEO and Director competences.*

Student experience and stress: Students are struggling increasingly with time management, anxiety, and stress, especially toward the back end of their MBAs that are increased by corporate work overload, making completion feel like mission impossible. COVID hasn't helped, but there is a long-term trend that may make the MBA less attractive 3 to 15 years out.

Besides more present uncertainty in the future shape, structure of delivery and segmentation, there are also more dynamic and changing uncertainties such as COVID, economic recovery, and slump, especially *the acceleration of innovation and change in businesses, a possible scenario.*

Even since beginning the project, while economic constraints already loomed and COVID still a threat, we now have the Ukraine invasion. On top of these uncertainty waves, we are threatened with a medium-term uncertainty flood through economic turbulence.

The public sector, which is not only huge but needy of strategic change and leadership and functional skills, on the one hand, but price sensitive and traditional in attitude, on the other, could be a latent ingredient in future growth dynamic.

Substitutes

- Executive development courses (curtailed in the pandemic) for example, mini-MBAs
- MSc's and MIMs (masters in management) (less challenging, generally cheaper)
- Internet learning for example, YouTube—often very digestible and convenient

These products have grown maybe faster than MBAs in recent years according to our knowledge.

In the longer term, DBAs could be a substitute at least in part (5+ years out?). This could grow both as a stand-alone product and also as a next step to take after an MBA. DBAs currently suffer from being PhDs in disguise with a bigger taught element and are extremely expensive.

What Business Are/Might MBAs Be in?

The traditional MBA is centered in functional disciplines with strategy and sometime leadership as integrative themes.

There has been less focus within MBAs on the hot senior management competences that are targeted by corporates. For example:

- Imagination and creativity
- Decision making
- Asking the right questions
- Influencing and advising
- Drawing out insights
- Strategic thinking (not to be confused with strategic analysis)
- Taking different perspectives

Many of these could form an overlay of learning applied to the functional topics as well as strategy, plus the project, which could be a playground for all of these and not some.

Probably the one competence that comes under this heading that has been featured more by some schools is leadership.

It isn't quite clear that change management is a "skill" here as this is often taught as a more cognitive, knowledge-based topic. Probably, it needs be included in the top management toolbox of competences too.

In an MBA scenario, some business schools redesign the MBA model to make these listed elements above far more central—to be practiced at every opportunity over the MBA: for example to case studies, MBA exercises, to the project, and also on the job to build the elite future senior or top manager.

Stakeholders

Most obvious stakeholders are:

- Students
- Business schools
- Faculty

Less obvious stakeholders:

- Society
- Media
- Businesses (sponsors and future employers post-MBA)
- Parent universities
- Families (partners and parents who might be a source of funds or loans)

High-profile MBAs are vulnerable to critical media pressure; for example, for corporate mismanagement and their value for money questioned.

Scope and Focus

Scope: This is the UK MBA market to map the main trends, past and future, and the drivers for change for mainly online MBAs being the main focus, especially emerging opportunities.

For example, highlighted through playful storytelling in Chapter 3.

Focus: Our key objectives are the following:

1. To understand the context in order to inform our sensing of future change (Chapters 1 and 2);
2. To develop some plausible scenarios of the future dynamics of the market, customer needs, and value, delivery, and competition *and especially for growth* in order to test and refine strategies.

Aligned to each are our guiding key strategic questions (cross referenced with the objectives):

1. From an "alien" perspective, what is the MBA market all about and why has it been so attractive? (Chapters 1 and 2)
2a. What obvious and less obvious changes might be around the corner (Chapters 2 and 3)
2b. What are the constraints and the opportunities from this? (Chapter 3)
2c. What are insights from a number of scenarios? (Chapter 3)
2d. What future growth trajectory might happen in the UK? (Chapter 3)
3a. What are our strategic options and their future attractiveness (Chapter 4)
3b. And their implications

We debated time horizons. There was much uncertainty at short term at a macro level economically and in the recovery from COVID plus any growth-dampening effects through UK fiscal squeeze, supply side effects in the economy, much higher inflation, and pressure on income, creating a break on career investment. Yet longer term, there were major uncertainties: what were students' appetites to work many hundreds of hours extra on an MBA when increasingly stressed by their day jobs?

The first three years would cover the post-COVID recovery (Future 1). Then, it is assumed that there would be a more rapid rate of business change and structural realignment of the supply side and market innovation (Future 2), years 4 to 6.

Key Targeted Deliverables

The key targeted deliverables are:

- A clear set of current and future issues ranked in importance, rated as positive, negative, or "mixed"
- Insights from any research: secondary and primary
- An account of the main growth drivers in the market with an evaluation of their relative strength and direction (positive or negative)

- Assumptions about the future and an evaluation of importance and uncertainty
- Future market constraints
- The scenarios of the future and insights (detail and alternative futures online 2)

Main methods

- Secondary data—reports and articles, for example, on UK and U.S. trends
- Focus group within UCL to Delphi "the future"
- A couple of HR Directors whose thinking is advanced and likely to inform the scenarios
- Networking at a conference with other MBA Directors
- Internal data from UCL on current position

Conclusion and Insights

The MBA market is complex, dynamic, and more volatile. Many scenario themes offer investigative potential. While the threat of maturity looms, there also seems to be pockets and maybe doors to growth in the longer term.

Key concluding insights include:

- The MBA is a complex product with multiple stakeholders.
- There are substitutes not just university courses but other sources.
- Top management competences are covered somewhere and could be made much more priority.

The rest of the project structure is as follows:

- Chapter 2 History, Current Context, and Current Position
- Chapter 3 Futures
- Chapter 4 on Implications and Options, Conclusions to be written

Chapter 2: History, Current Context, and Current Position

Introduction

In this chapter we cover:

- Historical development
- Current context
- Competition and costs
- Summary of industry issues and prioritization
- Key concluding insights

Historical Development

We wouldn't normally quote from Wikipedia, but this definition of an MBA is a good one:

> An MBA is a graduate degree focusing on business administration, investment management... covering ... accounting, applied statistics, human resources, business communication, ethics, law, strategy, finance, economics, entrepreneurship, marketing, supply chain, operations management.

It is a bundle of a huge variety of ingredients that span analytical skills, functional and soft skills, the latter being found in a variety of degrees of development today. The core traditional paradigm is scientific management, which pervades most schools. Invariably there is a heavy emphasis on applying MBA tools to formal case studies.

Applying an "I am an alien" thinking to this service industry could make it seem to resemble a supermarket of management skills and knowledge. *There is now so much content in an MBA so the alien might worry that it might pop?* But you don't have to be everything.

According to Wikipedia, the first business school dates back to Wharton in the late 19th century. In 1900, Harvard started the first MBA and was producing MBAs on an industrial scale by 1930. Europe was slow to emulate, but schools like the London Business School

(LBS), Cranfield, Manchester, and Henley followed in the UK much along that mode.

Major developments were IT (laptops, Word, Zoom). The online MBA and the part-time pathways led to increasingly sophisticated product segmentation designed around who the target students were and what they would be trained to do and how. They would get more salary afterward, but that premium may be eroded in future.

Estimates of the premium still range from 30 to 50 percent (the latter at LBS and prestige schools). Erosion is not helped by the increasing numbers of graduates and lower uniqueness, and maybe dilution of quality raising the questions of:

- Has the market reached saturation in the UK, and if not, what further growth might be possible and how? and
- Can "the supermarket style formula" still create new demand through reengineering the product, its style, and the teaching and facilitation skillset?

Current Context and Competition and Costs

In the UK, there are now no less than 131 business schools which have an MBA (see Find MBA, MBA Programs worldwide on Google), which again suggests a saturated market on the supply side. In that event of a market contraction or intense price competition, *it may lead to a scenario of market exits were there to a very adverse economic downturn caused by inflationary pressure post-COVID and a significant drop in demand.*

More positively, traditionally the MBA market has had far greater margins than other degree products and equilibrating the shape of the market might change. Presently players are integrated within universities to varying degrees, but there is potential scenario in which new entrants might team up with learning and technology companies (four to six years?).

These schools have several strategic groups, typically prestige LBS, and top, middle, and lower tiers all of these being distributed statistically in a double, reversed pyramid shape with medium numbers at the middle to top and in the same shape at the lower to middle, narrowing at the base.

The "so what?": *It is an extremely fragmented market*, and if it were not for university stakeholders for whom the MBA is, given the related revenue, a "cash cow." That fragmentation makes it potentially ripe for scenarios of alliances or even mergers maybe in Future 2, four to six years out.

On the cost issue, the vast majority of schools lose money these days on MBAs. It was a loss leader, enabling volume MSc programs and Exec Development courses. It may be surprising that the costs of acquiring new students and the costs of ensuring their placement are high. And there are overheads from the mother university.

This is a system with economic value independences (see the tailored "Business Value System" (Grundy 2018) and Figure 8.2 (cost is a part of the competitive mix, too)).

Current Position

"What obvious and less obvious changes might be around the corner?"

Growth

The number of students in the UK appears to be growing strongly at a compound rate of around 17.5 percent over the last few reported years. According to a search of the numbers, they report:

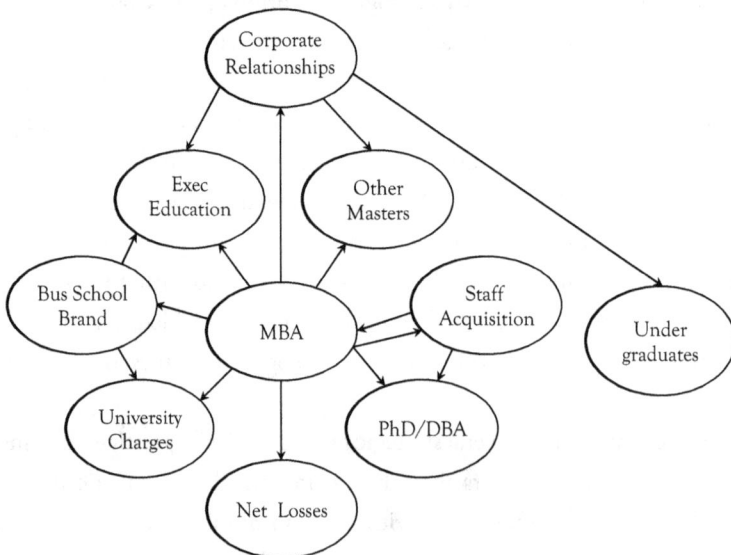

Figure 8.2 The business value system of MBA programs

Chart 8.1 MBA students by domicile 2014/15 to 2019/20: Hesta

Academic year	UK	Non-UK	Total MBA students
2016–17	8,670	6903	15,575
2017–18	9,580	7470	17,050
2018–19	11,085	8975	20,055
2019–20	12,665	12910	**25,575**

While COVID dampened the UK domestic growth, in the more recent past, growth in non-UK students was only 13 percent annually compounded, as opposed to 22 percent for non-UK. Could this be because UK schools were aggressively recruiting from overseas as these students shifted from live courses to online and were lured by reputation to the UK? It remains an unknown. If so, that growth applecart might be upset through a far stronger and more global set of business schools in Asia to severely slow or halt these heady rates of growth by year 6 and certainly over years 7 to 10, with an impact on classroom-based MBAs (see the "Introduction" chapter).

Rapid growth, especially online, also reported in the UK by the *Financial Times* in late 2020, is now reversing (www.ft.com/content/890c94f6-74ca-4a0d-ae32-fb44c3c4f371).

Is the UK local market "saturated"? Many industries would die for such growth rates of 12 percent. On the other hand, there could be still a future bubble in the second future years 4–6 of the scenarios. A rate of growth of 17.5 percent for the total MBA students as in the right-hand column would seem to be above the long-term secular trend. This is because a *compound rate of 17,5 percent would show a doubling in just over four years.*

The UK MBA market has thus exhibited healthy growth at least in the prepandemic period and foreign students have been a massive factor in the UK student growth. Both segments have benefited with the strength of the UK in online delivered through individualization. Post-COVID, online seems to have an edge where it is well executed and is of high quality.

Value Added and Value for Money

The MBA is not only very expensive but also the costs have been esca-lating in real terms. While some students have drawn some employee funding, there is some evidence that this external funding has been falling as careers become more fluid and punctuated with more frequent job moves, reducing employer payback.

This invites the strategic questions of: *Are we close to the ceiling on price?* and *are we overdue for better, cheaper entrants and cheaper courses generally?* (https://find-mba.com/articles/employer-funding-for-mbas-myth-or-reality)

Pricing and the value proposition may therefore suggest further scenarios.

MBA Supply Chain

This supply chain has always been primarily resourced by full-time faculty with only niche lecturing time taken by associates or visiting speakers. MBA projects now used by the vast majority of schools are provided with mixed sourcing, with more associates generally being deployed on online courses. This is an extremely cheap form of support and the result is often felt by the students at their most stressful stage of the MBA. Learning value is varied and this is an area where much greater value is needed.

Invariably the business school is the market front with very few instances of any other kind of organization as the main front or equal partner. Many other configurations are possible—this being a possible line of enquiry for the scenario work. For instance, could one have a core unit sourced by shared specialist units in which the lecturers are, for example, specialist strategists, finance people, and so on? (joint ventures?), say in 7 to 15 years' time?

Could four or five business schools join to share staff, even inter-nationally and operating in a virtual environment, effortlessly blending nationalities and cultures?

Summary of Industry Issues and Prioritization

Major issues:

- Will recent growth rates continue or will the MBA market stall (major)?
- Will the major schools wake up in time to reduce the gap between what students currently get versus what they need now and will need round the corner, through an agile delivery mode? (major)
- Even with all of that, how far are we away from saturation and maybe decline *as a scenario?* (major)
- What shape will the UK economy be in over the next three years and after with a new geopolitical and economic world adapting to Brexit and eco changes?
- How might the supply chain be configured, when and how quickly?

Minor issues:

- What does a leading and agile MBA of the future look like in the future (for a separate paper)? (Minor)
- Is there a need for a big mindset shift away from the MBA as purveyor of capitalistic, materialistic, and exploitative (planet and people) values (minor now, but increasing?)
- Media—what role will they play as a catalyst of change? (minor)
- What will the range of future value propositions look like?
- Could the public sector be a future engine of growth and how will this be delivered?

The lower issues may be "weak signals," but need watching still.

Key Concluding Insights

The MBA market in the UK is very complex and appears mature and maybe nearing saturation without further innovation. Online appears to be the dominant model now, but there is much scope for schools to innovate and freshen up. It has been a sellers' market and they have operated largely a knowledge supermarket model, which is ripe for refocusing, simplifying, and enriching to touch the soft spots that senior managers and entrepreneurs actually face, today and tomorrow. More detailed ones include:

- Content of some MBAs is bulging, yet less attention is paid to key competences and praxis.
- Value added: price pressure and costs may be more important.
- The MBA salary premium could fall with much further growth.
- Supply is very fragmented and may be tested for rationalization with increased price competition and any negative growth of class students.
- The resource base could be reconfigured.
- Recent growth is likely to stall even before Ukraine, energy crisis, and so on.

Chapter 3 Futures

Introduction

In this chapter we look at the following:

- The industry life cycle
- PEST factors
- Growth drivers
- Competitive forces
- UCL position (very briefly)

A fuller analysis would cover all aspects of the strategic onion, which frames this chapter (see Figure 8.3), but we will focus here most on the PEST and growth drivers.

PEST Factors

In February 2022, the UK was engulfed in a darkening cloud of rampant inflation, higher National Insurance and energy prices, higher interest

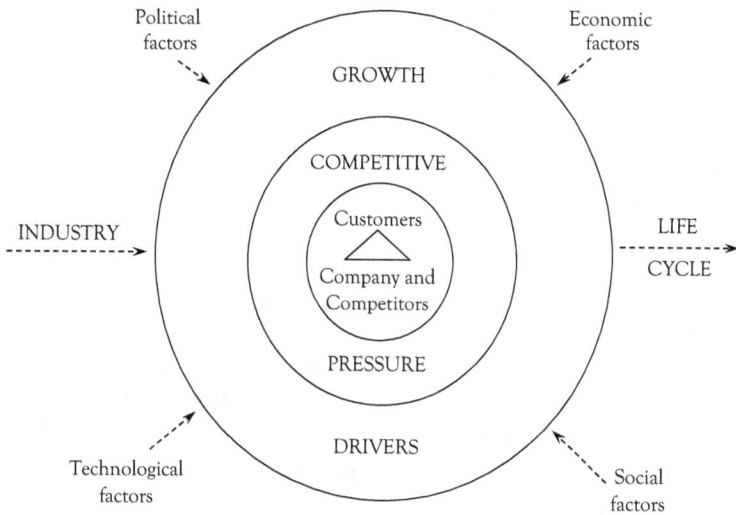

Figure 8.3 The "Strategic Onion"

rates, and political uncertainty internally and globally in addition to the Ukrainian conflict. Income per capita would be squeezed very hard in the short term at least. This was not a favorable backdrop to investing in an MBA, impairing the climate for MBA growth, hugely aggravated by the Ukraine invasion and knock-on effects.

Each one of the many PEST shifts could fruitfully be projected over time in terms of its impact over 20 years. (The social trends are likely to be smooth, slow burn yet increasing in impact.) The economic trends could be far more volatile in the post-COVID hangover economy. One saving grace has been the lack of obvious negative impact of Brexit, all things in sum amounting to limited instability.

There is clearly a lot to absorb in the "weak" signals, but in growth drivers, these factors have made us less bullish on the growth of the MBA market with the curve of growth of pessimistic, being more likely than in curve 2 ("saturation") in Figure 8.4 earlier.

Growth Drivers

Due to the very mixed picture April 2020–March 2022 with two intense years of COVID, we decided to depict the drivers for 2022 to 2027 (see Figure 8.5 for years 1–6).

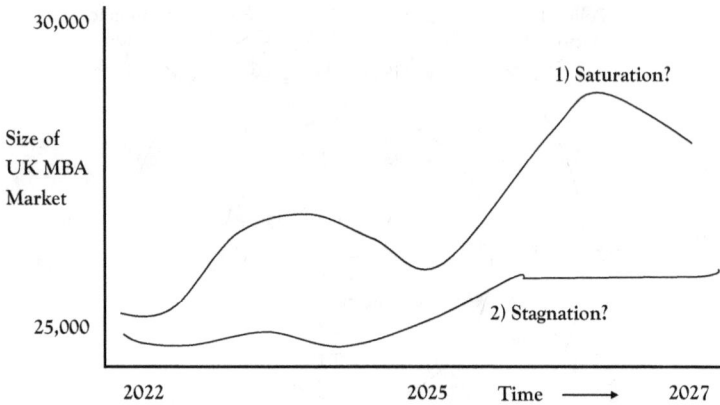

Figure 8.4 UK MBA market growth—(1) a possible projection assuming COVID recovery and (2) economic slowdown and MBA innovation (2022–2027)

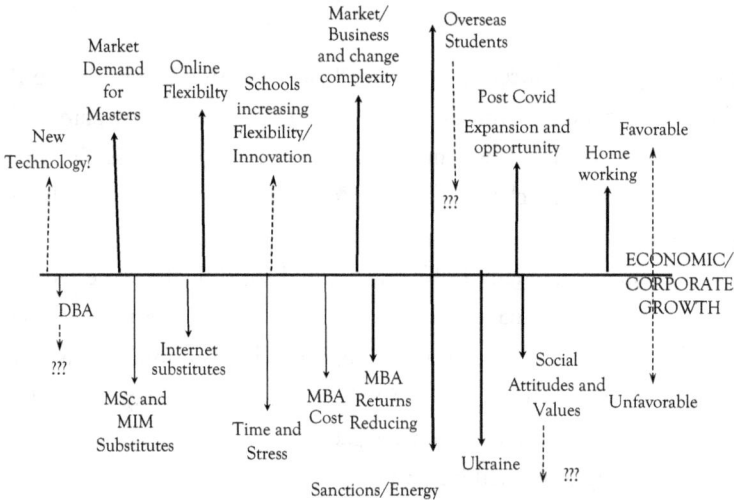

Figure 8.5 MBA market in UK growth/drivers and brakes

Overall, the growth drivers suggest:

- A very mixed picture suggesting it is optimistic to assume that the rates of MBA growth over recent years will be sustained.
- Unless the economic environment is benign throughout (unlikely in years 1–2!) and releases a strong virtuous cycle of

innovation, given the career opportunities amid continued business change challenges, growth will be lower as a base forecast.

- Continued growth in overseas students continues in years 1 to 3 but slower, not helping online as much.
- Achieving any real growth in years 1 to 6 will require much change and innovation.

In addition, we see the beginnings of shifts in social attitudes and values in the latter period years 4 to 6 that may run counter to MBA culture of extremely challenging workload and high commitment and effort, acting as a growth brake.

Let's look at the population of MBAs relative to the populations of the United States versus the UK. Their total populations are 332 million and 67 million making the United States five times bigger. We found one useful bit of statistics that there were around 195,000 MBA students in the United States in 2020 (see www.quora.com/How-many-business-graduate-students-are-there-in-the-United-States-each-year).

That is 7.5 times as many students in the UK (see earlier statistics), suggesting that currently in the United States, there are half as many students again as the UK proportionately. Our previous notions of the student population is that it was around double (the U.S. count). So that initially suggests a somewhat more modest assessment of the potential of future locally fueled growth in the UK, but half of these are overseas. So this suggests assuming that a few UK students go overseas for their MBAs a much more bullish picture! Lesson: Be really careful with data! The United States may have 14 times as many MBAs than the UK with UK students or two and a half times more relative to the population!

But maybe the United States will always outpace the UK in the relative market share of MBAs as the United States is the cultural home of the MBA and the country where capitalism has been traditionally more virulent.

We looked around for research and other commentary into medium- and long-term reviews on trends and discontinuities and drew a blank on anything with quality insights on future MBA growth in the UK. So, we were thrown back on our own "best takes" on the growth drivers and brakes in projecting growth.

The conclusion was that while there were many uncertain factors, the prospects up until late in this period would be relatively benign. Overall, we might expect at least 5 percent annual compound growth and higher growth with increased demand from offshore students assuming the economy stabilizes.

Market research is of patchy quality. For example, GMAC Prospective Candidates 2022 suggests preference for face-to-face and full time, but can students really afford that opportunity cost of time and money (income loss)? Are course candidates actually representative of the market generally?

There have been cases where a school has captured a large number of students from a corporate, which gives companies more influence on courses. This could be a fertile source of extra growth that a currently smaller player could target, especially if it had the credibility and agility.

Competitive Forces

Porter's five forces would tell us to be watchful of new entrants of a disruptive character and ones coming from other strategic groups as well as potentially harsher price and nonprice competition in the MBA market. Customers (mainly students) can only become more discerning and may demand smaller classes and schools might need to pay more attention to putting pressure on staff who may be feeling a burnout.

We haven't gone into detail here on the possible effects of any disruptive new entrants who may leapfrog the innovations attempted by ensconced business schools by reengineering the MBA product and its delivery. Such organizations may wish to poach those agile staff having the most commercial experience.

The key concluding insights are the following:

- The environment is very mixed and is dragged down with economic pressure and political turbulence.
- The recent growth in MBA courses even before the Ukraine looked about to stall overall and that looks worse now in the next 1 to 3 years.

- But a "prospector" entrant might still see untapped potential for UK-based students and much scope for innovation of product and market niche like corporate and civil service especially beyond year 2.
- Growth may still happen for online in the next years 1 to 3 and even more after 2025.
- Competitors might change medium and longer term in terms of how they compete and also who they even are

Chapter 3: Futures 3200

Introduction

In this chapter we cover:

- Primary data
- A systemic model of the MBA market
- Key assumptions and testing
- Scenario possibilities and choices
- Scenarios
- Key concluding insights

Primary Data

I was able to interview two former HR Directors both with strong business skills regarding the fit and value of MBAs, Nicky Burton and Stuart Reid. Space prevents us showing their rich quotes. Their combined output, which was remarkably similar, was that:

- MBAs in the past to them had not really fulfilled the image of being superior and value-added performers with exceptions.
- They didn't stand out as being particularly visionary, innovative, and wealth creators.
- The courses seemed too knowledge-based and analytical rather that being a great balance of hard and soft skills.

- Besides incorporating more hard and soft skills and helping
  the ability to take multiple perspectives on an issue, MBA
  courses could be far more value targeted, designed around the
  individual, flexible, and linked to ongoing lifelong learning.

This view was perhaps less of that from students and more corporate led, however.

A Systemic Model of the MBA Market

Figure 8.6 now gives us a visual picture that maps the main variables that will shape the market. We have chosen to structure it with demand on the right and supply on the left so that we don't just focus on demand. We can also get a better sense of future economic attractiveness through the interface of price and volumes. Supply factors are important too as with fast growth this could diminish quality and debase the MBA currency. Also, there would be supply side constraints, for example, quality teaching staff.

The supply side takes us through the hard and soft skills needed by faculty, their commercial experience, their style and agility, and lastly there are the new technologies, for example learning platforms and the frequency of renewal. In the past, programs would have a more fundamental review, say every 8 to 10 years. That could shorten to 4 to 5 years putting even more pressure on staff and costs (?), another possible scenario.

The demand side is even more complex in its richness with this splitting by market sectors. There are the competitive influences, the MBA halo (a giant brand), and substitutes. We haven't even mentioned the sustained driving influence of the MBA salary and package premium, which in turn depends on the perceived and real value added to businesses and the economy, which are vulnerabilities.

Note: Some things may not be central like DBAs and possible disruptive new entrants, but we felt it important to log these as others or ourselves in the future might take a different view.

Figure 8.6 helps to prioritize the issues without oversimplifying. It also allows us to revisit and adapt any scenarios.

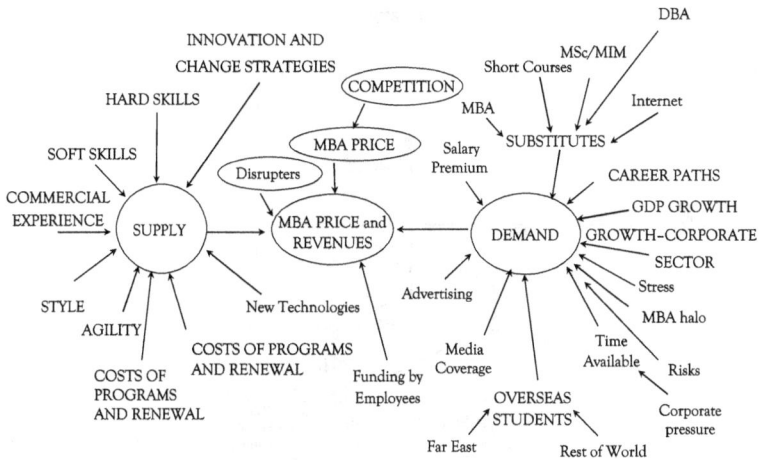

Figure 8.6 Systems picture of the UK MBA market

Demand seems to be a function of:

Perceived Tangible Value (MBA premium + career opportunities)
  plus
  Perceived Intangible Value (Value, Status, and so on)
  less
  Cost (financial cost + risk + time and stress)

Common Assumptions

Initial candidates for common assumptions were:

- No major war (now falsified)
- No major economic slump
- UK economic growth circa 1 to 4 percent
- Asian economic growth circa 4 to 6 percent
- Benign and positive media coverage of MBA and business schools
- Increase in demand from the public sector is not significant overall

See Figure 8.7 for a fuller Uncertainty Grid.

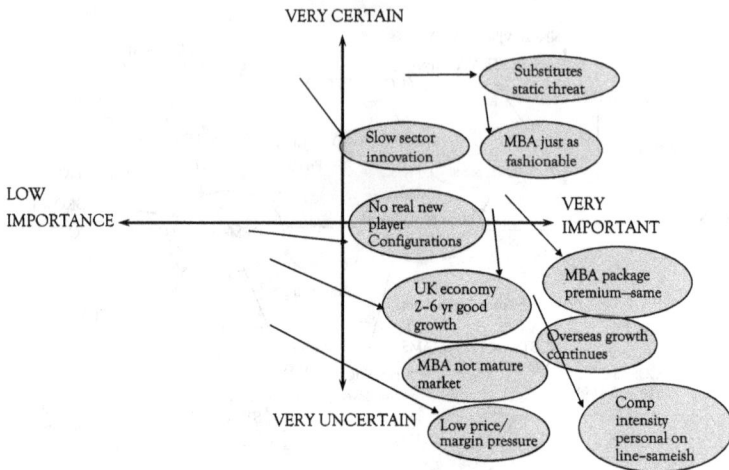

VERY CERTAIN

Substitutes
static threat

Slow sector
innovation

MBA just as
fashionable

LOW
IMPORTANCE

No real new
player
Configurations

VERY
IMPORTANT

UK economy
2-6 yr good
growth

MBA package
premium–same

Overseas growth
continues

MBA not mature
market

VERY UNCERTAIN

Low price/
margin pressure

Comp
intensity
personal on
line-sameish

Figure 8.7 The uncertainty grid—"zero/low growth scenario" (UK MBA market)

Scenario Shopping List

This list was compiled both from the scenarios highlighted in bold italics as we went and also some that we pulled from the Growth Driver and Systemic model pictures. Some of these could be mixed together:

1. More soft skills on the MBA and action learning; becoming more project and consulting based, with more focus on employability.
2. There are two further COVID variants over years 1 to 2 before vaccination worldwide reached saturation; these outbreaks add more impetus to the online model, also causing further economic disruption.
3. If there is a financial meltdown, the media blames MBAs; economic slump dampens MBA demand.
4. UK economic squeeze aggravated by global political and economic stability reduces UK demand (Russia invades Ukraine too?) (now a reality).
5. The UK market is saturated such that tier 3 players exit the market or consolidate.
6. Supply side reconfiguration—for example, corporates, consultancies, accounting firms get involved in JVs for MBAs; within this model less university influence: year 4 onward.

7. Radical and innovative change by a few schools to add more value to students and corporates boosts growth. Demand to do MBAs also increases through rapid business change in the corporate sector, producing a sustained boom in UK students, enabled by the fact the market isn't really saturated yet for years 4 to 7.

8. A much greater focus on what the value of an MBA is; its dimensions, for example not just money but career flexibility and agility, getting funding and financing, MBA project value to the organization, and an output being one's personal MBA portfolio, alumni, post-MBA advanced training, and so on.

9. A shift toward more longer-range MBAs 3 to 4 years out with greater practical application and more projects; the "Stretched MBA" and one which is more individually centered.

10. In a growth scenario, there is a race for talent that then challenges the assumptions about what resources are needed their sourcing, careers, and contracts and costs.

11. Fast overseas growth continues helped by UK visa advantages and by online strengths, advertising, and branding and assumed better engineering of MBAs for value.

12. Slow maybe no growth in overseas MBAs due to their schools radically catching up and maybe leapfrogging the UK years 4 to 10 for example, in digitalization, plus they create more global programs and the United States offers similar visa opportunities for work there that level the playing field.

13. Substitutes erode the market—Masters, short courses, the Internet. Plus the effort and the stress of doing MBA is off-putting to students, especially Generation X. Adverse media commentary begins to act as a turning point for MBAs being regarded as passe.

14. Counter to popular assumptions in the public sector, the UK Civil Service is subjected to a management revolution post-COVID and Party-gate that opens up that side of the economy to the MBA.

15. Growth comes more from programs that are more specialized—by sector, function, theme (e.g., digitization, advisory, and consulting) than the generalist ones.

16. The UK and later on the United States offer favorable visas to MBA students to work there during and for three years after MBA

completion, consolidating their skills pitting the two countries in a healthy competition.

17. A small number of major business schools become true multinationals and their strength enables them to pull students in from around the world wearing locally satisfied markets like the UK.

Online courses will be impacted by the retreat of COVID, enabling face-to-face courses to restart.

While we only have time to explore through storytelling only one or two in this list, it gives us a tripwire for detecting market shifts, discerning patterns in shifts, and enabling us to pull one down from the shelf for development, expansion, and evaluation.

Note: Some of these scenarios might be fused together to produce plausible and interesting scenarios. For example:

- Theme No. 1: Soft skills + No. 6 supply side change + No. 7 greater innovation + No. 8 greater value = "Growth"
- Theme No. 2 COVID + No. 3 financial meltdown + No. 4 economic slump + No. 5 UK saturation+ No. 8 focus on greater value + No. 12 slow/no overseas growth + No. 13 substitutes erode the MBA = "Slump"
- Theme No. 3: change in supply side + No. 8 focus on greater value + No. 15 specialization, visa growth = "Change of mix"

The first and the second themes for the future offer a polarity of views for testing the resilience and the upsides of the MBA. COVID receding is a growth brake for online demand across all segments of MBA.

Scenario Choice

Some important and uncertain assumptions are given in Figure 8.8 in dynamic context and these were framed to be positive on the basis that the world goes right:

- Substitutes are a static threat.
- The MBA is just as fashionable over the period as now.

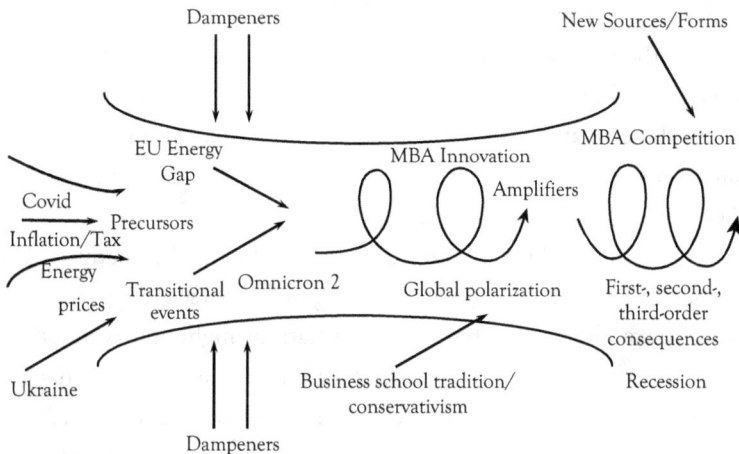

Figure 8.8 The uncertainty tunnel—low/zero MBA growth 2022–2025

- No real new player configurations.
- There is relatively slow innovation in the market.
- The UK economy will grow years 2 to 6 once NI, post-COVID inflation, and energy prices are digested.
- The MBA package premium continues around the same levels.
- The MBA is a mature but stable market in the UK with supply being saturated and not a lot of new, potential, demand, with a lower online growth.
- Overseas demand continues to grow but at a much more modest rate as Far and Middle Eastern schools build capability and reputation slowly though.
- There is low pressure on price and margins.
- Competitive intensity for more personalized online delivery is similar.

Testing was conducted using the uncertainty grid using two broad framings: (A) "modest growth" and (B) "testing the MBA model." Common assumptions were positioned for both (A) and (B). Further candidates like "there will be rapid innovation and increased complexity in businesses over 6 years" and "there will be rapid innovations and more focus on MBA value such that growth is accelerated across the sector with the UK leading internationally" were included in the testing.

Scenario A had many but not all of the 10 assumptions positioned in or on the borders of the "danger zone" of high importance and high uncertainty. This strongly suggests that there was a relatively high exposure to these volatile factors, for example, things like assumed UK economic growth and continued increasing demand from overseas students, albeit at a lower level than the recent past.

In Scenario A, there is high exposure to MBA market maturity, UK economic growth, and faltering overseas growth. These are aggravated in testing the model scenario B where such volatility might shift assumptions southeast (see the arrows). As some other assumptions enter the danger, southeast zone like "the MBA package premium will be the same," this might then erode the attractiveness of the MBA to students, especially if the value perceived by them were subject to increased scrutiny.

Regarding "competitive intensity of online," we see this as inevitably intensifying following the impact of COVID although most schools haven't value reengineered the product, which is yet to be as personalized as face to face. That assumption is at the very south edge of the grid, which is ominous feeding into the storytelling for the following two scenarios.

Scenario A: Zero to Low Growth 2022–2025 (Drafted April 2022)

The uncertainty tunnel translated the most volatile assumptions into a more dynamic sequence through to the future in Figure 8.9.

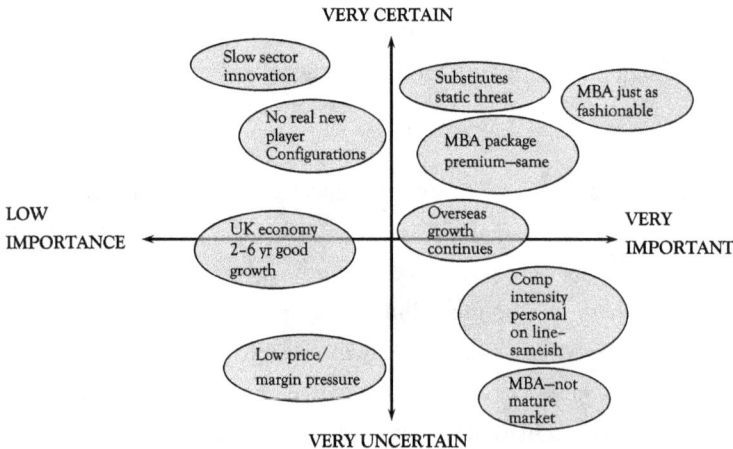

Figure 8.9 The uncertainty grid—"Modest growth scenario"

Story Line

Putin's army gets bogged down in the Ukraine after eight weeks of fighting and much territory is in his hands, but there is military and civil resistance and sanctions bite only gradually. In the winter of 2022–2023, his support crumbles as his energy revenues are dry and there is an army coup. This turbulence and energy prices have caused a medium global recession in 2022 to early 2024.

In the UK by summer of 2022, we have seen COVID waves become much more containable with vaccination and immunity. However, while COVID is less of a threat, unfortunately a somewhat worse variant blots raged through November 2022 to February 2023, although economic damage is much less than previously.

Economic growth falters with extra National Insurance and energy costs with bills doubling in a year, squeezing disposable income. This does not inspire confidence in prospective UK MBAs at all.

COVID has shifted for good the balance of online versus face-to-face on MBAs, but students crave real personalization. After the recession in 2022–2023 in the next few years, economic and business expansion through innovation might stimulate MBA demand. Gradually through continuous improvement, schools evolve into greater personalization although the remaining gap between the variable relevance, value of MBA provision, and real market needs do show up in reduced volumes and increased price pressure, especially as many online courses are cheaper.

A number of business schools realize that they need to accomplish scale of programs at the same time as enriching value for money, relevance, and marketability. Personalization becomes the marketing buzz word. A number of MBA Directors share ideas to rejuvenate the product and that the UK needs a makeover. They need to collaborate on a joint "learning platform."

As a first step to reconfiguring the resource base, they agree to share (bit like the player loans system in football) special skills within their partnership. This is also an attraction to overseas students, helping sustain the growth. Still, the inertia of the business schools as first and foremost purveyors of academic knowledge persists, and change is first slow and on the edges initially. This will gain momentum from 2024 to 2028.

This scenario seems plausible and mutually consistent. There are many alternative substories (tunes) that could be played. There is also big pressure for change, but there is countervailing inertia, mind sets not conducive to change, and industry fragmentation. So there are wobbles here.

The key concluding insights are as follows:

- There are many diverse possible scenario themes; so there is much uncertainty including accelerated innovation, offset by industry traditionalism.
- There are issues about what the real value of an MBA is in the contemporary world and the halo effect cannot be taken for granted.
- The future may lie in more flexible and more personalized MBAs with more focus on application.
- Demand and supply drivers are complex and interplay in complex ways offering much change that traditional business schools may struggle with.
- Growth prospects overall are weaker for 2022–2024 and maybe 2025 too, although online could grow.
- With price pressure, weaker schools will be squeezed and some might exit or collaborate.
- After 2025, there may be growth for more innovative schools, but its timing has been pushed out into the future by economic conditions; there are opportunities for niche market development, for example, corporate and public sector MBAs.

Implications and strategic options are omitted due to space constraints.

Final Concluding Insights

- The MBA market is in a state of great flux through external shocks, a corporate environment of probably doubling of uncertainty, and potential questioning of the real value of the MBA.
- Before the recent inflation and hikes in energy prices and Ukraine, there seemed to be a large potential for innovation

and change building up, but some of that is likely to now be lagged.

- The online market may still grow through convenience and so on. However, the scenario work already suggests lines of enquiry for widening that advantage through individualization and practical application.

By Dr. Tony Grundy (opinions are his own)

Conclusion

The simulated MBA project mentioned earlier was a rich learning experience and highlighted the importance of progressive focusing and of prioritization as well as being open to unexpected findings. Although shortened, hopefully it will give an insight to the practice of scenario building and storytelling.

Key Concluding Insights

To develop quality scenarios requires the skillful, structured, and imaginative integration of many tools, thought processes, and evidential support, prioritization, and insight.

It is worth emphasizing separately to be mindset aware. In the course of this exercise, I took a student (being an MBA graduate myself) mindset, a business school (a corporate mindset), and also lecturer mindset. I saw the market through all of these mindsets (and also an alien mindset that I was able to get a more rounded a challenging view of the futures). This alongside the different views of the future necessitated a very agile approach and mindfulness, which mindset was now in play.

CHAPTER 9

Conclusions

Introduction

An urban myth has it that if you put a frog in a pot of boiling water, it will instantly leap out. But if you put it in a pot filled with pleasantly tepid water and gradually heat it, the frog will remain in the water until it boils to death. The frog is not able to detect the gradual increase in temperature until it's too late.

—The National Library of Medicine. December 7, 2004. *Canadian Medical Association Journal* 171, no. 12, p. 145. https://doi.org/10.1503/cmaj.1041718.

My take on this is that slow environmental change can be more dangerous than a rapid change as one has no choice but to take notice and act! This highlights the need to fine tune the sensing routines and processes of organizations, particularly whose agility and internal clock speed is sluggish. *So, uncertainty is not all out there in the environment, but it can start at home.*

This chapter is very much on our implementation of better approaches. In the final chapter, we will be covering a number of areas:

- Bad cop or good cop: is uncertainty mixed?
- Applying scenario and related approaches in practice
- Using it in everyday life
- On uncertainty and scenario theory
- Toward an energy theory of strategy
- Key concluding insights
- Summary of the book

Bad Cop or Good Cop: Is Uncertainty Mixed?

I now ask the question of whether uncertainty is all bad? It's threatening to us all as it stirs anxiety fear and even dread (a huge concern to humans in existentialistic philosophy; Heidegger 1927). I reckon that a large part of it is tied up with the need for humans to hang onto territory and to defend it, thus provoking a closed and negative response. One of the limiting constraints on the use of scenarios and thinking about uncertainty generally is our capacity/ability to cope with dread, allowing us to manage the deep and dark, swirling feelings of loss that are generated by thinking the virtually unthinkable. This is even more threatening than in a strategic thinking session as these turbulent feelings, even if at this stage, are only in the imagination and are stirred up far more head on.

Heidegger also talked about the sense of "falling" as resulting from the perception of experiencing great vulnerability and helplessness. This is what one experiences with acute uncertainty.

On the BBC Sunday TV program May 22, 2022, for example, the Head of Press Communication at the White House, when asked whether the United States "got" the real threat from Russia before the war, admitted that they had been preoccupied with other wars and potential threats from elsewhere in the world. Combined with that, they had not been ready to think that European stability was truly exposed to a war threat and especially that it would be prosecuted in that brutal way. Simply that was too hard and horrible a thing to imagine. *But the lesson on us all is that you can't blow hideous possible futures away however tough they are.* That means being acutely mindful of the overall mindset and the assumptions and beliefs web that underpins uncertainty (see Figure 9.1).

A wonderful example of the effects of this "dread" is Kotter's book with penguin characters, *Our Iceberg Is Melting* (2017), who need to find a new home.

But uncertainty can offer opportunities too. For instance, climate change offers huge growth opportunities through green investment. Such threats provoke change, which stirs up practices and mindsets, making organizations more alert, agile, and responsive. That's all "good cop" stuff.

One of the wisdoms that is buried in SWOT analysis is:

"There is invariably an opportunity buried in a threat."

Even where uncertainty posed nail-biting threats, not only can we see further ahead into that than we thought possible as demonstrated in this book, but we can increase our resilience and agility as seen later in this chapter. It is far from all being "bad cop."

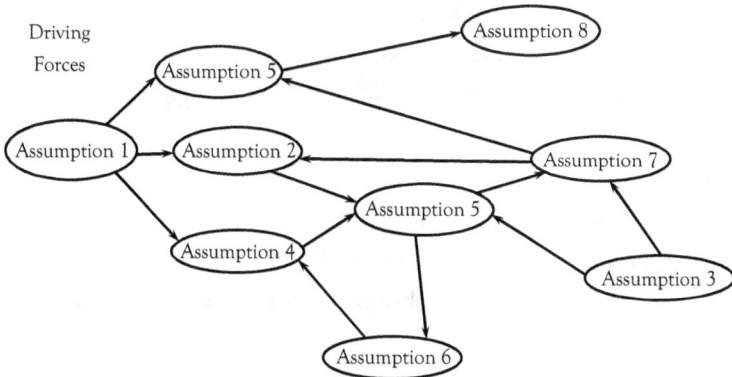

Figure 9.1 *An assumptions and beliefs web*

Applying Scenario and Related Approaches in Practice

This book has a toolkit that will go a long way toward shining a brighter light into the fog of the future. Whilst inspired by the founders of scenario thinking in the 1970s and the 1980s, the tool kit has been pushed way beyond using a mix of PEST and Porter through the uncertainty grid and many other tools to become a much more sophisticated, integrated, and effective process. Indeed, those early proponents were probably a little ahead of their time in that since then turbulence has become endemic rather than episodic.

In the last century, there was no Brexit, there was no massive pandemic, no direct threat to European peace, the UK was a member of EU for 30 years, and there was considerably slower and relatively pedestrian ecology change.

Other than the secondary banking crises in the UK in 1973–75, there was nothing like the credit crunch of 2008. What matched the 7/11 terrorist attacks? In my hazy memory of those times, climate change was a distant and vague threat. Social media did not exist. Stagflation was assumed beaten. *Truly, scenarios were born before their truly biggest hour of need 40 years later!*

If there were ever a great example of accelerating uncertainty, it is the story of the British Prime Minister's eventual eviction for a stream of incidents when his truthfulness was challenged. There were 45 resignations on July 6 and 7, 2022. At one stage, there were 10 resignations an hour! His rate of appointments couldn't keep up with the rate of resignations! I had written a stream of letters to him, giving a strategic steer over 2001–2002. In the last one three months before the eventual coup, I suggested he was *doomed* and that he might consider a film acting career, which is something he might do well. Even that sixth one had no reply. It is a tongue in cheek, but still a pertinent example of how one can sense over the horizon using scenario storytelling (see online case study 5).

Since this book was finished, Liz Truss became Prime Minister and within 43 days (in 393 hours assuming ten-hour days) nearly managed to bankrupt the UK at a cost estimated at £40 billion or around £93 million an hour estimated work by Liz Truss, treating us to a remarkable experience of Heidegger's falling unparalleled since probably Dunkirk!

As the worlds of business and management are spaces for sexy sounding, idealistic movements like Total Quality Management (TQM) and Business Process Reengineering (BPR) once upon a time and Six Sigma, Lean Management, and Performance Excellence now, new generations thirst for the next craze. So, a book like this with scenarios as its core can face a skeptical audience, which is a pity. Having business foresight and thus sensing and thinking about the future is not a fad that has gone away; it's an integral part of our evolutionary process.

Perhaps the most challenging issue is climate change. What could be more applicable to the boiling frog story than that? We have not had the time and space to deep dive into that one here, but arguably present war and economic turbulence are minor if we were to be like H. G. Wells and are prepared to visualize 125 years into the future.

We will need scenarios like its bigger sister—strategy throughout this century. I hope that the toolkit, the case studies, my bouncy narrative, and the readers' exercises (if you haven't done them, you must, even if after you have finished this chapter) have induced you to see that scenarios as exemplified in this book truly help you to manage uncertainty strategically.

So, what are the issues of putting the process into practice?

- Defining the scope of a study and its focus
- Planning the time and timings

- Finding the right people
- Defining the stakeholders
- Positioning
- Facilitation
- Overcoming skepticism and resistances
- Strategic positioning papers
- Testing against fragility and resilience

Defining the Scope of a Study and Its Focus

The scope is determined by three main things:

1. Space (business and geography)
2. Time
3. Issues (e.g., regulatory, economic, social, markets and competition, technology, operational, organizational, implementation, stakeholders)

"Space" can be broad or narrow—the choice depends on interest, objectives, variably and time and need. "Time" can be a little as five minutes (a conversation),ninety minutes (a football match), 18 months (the Ukraine war?), five years (MBA scenarios; Chapter 8), or 20 years for electric cars, 50 years for the circular economy. It is "horses for courses."

Short Case Study—From Family Life

To illustrate just how short that time horizon can be, many years ago I took my young kids out for a pub lunch in a quiet Cambridgeshire village. They could be quite noisy and difficult when I had them together and I had had some difficult and bad experiences. So, I did some preparatory storytelling with a 60-minute time horizon, leading to things going down and what I would do about that and when.

We had just gone into the pub and my kids (seven and nine) took one look at it and decided that it just wasn't for them. "It's really not nice," said one and the other. "This place smells," said the other. They were beginning to argue and fight with each other and clearly had embarked on a path of disruption.

I sensed myself being sucked into a turbulent uncertainty tunnel like being sucked into a jet engine of uncertainty or even a black hole. I stopped in my tracks, got hold of their arms, and said "Stop" and "We are going home," thus avoiding a near certain disaster.

My reaction speed was 1.5 seconds, enabled by my earlier scenario work. *So my storytelling had successfully set up the trip wires that told me "This is about to happen again,"* underlying the value of scenarios through cognitive and action agility.

The case underlines the point that very short-term time horizons can harbor high-impact uncertainties and thus are very amenable to storytelling. *They are very good now (in their thirties).*

More generally, the duration of the time horizon is set by considering how far can one foresee with reasonable plausibility, what might emerge, and how and with what results. In addition, this can be influenced by what the investment time horizons are like plus what proportion of the NPV of the business is tied up in its "terminal value," that is, the NPV of the sustainable free cash flows per annum after the point of the time horizon. In some cases, it could still be 30 percent of the total NPV so that is still material.

As emphasized earlier in the book, it can be helpful in setting some horizon to define what phases of the future there might be, or maybe even in a bolder way slice time up into two or three futures.

The breadth of the issues chosen will depend on context, complexity, the interest, the objectives, and needs. There is a trade-off between painting a more complete, rich, and dynamic picture and spreading oneself too thinly.

Another thing to consider is setting the boundaries to the study: What things are you not going to be doing? Where it is difficult to be black and white that you can still differentiate primary and secondary targets for a scenario?

Finally, to make things even clearer, it is useful to define a few key objectives such as:

- To explore the future major changes in the pay-in-advance funeral market and their impact in order to assess the threats

- To understand how resilient that is to two or more scenarios to provide a health check
- To project the implications of such shifts into the future over time and to create some new strategic options to deal with them

It may even be useful to define a small number of strategic questions to inform the study such as for example.

What might be the cunning plan for getting people to sign up for a pay in advance for a service that is something that they really wouldn't like to think about (like for prepaid cremations)?

Planning the Time and Timings

Time: I have more commonly done scenario development within a two-day scenarios and strategy workshop with the advantage that two days allows enough time to get into helicopter thinking space as a platform for the time travel, scenario context building, and of course some strategic option grid evaluation and work on any implications.

With standalone scenario work, then one day can sometimes at a pinch be feasible provided the futures are not terribly complex and diverse and a fair degree of knowledge about them is already available. For instance, Tesco Direct was accomplished in a day. I also facilitated one for Tesco Metro, which resulted in considerable thinking around the existing strategy and, in all fairness, another day would have been much better.

If there is a lot of build-up work required as in Amerada Petroleum, a full two days would be needed. The best advice on duration from my experience is "don't skimp on time." Besides a two-day workshop model, a really good approach is to meet up at 4 p.m. and work for two-and-half to three hours to get tuned in the night before the main sessions, and thus to have done some sharing of preparatory work and development ahead.

A scenario dinner would be a great unfreezing process with maybe some ice breakers and some war stories and getting people to do some storytelling from their personal lives. Then on the next day, you can hit the ground running with the main event. Within the next two weeks, there needs to be a three-hour washing up event to distill lessons learned and extract the insights, the key decisions and rationale, and to arrive at the action areas and responsibility. If you were wanting to refresh the vision as a secondary output, then that could be the day two or at least until midday.

With regard to detailed timings, a good process for arriving at it is as follows:

- Define the objectives and any research questions;
- Define the targeted outputs;
- Define using a list of questions to guide each exercise (typically intro, 10 minutes; work, 50 minutes; feedback, 40 minutes (two or three subgroups)—1 hour and 40 minutes). With four cycles of exercises in a day with breaks. That's a day's work.

Once the questions and the process of enquiry are devised, then you can pick from the toolkit which tool to use based on what you are asking in the sessions.

Time and scope: In such an uncertain world, there is *a strong case for combining strategy and scenarios in the same event and process it as an "SAS" exercise.* That also emphasizes clinical activity, decisiveness, and battlefield alertness.

Finding the Right People

First of all, however knowledgeable and experienced you are in scenarios, there is still no substitute for involving someone why should be "in the know" and thus gather some fresh, primary data from, rather than just googling the topic. Even just one or two formal or totally informal interviews will enable you to think about the issues a lot more objectively. Interviews give you a lot not just about the present and trends but also about discontinuous futures.

Better still is a proper workshop with at least three people in each subteam so that there is more chance of generating rich ideas. The best number in a subteam is four or five. If you had three subteams, then the ideal total number is 12, but you will need to allow for more reporting back time. It is good to have one person with a more creative bent in each subteam or it may run dry. All need to be interested and motivated, but not all need to be divergent thinkers. There is a place too for the reality checkers and the shapers who can put more structure and sense into the flow of ideas. There should be a balanced team mix.

As there should be enough knowledge of the status quo and strategic issues, that calls for some senior people. Equally, there is a very real and important role for newer and younger people to provide a different and fresher view.

Defining the Stakeholders and Positioning

Stakeholders were covered in Chapter 7. Stakeholders vary in their importance, attitude, and influence and across different issues. So, some would be very involved in formulating strategies and less so in the "how" of implementation, while some implementors can be good too. So, there might be a number of stakeholder grids with people appearing at different places on different issues. This mapping can give you insights not just who is best to invite *but who it is politically correct to invite.*

A "stakeholder" is defined as "someone who is a decision maker, an influencer or an implementor, or a victim." Also, influence or, more brutally, "power" can be positive or passive, and also defensive.

Of course, we may want people with no particularly special power but who can inform, direct, and shape the investigation, ones who can get things done, ones who know things, and ones with vision. Such people were called "seers" in ancient times.

Once the objectives and expectations are settled, the exercise can be then communicated to both stakeholders and participants. This can be overlapping between groups. Of course, people not invited may be put out unless they are managed skillfully by positioning it well, in order to gain buy-in. When the output is finished, it can be sent to them either raw, as a summary, or a strategic position paper (see below). That communication should have at least:

- What it is about
- Scope: what's in and what is out (very important)
- Why we are doing it—the key objectives and intended outputs

- The process and any rework
- Timings and key strategic questions
- Targeted outputs
- Facilitation
- Who is invited and why
- Prework
- Other expectations
- What will or might happen next

Facilitation

In the BT case, I told the story of a facilitator who didn't appear impartial, which triggered a big upset in the group. It is hard for an internal facilitator to do the job by appearing impartial. The very fact of being employed there makes it extremely difficult to be a strategy facilitator (for more see Grundy 2002a).

Also, one really needs some training both business-wise and process-wise, not just for competence but credibility and confidence too. The facilitator may be an MBA, possessing organizational behavior ("OB"), project management, and consulting skills, but practically orientated courses to impart this training are rare.

All too often, planners tend to be set in a "expert" paradigm rather than a facilitator and its dynamics, especially those who have come from a financial background. So they may lack some of the skills.

Scenario building is about being able to model all kinds of industries in one's head so that you can ask the probing and the incisive questions and the ones that challenge assumptions and mindsets. It also requires a stance which is all about integrity—you align with the organization and care a lot while maintaining a strong independence and detachment. When it is really called for, you can say what's your own take on it.

I once helped an MSc student who was doing his project on facilitation. I was interviewed to inform how I added value through being a strategic facilitator and many things came up:

- Defining scope and objectives and advice on stakeholders, participants, and positioning
- Detailed timings and exercise planning
- Designing prework

- Conceptual input and setting up exercises
- People management (there can be difficulties!—see below)
- Observing and nudging group work and posing questions
- Time and activity management
- Dealing with difficulties
- Facilitating feedback
- Summarizing and evaluating and drawing out insights and implications
- Process management throughout
- Assistance in the storytelling
- Project managing next steps
- Asking "what's the one big thing we forgot?"
- Landing the thing at the end

This is quite an intense list as you can see. Even though I have had thousands of hours of flight experience, yet there is always something to keep you on your toes. On one occasion, the groups were split into pairs and I just had the inkling that I needed to check with one pair. They were talking very quietly, so I approached them slowly and when I tuned into the conversation, I realized that they were having a fierce and personally charged argument! One of them was just on the brink of giving the other a smack across the face by Will Smith! It was almost like a night at the Oscars.

I just managed to avert a massive problem. We were all two minutes maximum from an uncertainty tunnel!

Overcoming Skepticism and Resistance

Working with my UCL MBA students on their Futures Project reinforced my past impression that there are some deep-seated resistances that inhibit any transition from trend and discontinuity analysis, which is embedded in conventional planning. This might be down to

- Fear that they will get it wrong and thus look silly (but scenarios are about sensing pathways rather than projections?).
- Difficulty of shifting from a descriptive and analytical cognition to a much more creative one.

- Stepping outside the currently shared beliefs of the prevailing planning mindset of the organization—the strategic furniture that they have been socialized in.
- The present is a tangible and confers security (unless you are being sucked into an uncertainty tunnel, for example, seafood toxic reaction!); as the future is fluid, the mind thus defaults us away from that to the present.
- There is thus an understandable reluctance to experiment with a new way of thinking like scenarios. Managers disbelieve that even two or more scenario stories will give a meaningful range of outcomes that decisions can be based on. But this is to say "it's better to go around blindfold than to walk around with two eyes as we can't see everything everywhere all at once." But each scenario is a test and it will create learning and triangulate the shape of the phenomenon. Why compartmentalize storytelling as just something that you do for your kids at bedtime when it could be such huge value? You can always rerun it too.

Strategic Position Paper

This document is a write-up of a piece of future thinking, which gives a first take on the future, developing the analysis from the present and the past. Typically, it isn't very long—maybe five pages with supporting pictures. It is positioned as a paper for discussion to record the thinking so far and to trigger more thought and learning.

It is also useful for getting buy in from stakeholders:

- To gain interest and attention (that this issue is worth thinking about);
- To open up more thinking about the future;
- To provoke thought on possible different storylines (at least two—that's really the minimum);
- To begin to think that we should consider some fresh strategic options to pre-empt or react to future change;
- To keep any of them not invited at the workshops so that they don't feel that they are excluded.

Testing Against Fragility and Resilience

Having assessed the impact of any new scenarios on the existing strategy and possibly having looked at the array of contingent strategies, there also needs to be some thought about the implications for the environment, the business model, change, and mindsets. This can be done either in the main scenario workshop or in a subsequent smaller "washing up" session.

But more fundamental is to add on some time to explore fragility and resilience. These two factors are very important and yet underdeveloped in mainstream strategy. They have a huge role to play in exploring the impact of uncertain scenarios. Fragility and resilience both seem to be a blind spot when managing uncertainty.

I define "fragility" as "the extent to which a group or business or a part of it is vulnerable to external stresses and strains."

I define "resilience" as "the capability to withstand external and internal stresses and strains either through sheer strength (of the business design), flexibility, or agility."

Fragility and agility are thus polar, one being bad and the other being good. Thinking about them in the same breath does seem to be on a continuum in the same way as strengths and weaknesses are in a conventional SWOT analysis. However, fragility can be a weakness, for instance, through organizational brittleness. For example, when a new top team hits a bump early on and struggles to make decisions, it suggests a high level of suspicion in the group. Just like the rivets in the *Titanic* (see the earlier case study), this brittleness could be under the surface, and internal and magnify external vulnerability. So there's an accident waiting to happen. That's a contingent thing, still not a measurable "weakness."

So how is the analysis of fragility and resilience any different from "weaknesses" and "strengths"? For me, the natural meaning of these factors is richer than a broader SWOT. They don't just explore a state through a set of properties but are about a dynamic capability to withstand, to minimize, or even avoid damaging impacts. So we are not just dealing with a "hard crunch" or a full on "car crash" scenario. In the following suggested analysis, you would be testing fragility and resilience. This would not just relative to an expected future, but potentially to a range of potential futures and at least to specific threats too.

To give SWOT analysis something of a makeover, I propose a better tool than SWOT—"FROST" analysis:

- F for fragility
- R for resilience
- OS for opportunity scenarios
- T for threat

As you can see, in Figures 9.2 and 9.3, I have used the same format as the strategic option grid for displaying this framework. Both fragility and resilience are broken down using some generic themes—do feel free to tailor to your own circumstances. These are

- Strategy
- Leadership
- Capabilities
- Processes
- Other resources

These seem to capture most of the really mission-critical, strategic assets of a business that could make it more or less vulnerable to uncertainties. "Resources" here will include both finance and people.

Options Criteria	Threat 1	Threat 2	Threat 3	Threat 4
Strategy	★ ★ ⭐	★		
Leadership	★ ⭐	★		
Capabilities	★ ★ ★	★		
Processes	★ ★	★		
Other Resources	★ ★ ⭐	★		

Figure 9.2 The fragility grid—against major threats

Score: 3 = very low, 2 = medium 1 high exposure to fragility (NB reverse scores for Opportunity Scenarios)

See Figures 9.2 and 9.3 for mapping the five key drivers of fragility and then those of resilience against major threats.

In addition you can also map the five key drivers of fragility and then those of resilience against major opportunity scenarios, which can be as broad or as specific as you like (not shown for brevity).

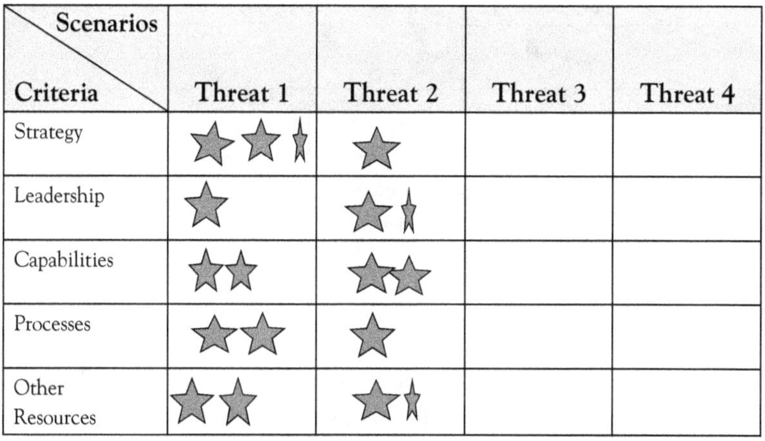

Scenarios Criteria	Threat 1	Threat 2	Threat 3	Threat 4
Strategy	★★⭐	★		
Leadership	★	★⭐		
Capabilities	★★	★★		
Processes	★★	★		
Other Resources	★★	★⭐		

Figure 9.3 The resilience grid—against major threats
Score: 3 = very high, 2 = medium 1 = low resilience

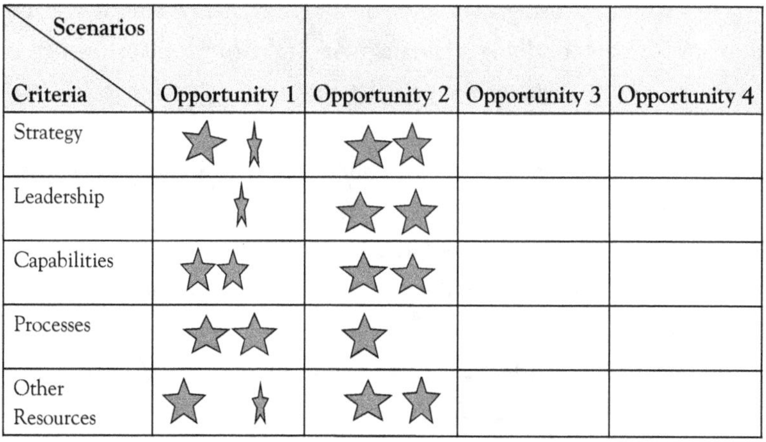

Scenarios Criteria	Opportunity 1	Opportunity 2	Opportunity 3	Opportunity 4
Strategy	★⭐	★★		
Leadership	⭐	★★		
Capabilities	★★	★★		
Processes	★★	★		
Other Resources	★⭐	★★		

Figure 9.4 The fragility grid—against "Opportunity Scenarios"
Score: 3 = very low, 2 = medium 1 high exposure to fragility (NB reverse scores for Opportunity Scenarios)

Scenarios / Criteria	Opportunity 1	Opportunity 2	Opportunity 3	Opportunity 4
Strategy	★★⯪	★		
Leadership	★⯪	★		
Capabilities	★★	★★		
Processes	★★	★⯪		
Other Resources	★★	★		

Figure 9.5 The resilience grid—against "Opportunity Scenarios"

Score: 3 = very high, 2 = medium 1 = low resilience

Reader Exercise

Then, for a couple of threats and opportunities, how do these look in the context of both fragility factors and resilience factors?

In terms of the scoring of the resilience grids, notice the reversal of the scores so that, for instance, where there is no resilience against either threats or opportunities, there are low scores rather than high scores. This is because fragility is a negative thing.

To test strategy using all or some of "FROST," help is already at hand through a process of doing a "Strategy Audit" (Grundy 2018), which is a strategy health check of the completeness of the strategy in its present state and of its processes. Capabilities might be addressed in some organizations through, for example, succession and development plans and engagement studies, but that is typically patchy and not really very testing. "Leadership" can be sensitive as this might be completed by the leaders who might think "oh, dear that's us, but if I am a turkey how can I vote for Christmas?"

In terms of the grids themselves, I show for fragility against threats and one for resilience against threats; in addition, I have one for fragility against opportunity scenarios and another for resilience against opportunity scenarios. Do make sure when you flip from threats to opportunities that you adjust the scoring basis so that when you are very resilient in the face of an opportunity scenario, this is a good thing.

Not only should we look at the broader implications of change for any scenario, but it is also important to compare that with the organization's fragility–resilience so that we can get a better feel not just of brutal impact of change but also its vulnerability. For instance, Amazon was in better shape than regular supermarkets when COVID struck and even better relative to non food retailers who were locked down.

To get a vivid picture of real resilience, there is nothing better than to get familiar with the Honey Badger, a fierce and awesome animal half-scavenger and half-lion (look up YouTube). Two of them (they work in twos) can make a really good showing against a lion! They are very strong, have armor-plated thick skin, savage teeth, and great agility matched only by their fearlessness. If all fails, they break wind and no animal within 25 feet can hang around. They are problem solvers and innovators; in football we would say they are "complete players" (Grundy 2018—case study).

I once made them center pieces of a corporate seminar at Henley for 50 managers who were suitably impressed! Seriously, search them on You-Tube. That will give you an idea this is not just like SWOT but serious! They would survive a nuclear war.

In addition, the resilience and fragility of an organization will be pivotal in navigating any choppy sense ahead. But as we saw with story of the boiling frog at the start of the chapter, in addition we need fast responsiveness and speed—what is the time to react, which is dynamic? A useful model here is in Figure 9.6 which separates the process into six phases that will blur into each other:

- Recognition
- Prioritization
- Decision making
- Resource mobilization
- Implementation and change

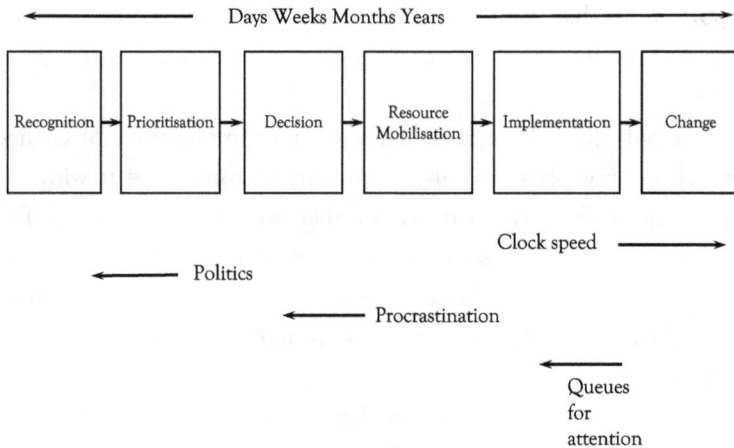

Figure 9.6 The reaction to an event—possible process

I added "change" as the last one as that can be longer and more difficult.

I have also added in "politics" and "procrastination" as subterranean processes that act as a hand brake or worse to check speed. Another constraining force is queues for attention as there is always competition for that. Finally, I show clock speed (at the corporate and maybe industry level for adding momentum as a kind of "jet stream").

To go through the phases takes time—maybe weeks, months, or years. However, what time do you have to react? What if there is a Gap, between the Window for Action and the Reaction Time?

Could you be, as what Sir Alan Sugar, the entrepreneur, said in a TV reality show with the Chicken Pizza Project, "doomed"? The message is clear. You need an organizational shake up (now politely called "transformation" as if it were a makeover!)

Finally, I have included my simplified version of a streamlined scenario process that takes you through it in five key stages (see Figure 9.7):

- Define scenario
- Develop assumptions
- Storytelling
- Create and evaluate options
- Implications

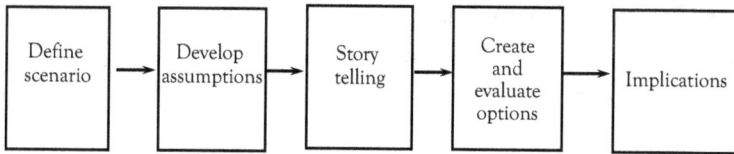

Figure 9.7 Scenario development—process (Grundy version)

Using It in Everyday Life

Here's a very quick story to illustrate the application of scenarios in everyday life.

I recently went on a couple of days writing holiday to Amsterdam and was using everyday experiences to inform my notions on our taken-for-granted ways of mentally processing uncertainty. The highest risk of the trip after trams (very important and very uncertain) was bicycles (medium important and extremely uncertain).

Tony Versus Amsterdam Bikes

Despite my best intentions and attempts at mindfulness, I did have quite a near miss. With the Bee Gees song "Stayin Alive," in my head, I did a quick take on the root causes of this grave danger, which in U.S. military terms is a "clear and present danger" with random streams of them coming at you at a speed of 15 to 18 mph (at the latter speed, that would mean with a two and a half hour second warning). One's "Bike-Dar" needs to be around 60 feet or 20 yards and also maintain visual angles of 360 degrees!

My fishbone highlighted six major root causes of the problem of bike danger:

- In Holland, bikes rule over all, including cars and pedestrians, in terms of their right of way.
- The mindset of cyclists is that "We are the kings of the road."
- Instead of being cautious and breaking if they see a pedestrian, they don't seem to break proactively; indeed their technique seems to be a small, last-minute swerve!
- The road layout is the mirror version of the UK and one's brain constantly places attention in the wrong directions.

- The color of the cycle lane is the same as the pavement and there is no clear demarcation.
- Scooters that move even faster than bikes and randomly mix with them.

This does mean that there is a continuous state of high risk. There are accidents waiting to happen. Other sources of threat, for which I used my fragility–threat grid, were:

- Losing money or my phone
- Being mugged
- Having my laptop stolen
- Getting COVID-19 for the third time and having to stay in Amsterdam for another week

You might think I am overthinking, but I can assure you that I am not always as mindful as I might be. So I should be rated as "fragile" in the face of such threats. Indeed, I set a project for myself to be hypervigilant and to adapt my scanning for bikes and directional awareness over a two-day period to reach a new level to stay alive and unbruised.

I was doing well on Day 2 until I had a near miss that could have been pre-empted by asking "What is the one big thing I missed?":

In one scenario I could get distracted.

I had a very quick interchange with someone in a car for a second and a half and turned to find a bike bearing down on me!

Such stories illustrate the extent to which both uncertainty and risk have an inherent structure that we can surface as a part of the process of managing uncertainty. More specifically, that event also illustrates the need to consider relative speeds not just in terms of movement in the real world but also speed of recognition, decision, and reaction. *So, there is a dynamic dimension too and which is part dependent on you as the observer.*

Another example of scenarios in everyday life also involves an accident and illustrates the value of having a picture in your head of not only future but also what you might do about it.

Tony Versus a Four-Wheel Drive

Years ago, I was watching a war film in which a soldier gets run over by a tank. Actually, that prompted me to think about the danger of being run over by a car. It had come to my attention that I was sometimes so overdetermined at crossing roads, especially in London and I could be playing a long game of Russian roulette. So, after the film, I asked myself the strategic question of "Could I minimize injury if I was hit by a car?"

My strategy was to, if at all possible, to leap up and bounce off the bonnet. To go under car seemed a very bad idea and landing on the bonnet would be lower impact as it is angled and softer too. I do Hot Bikram yoga each week and my muscles are truly strengthened in the feet in three of the postures on tiptoes for three minutes. This gives me real leaping powers, which would, of course, increase my resilience faced with the challenge of jumping on a car bonnet.

Well, two days later, I was on a trip to a meeting with Honda who then still made 4WD cars in Swindon. I decided to stop off for five minutes to post a parcel in Farnham Post Office Bucks, close to the scene of the incident. Later on, I was to spot that the pavement was cobbled as was the exit to a concealed car park at the side of the Post Office.

The queue took a lot longer than expected, and I felt I had lost time. So I decided to do a slow run back to my car 30 feet away. *I was going at about 8 mph when I saw a four-wheel drive bearing down on me at a similar speed! Instinctively and instantly, I leapt.* My bottom caught the horizontal of the bonnet cushioning the impact and I swerved around and dropped off the bonnet looking at the by now static car balancing on both feet with arms out to steady myself. Like a Kung Fu star. *Yes, that really did happen.*

I will never forget the look on the lady's face who was the driver as she digested first that her car had hit me, second that it was her fault, and third that third the damage seemed to be averted through my stunt.

Several people asked if I was okay. "It's only a scratch," I said. There is a moral to the story in that when you do futures work sometime the future you have foreseen comes along quicker than you think! Also, timing is key. A second earlier or a second later, it would have never happened. But as this case underlines, that doesn't mean you don't do the work anticipating misses or near misses.

If I had got hurt, I would never have made to my meeting or at least could have broken something or ended very bruised. The lesson is that scenario work in everyday life can be prefocused or associated with the development of your strategies and resilience and reducing fragility. Having practiced the art everyday also enhances scenario work in business and work, too.

My final online case study 7 is a story of deliberately courting uncertainty when I and my wife set off on an experimental mission to explore how agile we could be and resilient by embarking on a Random Weekend—a Field Study of Uncertainty. Besides highlighting the positivity of uncertainty as it stimulates innovation and creates surprise through the activity of the environment and by random choices (here chosen by cards and by tossing a coin), it is a must.

Tony Versus Oysters and Paella in Elmers End

After a few days in Barcelona where I had some fantastic paella, I went out for a meal in Elmer's End, South London. I was on my own to explore places to take my wife. There were two restaurants next to each other serving seafood and I hovered outside thinking "which to choose?" It was rather like the film *Sliding Doors*, but I thought "can't matter that much really, so I will go left."

It was a Wednesday night and I chose from the menu: bread and olives with vinaigrette, oysters, *and* paella. I fell into an uncertainty tunnel.

Future 1—The precursors and some "weak signals": The oysters were delicious and the paella cheap at £12 was huge, but I have to say the giant prawns seemed tasteless and I remembered thinking of the rest: "Any one of twenty-five of this sea-life including mussels could be off…."

Future 2—The transition: I pushed myself to finish the lot and the fuse was lit—within two minutes, I began to feel very sick and very weak and disorientated. Was I about to be sick?

Future 3—The journey: Having realized I might be sick, I staggered to the toilet.

Future 4—The fall: I tried to get to the sink and fell into the toilet wall and collapsed to the floor. After about two to three minutes, I decided

I had to get up. I had not been sick. Wiping the blood of my forehead gingerly, I got back to my chair and recuperated for 20 minutes before somehow getting home.

Future 5—The knock-on consequences: My neck was very swollen and I had mild concussion for six days.

Here are the lessons learned:

- An apparently trivial decision or event can produce wild and unexpected results (the "butterfly effect").
- An event chain can occur extremely quickly.
- Through being mindful, many adverse events can be headed off: to have ordered paella in Elmer's End in a slow-moving mid-week was asking for trouble and I should have spotted it on my uncertainty grid. To be fair, my unconscious mind did flag that up.
- One's resilience is a key variable and one can be far too optimistic in that department!
- Taking care isn't boring or overthinking, but a balanced part of managing uncertainty strategically.
- Our worlds are riddled with *Sliding Doors*.

Reader Exercise 1

For a regular issue of your choice in your personal life, ask the following questions:

- What are the assumptions around "the world going right?"
- How important and uncertain are these and where are they on the uncertainty grid?
- Based on the ones in the Southeast or "Danger Zone," what storylines could pan out?
- Using the uncertainty tunnel of the event chain, or both, flesh the storyline out.
- What are the takeaway insights or what's, for example, anything we need to do differently, not all, do in addition, and so on?

As far as doing this exercise for your business life, the concerned possibilities include:

- A new role;
- A new job in a different organization;
- A relationship with someone;
- A crucial meeting;
- A restructuring;
- A new project;
- An area of change;
- An attack by a competitor;
- A new entrant;
- A product launch;
- An acquisition or alliance;
- An organic strategic investment decision;
- Regulatory or political change;

and so on.

Reader Exercise 2

For a regular issue of your choice in your business life, repeat the process, maybe picking one from the previous list.

Now take a quick look at the positive impact of exploring uncertainty by deliberately introducing a random element through online appendix 7—the random weekend.

On Uncertainty and Scenario Theory

I said at the beginning that this is mainly a practical book and not abstract theory. There are therefore some books listed at the end, including those on scenarios, that there's little space to deep dive into. I will just reference some of them here:

Cairns, G. and G. Wright. 2011. "Scenario Thinking." Palgrave Macmillan. A similar, systemic approach to this book with some useful models and processes linking back to basic principles like Delphi methods of sampling expert views.

Hertwig, R., T. J. Pleskac, and T. Pachur. 2019. "Taming Uncertainty." Cambridge, MA: MIT Press. A theory-based set of cognitive and behavioral studies which are deep and rich indicating real progress in that understanding.

Hines, H. and P. Bishop. 2015. "Thinking About the Future." Houston: Hinesight. More a snappy consultancy guide and a good starter reference for trying to do your own scenarios.

Schwarz, P. 1996. "The Art of the Long View—Planning for the Future." NY: Penguin. Classical text going back to foundations of scenarios, more discursive, anchored in a learning process like this book.

Van de Hayden, K. 2014. "Scenarios—The Art of Strategic Conversation." John Wiley & Sons. Also a classical text going back to foundations of scenarios, more discursive, anchored in a learning process like this book.

Toward an Energy Theory of Strategy

As we are now getting to the end of the book, it calls for integration in these last couple of sections. The unexpected catalyst for this came through my wanderings around Amsterdam. I stopped to browse in a shop with funny objects in it and found an Einstein mug. I nearly bought it, but at €20, it was beyond my price point, despite the fact it had his famous energy equation $E = MC^2$ on it.

During my day, the Einstein mug kept bubbling up back at me in my thoughts. Later in a bar, the equation came up and it wasn't just about my regret at not forking out an inflated tourist price (I might have paid €20). My subconscious strategic mind (Figure 1.1) was clearly up to something and I have learned to listen in case it yields a useful insight or new "line of enquiry."

The thought came to me, "What if there is a conspiracy at work? Is that just what someone made up to put Einstein on a pedestal and that is not the right equation?"

I googled and found that $E = MC^2$ was an-oversimplification as the terms needed to all be squared again:

$$E^2 = (MC^2)^2 + (PC^2)^2$$

And not only that but there was an extra term PC, *and that was momentum.*

But that's not all. In the terms M and C, you had parallels with the world of strategy. M or mass is a static quality and it has a structure. Even if we are looking at it as liquid or gas, there are heaps of stuff at molecular, atomic, and particle levels. That is parallel to all the positioning work to understand an organization's current strategic posture. But C here is the dynamic, the speed of light, 108,000 miles per second. I have come to hold strategy dynamics as of equal importance to the more structural in strategy as it has thus featured a great deal here and in my last book, *Dynamic Competitive Strategy* (Grundy 2018).

"E" here has a parallel with "organizational performance" as an output to strategy.

And where does "momentum" fit in then? Well, is that not about the momentum a business has built up, which is delivering cash flows just now? We can understand that most easily in the context of lockdowns where the disruption caused loss of a huge amount of economic and social momentum.

So, a way of thinking about strategy is to see it as the product of structure and dynamic factors and the sum of this and that of business momentum. (Anyone who ran a business through COVID would tell you how difficult it is to rebuild the momentum lost through lockdowns as in the health club industry).

The first terms M and C are likely to be far more important if only because C is so big, maybe accounting for the oversimplified version $E = MC^2$.

So where does uncertainty fit in? Well, if I was forced to choose, I would say it is 20 percent structural and 80 percent dynamic—essential in getting a better grip on it. For instance, the fishbone of why bicycles are so dangerous in Amsterdam is structural. These are solid dangers in a material world (Madonna 1984). Things like the change drivers and the uncertainty tunnel are dynamic and event chains likewise.

It is truly most interesting to find parallels like this between the natural and the business worlds, but as both exhibit energy that's not so surprising (in the case of business, energy means growth, cash, performance, transformation, and so on). Also, while both appear complex, things can be simpler than you might think. Thanks so much and once again for the strategic unconscious mind. It can be your strategic friend!

So, imagine now that we are on a jet, which happens to be flying to Colombia. The pilot announces, "We are nearing our destination and beginning our descent to Bogota." Or at least *the end of business foresight and scenarios for managing uncertainty strategically.* So where has our flight taken us?

More importantly, it's your turn now to see and experience the world differently after landing—use these thought processes, ongoing!

Concluding Insights Split by Chapter

From Chapter 1

- Contrary to what some think, uncertainty can be managed.
- A great way of starting to manage uncertainty is to do a scenario skeleton, which can be done quickly and yields rich insights.
- The scenario can be built especially by looking at stakeholder intention and the option set of the players.
- Scenario processes should be tailored to the issue and context and are rarely "set piece."
- Successful scenario developers are more likely to have well-developed psychological and behavioral skills or economic analysis skills, or both.
- Central to the process is identifying the key factors, variables, or assumptions and evaluating their importance and uncertainty to pinpoint the areas of most volatility and as a precursor to identifying transitional events and storytelling.
- Scenarios, while being very intuitive, can still be informed by and guided by some quantitative forecasting, targeting, and doing "what ifs."
- Scenarios don't necessarily have very long-term time horizons—remember, the COVID projections were just for a month.
- Scenario storytelling can help reduce the emotional difficulties of dealing with acute anxiety, fear, or dread associated with deep uncertainty; and they can also help minimize the time lag to react.

From Chapter 2

- "Uncertainty" is used often for issues that appear singly too hard or worrying to think about and all that doesn't have to be the case.
- One can address uncertainty by defining the key assumptions and prioritizing them with the uncertainty grid.
- Each one of these assumptions may need breaking down into micro, "subatomic" assumptions.
- Uncertainty is dynamic and will change over time, so we should see this as being curved and draw it that way accordingly.
- Fishbone analysis can diagnose future causes of an outcome as opposed to its traditional use either for a present or past problem.
- Root cause systems analysis can be used to understand the interdependences between uncertain variables and assumptions.
- Sometimes there are more than just one game going on, amplifying uncertainty.
- Finally, scenario storylines can also be generated from the event tree or event chains as different causal clusters.

From Chapter 3

- It is important to have a clear and structured scenario process that will enable the more fluid and creative aspects of the exercise, as in the Shell process.
- To start with, do a quick and dirty analysis of the issues using the strategic onion model, applied dynamically, and with some thinking around changing clock speeds, and shifts over it.
- Or dynamically, maybe with an from–to (FT) analysis.
- Set boundaries, for example, geographic and market space and time horizons.
- The PEST, growth drivers, and competitive force models both as snapshots and dynamically as curves over time can help with both the assumptions on trends and also in highlighting possible discontinuities.

- A systemic picture can help generate the critical assumptions, particularly those that are most important and uncertain as a prelude to scenario storytelling.
- Where the industry setup might be challenged or there is some new field of opportunity beckoning, then it may be useful to hone in on the business value system model.
- Transitional events, possibly generated out of one or more assumptions that are particularly uncertain and important, can act as the start of the storytelling and form the uncertainty tunnel.
- Or you might decide to start your mental time traveling with some future and different worlds and work backward from that with the uncertainty tunnel.
- When constructing scenarios, pause time to think what the most limiting constraint is.
- And also ask, "What is the one big thing we have missed?" and "the second big thing we have missed?" for all the scenario(s).
- With any business value system that is hypothesized, ask the following questions: how workable will it be, who will be best placed to exploit this effectively, is it over complex, actually underdeveloped, how sustainable it is, and what clock speed can we expect?
- The reliability of the process will depend too on the background economic and psychological analysis and thus your skills and the richness of any data.
- When sense-checking the existing strategy at the end of the process in Figure 3.1, or to embark on new strategy or any new scenarios, it is important not to see that as a new if there is a linked piece of work and allow time for digestion.

From Chapter 4

- Storytelling can be remarkably accurate even though its intent is more to explore plausible future scenarios rather than to make specific predictions as in the War in the Pacific.

- Storytelling works best if there is chronological development with one event leading to another and with specific times and actors to color it.
- Future slicing can add more plausibility to the time dimension.
- Workshop design is crucial and needs to have structure, timings, background work, key tools, key strategic questions, and facilities that are congenial to creativity with low distractions.
- Facilitation is a must and needs to be handled behaviorally and politically by a business and strategically savvy person who is naturally creative as well as good at distilling insights and landing the process and its output.
- You are a cause of your own uncertainty mediated by bias mindfulness and dragon-eyed vision can mitigate your biases.

From Chapter 5

- Organizational change is particularly uncertain as the strategy mix for change is often emergent and ambiguous and there is no set, best change process.
- A number of tools can help to deal with uncertainty, including wishbone analysis with uncertainty grids overlaid, FT analysis, and difficulty-over-time curves, with processes as per Figure 5.9.
- Storytelling is a really rich way of deep diving into some dynamic possibilities.
- This is made harder when there is some event that is particularly sensitive to think about like the Queen's death; nevertheless pushing through that discomfort barrier can be very helpful.
- Such stories may well break into subscenarios.
- Scenario storytelling is an essential ingredient in strategic visioning.

- With an effective process, a good team, and a suitable facilitator, much value and insights can be derived surprisingly quickly.
- Storytelling can then inform to decisions as to what you need to do differently.

From Chapter 6

- The positions of assumptions on the uncertainty grid are very likely to be informed by other tools like the strategic onion for determining value and cost driver analysis.
- Sensitivity analysis should inform the positionings of assumptions on the uncertainty grid as true stress and resilience testing.
- Uncertainty around acquisitions can be targeted using the three Vs of acquisitions—the inherent value of the strategy, the value added/lost in the deal, and the value added/lost in integration value.
- For both alliances and acquisitions, there are likely to be a lot of assumptions that are behavioral and need testing on the uncertainty grid.
- International strategies are relatively uncertain as they have not just the imponderables of strategy but also those of international strategy to deal with, making them disproportionately uncertain and even made worse for acquisitions or alliances.
- Marketing strategies generally are often rife with uncertainty due to behavioral factors.
- Innovation and technology strategies are also very susceptible to uncertainty both externally and internally.

From Chapter 7

- Stakeholders are a major driver of uncertainty and this invites in-depth analysis to pick out these major drivers.
- A three-level approach may be needed to get a clearer picture of stakeholders through (a) positioning them on the high-

level grid, (b) through the vectors of the stakeholder agenda
analysis, and (c) through fishbone analysis of the causes of one
particular agenda analysis.

- This should be accompanied by storytelling of their moves as
  a group, or as individuals, or both.
- Throughout this process, it is essential to *become* them via the
  "out-of-body experience."
- There are very important inputs from verbal behaviors and
  nonverbal behaviors alike.
- The process of profiling is also important.
- Game theory and role plays bring the stakeholder dimension
  to life, adding vital behavioral color.
- We are often concerned as to whether we can trust particular
  stakeholder; try the "trust-over-time curve"—what has trust
  been like to date and where might this go in future?
- Sometimes apparently minor and trivial data may be
  disproportionally important.
- Mood-over-time curves are another important variable.
- The various case studies demonstrate how essential and
  valuable is stakeholder analysis in live scenario building.
- This book will add the missing dimension of uncertainty to
  any MBA.

From Chapter 8

- Developing quality scenarios requires the skillful, structured,
  and imaginative integration of many tools, thought processes,
  evidential support, prioritization, and insight.

From Chapter 9

- Workshops are a very powerful way of providing the thought
  space and the emotional space to explore the future.
- Facilitation is essential plus sufficient design and preparation.
- Visual tools are a must, too.

- Time traveling is strategically and politically sensitive and you thus need to take care with who you invite and who you don't and maybe separate out the main strategy development time for a later session, and write a strategic position paper in the meantime.
- Make sure that distractions are minimized.
- Fragility and resilience testing can be useful if existing strategies or future options might be vulnerable in the face of uncertainties; or indeed suggest big upsides too, especially with my SWOT after a makeover with "FROST" analysis.
- Not only does applying scenarios to everyday life add huge personal value but it also encourages that as a habit so that you are then able to improve their your use in business, too.
- As a high-level framework, the $E = MC^2 + Momentum^2$ for a business may help you overview a strategy to bring together its static and dynamic elements.

Quite a journey?

Summary of the Book

This book took you through what is uncertainty and why it is important and difficult to manage. Besides being dynamic, uncertainty arises from complicated causes. Behaviorally saturated and wicked, it can be mostly untangled through a combination of tools and processes to get a much clearer sense of the range of possibilities and outcomes. Scenarios and storytelling shine a very effective light through its fog.

They can be applied to geopolitical events like wars and pandemics, economic turbulence, all kinds of strategic and tactical decisions, to organization change, your businesses, your role and challenges, and to your personal lives.

To illustrate how scenarios and storytelling can be applied to personal life, in the past week for example, I have gone through several uncertainty tunnels such as several very near misses by bikes in Amsterdam, a monumental queue to catch the plane after a two-hour queue—all uncertainty tunnels which tell me something of my agility and my resilience. Much of my resilience also comes from thinking about the future and possible futures, and practicing the following dictums:

Don't be afraid—confront uncertainties.

To the question, "Why think about the future?" the best answer I know is "Because we are going to spend the rest of our lives there" (Charles Kettering).

If we could only predict with 90 percent accuracy what's going to happen just think what advantage that would give you.

In the penultimate online case study 6, I foresaw the deposing of Boris Johnson five months earlier in a letter warning him, for instance.

Contact me Dr. Tony Grundy, London tony.grundy101@gmail.com.

Do e-mail me for slides of the figures (my copyright) for everyday use; this offer excludes consultants sorry.

Case Studies

1. Russia Invades Ukraine and Putin's Motives
2. COVID-19 and the Initial UK Pandemic
3. Tesco Scenarios
4. International Strategies
5. BT Case and Behavioral Uncertainty
6. Letter to Boris Johnson (then UK Prime Minister) Regarding His Future and Career
7. The Random Weekend—a Field Study of Uncertainty

https://neuroleadership.com/your-brain-at-work/the-neuroscience-of-storytelling/

CASE STUDY 1

Russia Invades Ukraine and Putin's Motives

To kick off, I will cover a complex case that at this juncture is extremely topical—the Russia versus the Ukraine conflict. This ranks as a historically volatile situation similar to the Cuban Missile Crisis, the Invasion of Kuwait, and for the UK, the Falklands war.

Two days before I began to write this book, I was beginning to do scenarios for a possible Russia–Ukraine war. I was increasingly concerned about the slow but most concerning build-up of tensions and military mobilization that were more than disconcerting. I thought it would be a great example of scenario storytelling and in real time for teaching in class on the Futures project at UCL School of Management, but I was also concerned that such a conflict also would drive oil and gas and electricity prices up, trigger very high inflation, and lead to European and maybe global recession.

I did a bit of googling to make sure that I hadn't missed anything of obvious importance. Using the tools and structures that I have facilitated senior managers' thinking about uncertainties and futures, I did a sketch of a structure that could become a platform for managing this uncertainty strategically on just over a page (see Box 1). This is very much a "Plan for the Plan" (Grundy 2018).

Box 1 A Draft Structure for Exploring Uncertainty in a Russia–Ukraine Conflict

February 13, 2021 Ukraine–Russia

Example of the Structure of Scenario Storytelling

The building blocks of these are: Putin's motives, options, tools, and processes

Possible Putin Motives

- Defensive: to distract his country from hardship by configuring an external threat
- Defensive: to prevent Ukraine from either shifting more to the West or even joining NATO
- Defensive: to get a go-ahead to a gas pipeline project Nord Stream 2 from Russia to Germany to secure that lucrative business
- As a first step to extending control over those countries formerly satellites of Russia, blunting their Westernization
- Offensive: Ukraine is the major conduit for Russian gas to the West; to secure control
- Offensive: to erode the geopolitical influence of the West especially, the United States, while the United States is seen as having weaker global resolve, especially in the light of the Afghanistan withdrawal in late 2021, and as a prelude to even closer relationships with China
- Stress testing: to wedge open the differences of opinion between the NATO countries
- Personal: to be seen as having left his mark on Russian history as a great leader (megalomania?)
- Or a combination of these

Putin's Options

- To negotiate a minimalistic agreement (on what though? territorial claims? and agreement to go ahead with Nord Stream 2; also a statement of intent by Ukraine that it does not intend to join NATO—would the Ukraine agree to that?)
- To stage a minor incursion on some pretext—and then either to use that as a bargaining counter for peace
- Or to do further step-by-step incursions and then finally a total invasion of the country, thus to gradually escalate the conflict

- To not invade but to saber-rattle, thus shaking the West with fear: could he keep his army hovering until late spring? Also, that would aggravate economic uncertainty in the West through inflation and economic slowdown—painful
- To do a full invasion either in a predictable way like now in mid-February 2022, or to strike later with the best possible surprise and maximum deception
- Unlike popular belief that even with sanctions, he will not turn our gas supplies, or he actually *does* turn them down or off threatening to trigger a Western recession with gas prices doubling yet again
- To launch nonmilitary and noneconomic aggression: for example, cyber attacks either with anonymously or by disclosure that it is indeed launched by Russia as a counter to economic sanctions

These possible strategies above might be launched if and only if certain conditions are met ("contingent strategies") to be flexible and agile. Scenarios could be developed for each of these options and also for how these might cause shifts in the Western alliance as agendas, for example the United States, the UK, Germany, and France, are possibly divergent.

Personal: Putin is a very cunning man and has gamed a number of scenarios and for sure is enjoying all the attention. Interestingly there seems to be little media coverage of Putin's personal agendas.

Verdict: Putin has far more options than just the all-out full and immediate invasion and may well have more up his sleeve than just the obvious. The biggest clues are to be found in a deep understanding of his agendas and their weightings of importance. A saving grace might be that he might wish to avoid a "lobster pot" strategy—where once committed, he can't easily get out. One possible outcome is a renewal of the cold war with the West, strengthening the military shield around countries like Poland.

Tools and Processes

To facilitate managing these uncertainties strategically, these might include:

- Doing a mind map of the systems that might impact on the conflict, for example, political, stakeholders, economic, military, social and psychological, mindsets, and personal agendas
- Game theory: a model for exploring the trade-offs and the pay offs especially due to cooperation versus aggression
- Storytelling and mental time travel so that we work our way forward and backward in time to plot possible causal chain effects
- Transitional events that cause the future to change course, for example, Putin, Biden, or even Johnson in the UK have heart attacks! *(These are events that if they happen take us from one state of the world to another one.)*
- Getting expert input from informed sources, for example. Which I did—not disclosed.
- Using what I call later on the "OBE," having the "out of body experience," by imagining that you are someone else (literally), for example Putin, you absorb their agendas—their thoughts, beliefs, feelings, and values before role playing them

(Written in February 2022.)

This initial work took around an hour including some googling. That underlines a central theme of this book: that scenario storytelling need not be overly time consuming and rich insights can be gleaned even at an early stage. Here, for example, it did lead to a number of interesting insights even with rather minimalistic effort.

One of Putin's great advantages was to be able to keep everyone guessing. I visualized him actually keeping himself uncommitted and oscillating according to incoming stimuli and mood so that commentators and intelligence experts would truly have no clue. Given the range of options he has (many "strategic degrees of freedom"), he would have no difficulty mixing together his messages and moves and their timings to confuse and distract Western analysts. So, we need to find someone (an informed actor?) to role play him.

Other insights were:

- Putin has many shades of options available so he can play tunes on the ferocity of any aggression, its mode, and timings.
- His apparent equanimity to sanctions suggests that Russia can't be hurt as much as Western commentators and politicians suppose or that he has tricks up his sleeve like guerrilla computer hacking that can hurt the West as much or more than sanctions. That prospect is scary. While it might smack of an action thriller film, where power plants or computer networks are closed down, there have been prescient films on other macro threats like pandemics. For example, the film *Contagion* (2011) depicted a deadly virus that originally came for bats (sounds familiar?). The film was removed form Netflix in 2021 after "causing too much distress." (After my initial draft, there were reports on unidentified cyber attacks on Ukrainian banks on February 15, 2022!)
- I rapidly stubbed my toe too against the critical role of the supply of gas to the West and the related issue of the price of all and the vulnerability of the West through recent inflationary surge post-COVID plus gas price hikes only in the pipeline.

Generally, my sense that Russia might stage some military action went up from 40 to 60 percent and my perception of its impact on all sides, especially the West, doubled. Just one day ago, I had just parked my car at Waitrose and was reflecting on these shifts and concluded as I walked:

"This could knock the stock market back by 2–3 percent for a while, but I would take a drop of 2 percent happily." When I got to my destination, I discovered it had dropped by 1.7 percent! It is nice to see around the corners and becoming more farsighted certainly pays. My emotional state was less disrupted too.

Another interesting insight came up through weighing the number and plausibility of options on both sides. Russia had many tricks in the bag, the West apparently a few, maybe only sanctions, diluting potential power. The West seemingly ruled out putting troops in. But that was still a theoretical option as were air strikes. Of course, that would be direct if in a limited war and if we doubted Putin's sanity, maybe a precursor to nuclear war. In scenario storytelling, you may need to think sometimes about the unthinkable.

It is worth noting that I experienced an initial emotional effect originally when I was beginning to think about the problem that I also had with the onset of the credit crunch in 2008 and the pandemic in February 2020. Initially the experience is fear when uncertainty is recognized. Then there is the thought: Can I influence this happening and with what effect? I know that influence is low. The third step is "Can I be bothered to think about it and do I really want to, and now?" If the answer is "no," then that is so often the end of it. We can call this the "look away from it" bias or LAFIT-off bias. That is an instinctive reaction that is perfectly understandable, but potentially very damaging. I believe that it is a big deterrent to doing scenarios and thus becoming farsighted.

Finally, an important insight here was the importance of the psychological and behavioral perspective in understanding human behavior and decision making and the economic perspective in understanding the ultimately monetary-based drivers of key players. These perspectives, of course, interact. It also follows that the better you are at both those skills, the richer and more reliable your scenarios are likely to be.

We return to Russia and Ukraine later in the book in Chapter 2. This just gives a taste of game theory (Von Neumann and Morgenstern 1944).

COVID-19 and the Initial UK Pandemic

Storytelling the Trajectory of COVID-19

One of the reasons for doing this book was to help CEOs and their Directors to navigate hard-to-foresee events that could cause unforeseen disruption. Aside from the credit crunch fueled by dodgy lending, monetary largesse, unwise innovations in securities, and so on, the obvious example was COVID-19, which appeared as a "weak signal" in the West in very early 2020.

I recall beginning to think in February 2020 that this could be very serious in its impact. Years earlier, bird flu in the Far East was a threat and had been a near miss in terms of wreaking havoc on society and business. We had a narrow escape as it withered away without taking off. So, when COVID registered on my consciousness in early 2020, I was alert but just as I mentioned earlier, it was one of those things bad to think about, but something I could do little about.

But by March, it was clear that this syndrome had very real momentum. On March 18, there were 2,500 cases a day and it was doubling every three days. I did some workings that suggested we were in for a very rough ride indeed. In a "do nothing" environment within 30 days, we were facing a disaster, especially as the death rate from COVID was around 2 percent. Here are the figures with the second column have a far gentler impact, emphasizing the important driver of the reproduction rate (later known as the "R" factor). In the second columns, the growth rate drops after six days (see Table 1).

These trends might have resulted in a very worst case of deaths at an approximate 2 percent rate of between 5,000 a day and around 50,000 a day in the UK, obviously with no change in lifestyles, no lockdown, and no vaccinations.

Table 1 COVID-19 Extrapolated Infections from March 18, 2020

Infections a day (doubling each 3 days). Infections a day (50% increase per 3 days)—higher range

	Higher Range	**Lower Range**
Base rate of infection	2,500	2,500
After 3 days	5,000	5,000
After 6 days	10,000	10,000—the starting point
After 9 days	20,000	15,000
After 12 days	40,000	22,500
After 15 days	80,000	33,000
After 18 days	160,000	50,000
After 21 days	320,000	75,000
After 24 days	640,000	110,000
After 27 days	12,800,000	165,000
After 30 days	25,600,000	250,000

I found these figures that I did on my mobile phone in 15 minutes truly scary, yet around this time our Prime Minister Boris Johnson was minimalizing the scale of the threat and on his public visits, he went out of his way to shake as many hands as he could and in the same breath suggesting he wasn't afraid. *He did get COVID.*

Just with very basic forecast and no clever modeling, it was possible to sense a rather nasty path ahead. The UK government dallied and it was only on the March 23, five days later, that the first lockdown was instigated, by which time COVID was out of control. Way before the March 18 that should have been plain and clear. *Those five days lost might have increased cases by 10 percent or more and thus deaths and also cost time in mobilizing the government and the NHS. Delays are costly.*

This would not be any surprise to decision theorists who would suggest that much of this delay was down to recognition lags, not just cognitive but emotional—my LAFIT-off factor as in the Ukraine case study. But even so, you would think that all the government policy makers and minders could have done similar calculation to the one that I did above. Indeed, after repeated policy failures in one of several letters I wrote to Boris Johnson over 2020–2022, I suggested that I could be his "Minister for Common Sense." No answer.

In addition to this old style, but solid projections, I did something else that scenario theorists would highly recommend: to immerse myself deeply in the technical and behavioral fundamentals of pandemics especially their dynamics, their histories, and the effectiveness of counter measures. In March, I found on the Internet a concise and comprehensive report by the "SPIM Vaccination Group" in 2018 on modeling, telling me much not just on countermeasures and their effectiveness but also giving me illustrative profiles of past pandemics, which helped me form the story from 2020 through to 2022. From that, I observed that multiple waves are the norm.

PANDEMIC RESEARCH 2018 SPI-M_modelling_summary_final .pdf

I was interested not just from a health or an academic point of view but also from a business angle. I am a strategic adviser to CEO, Matthew Harris, of a fitness club chain, Fitness4less, over this terrible period and Matthew suffered great stress especially through the lockdowns. The impact was a loss of strategic and operational momentum that is akin to a fly wheel. I also found this term to be the hidden variable in Einstein's $E = MC^2$ equation in Chapter 9.

I have tried to help Matthew to second guess government policy and the dynamics of COVID-19 and its mutation Omicron.

These lockdowns and the impact that these diseases have dynamically on the client base have led me to propose much more agile thinking, sometimes suggesting patience and sometimes more impatience to get performance nearer to prepandemic levels. A key insight for him in the lockdowns was to have a "mothballing strategy" operationally while using the time to think what post-COVID strategies might be in that future environment and how to damage limit in between pandemic waves. I encouraged him to slice up the future by quarter through 2021 and to overlay his business planning and initiatives along these time frames.

Even from an early stage, it was possible to get a sense of the sort of modelling that might be appropriate. For instance, in one scientific source, it went through the shape or previous epidemics and in each case, there were multiple waves. When the UK went into its first lockdown in second quarter of 2020, it was a common assumption in the country that we would be back to near normal after three months, but we were to experience a very large wave in late 2020 and early in 2021 with another variant and another wave in December 2021 to April 2022 due to yet another variant—Omicron.

In February 2022, the Lead on COVID from the WHO (World Health Organization), Dr. Maria van Hove, suggested on the "Sunday" BBC program that we were likely to see another wave before COVID became much more containable ("an epidemic") and that while another variant might be less dangerous, there was a chance it could be more dangerous as well. We are still facing uncertainties with upsides being immunization and boosters. But the downsides are infections to the vaccinated have become quite common, and also possibly greater transmutability along with perhaps again abandonment of restrictions and many precautions. In her view, the COVID show would continue through 2022 and into 2023.

Insights from the COVID story are that:

- Sometimes even basic extrapolations of trends with some possible adjustment for shifts and changes can give a good starting point for understanding the scale of importance and degree of uncertainty and sensitivity or outcomes to input variables.
- There is often a wealth of data available, and sometimes even theories and models are available on the Internet to facilitate your thinking, but before deep diving in, pose the right questions.
- Much of the foresight trick comes from an acceptance of and a willingness to embrace the dynamics of uncertainty and to accept that like history, the future will have phases too. So we should split it.
- There are invariably lags in processing and dealing with signals and these very lags shape the way the future unfolds (see Figure 9.6).
- Braving the anxiety, fear, and discomfort to face new uncertainty through active investigation reduces the response time and also gives more of a hold over that angst.

The COVID case study illustrates the dynamic nature of uncertainty. That in turn inspired me to stretch out the COVID curves of the disease spreads and the consequential disruption caused to decipher three waves of uncertainty in the UK between November 2021 and March 2022, namely

- Omicron
- Party gate (Boris Johnson and nearly 50 staff investigated by the Metropolitan Police for possibly breaking COVID rules)
- The Russia–Ukraine war

Uncertainty washes over us as waves impacting over both the government and the rest of the population. Imagine what adding the magnitude of these Uncertainty Waves all on top of each other would give you. And it is far from over yet: setting aside the Ukraine situation, the UK Prime Minister still faces the awkwardness of facing up to the evidence in a matter of weeks! In fact, what we experienced in March–April 2022 (Ukraine and economic turbulence) and 2020–2022 (COVID) *were uncertainty floods generated by the cumulative uncertainty waves* (and which are a follow-on consequence). Indeed, acute and particularly uncertain uncertainties seem to call for a new language so that we can capture this wild turbulence.

CASE STUDY 3

Tesco Scenarios—Selling Through the Internet Without Cannibalizing Ourselves

This case study graphically illustrates the development of a strategy that created a new overall system of adding value besides illustrating the role that the process of scenario development can play in strategy development.

Very many years ago, I got a call on a Monday asking if I would like to facilitate a one-day session to re-examine the strategy at Tesco. In common with Tesco Metro, Tesco Express, and to a lesser extent, Tesco Non-Food, the home-shopping operation lacked a focus, as I found it, without a really clear idea of how it was going to compete better than its competitors, what value it would be bringing to its customers, and indeed who they would be.

It was also unclear as to what their product offering would be and how logistics and IT would work: it was an "emergent strategy" (Mintzberg et al.1998) or one whose logic may emerge only really through experimentation as a pattern during implementation, which is not quite ideal.

Tesco Direct (now Tesco.com) was definitely a big step. But was really nothing really like it around at that time, so the element of future thinking was even greater. The natural choice was to use some scenario storytelling to explore the future and to generate and flesh out strategic options. We were then in 1996 and the dot-com market was embryonic. Indeed, the boom in dot-com was around the turn of the millennium. Amazon was just two years old then!

The starting point, or the "current position," was that Tesco was home delivering a few rather random products to a few random people—at that time things like gift cards and flowers. Indeed, in this case whatever they were doing then was a distraction. So, I asked the two subteams who worked on the issues to imagine we had a zero base—in effect to think of this as a startup.

First of all, we tried to time travel five years into the future and that proved very, very difficult. Basically, even if we tried to take orders for most if not all of Tesco's products (that's another issue) as a mass process, we had to make it operationally do-able. When I enquired how they were currently doing it and might do it in future, the answer was: "Well, to start with, we were taking orders over the phone as we were only selling a few things *but we think we will have to get people to fax it in when they need a proper shop.*"

I identified this issue as a limiting constraint that would be a major dampener to slow if not halt the progress of the new business model as a key "line of enquiry" in detective terms. The concept of the limiting constraint comes up time and again is scenarios.

Illustrating the value of asking the right questions in scenario work, I didn't allow myself to be distracted by that assumption and I asked: "So what do you think we will be doing to take orders much further into the future?" The answer was, of course, that people would be eventually be just as used to using the Internet as going into a shop. But it would need to be low effort and lower cost. As they would be making home-shopping purchases from home that would require a home computer and better still a laptop for armchair shopping. It's all obvious now, but not then!

So, I hypothesized that at some future stage, a laptop would be used by a sufficient number of consumers in order for grocery home shopping to really take off. But by when would that happen, and was there any transitional event that could bring it closer in time? (This illustrated the value of positing a future state and working backward though the event tree to see how that could work.)

At the time home computers and laptops were still quite expensive in the range of £700 to £800 (probably over £2,000 at current prices!), *but I felt that if the prices were to drop say by a third to be around the price of a half-decent color TV, then the market could take off.* So, I then asked: "So what might bring that about?" There was a very plausible event: one of the big PC manufacturers would drop prices by 20 percent or more and go for volume so that they would rapidly recover to profit. Maybe an IBM or an HP. *This was a really key insight.*

I then visualized that happening within two years, which would be perfect as that would be around the time Tesco would have established critical capabilities and a critical mass. With hindsight, it all happened about 18 months later and there was a further boost to demand as the Internet became talked about and trendy. It began to really change all our lives in a nonlinear and steeply rising, linear curve. The rest is history.

This chain of reasoning happened in about 45 minutes; sometimes a scenario comes through very quickly. And the crucial thought breakthroughs were there in around 5 to 10 minutes. So, we had a most productive one-day strategic thinking to lay the foundation for Tesco.com, now a huge business. But was that enough? Well, probably not, or at least there were some loose ends. Toward the end of that day, I shifted from my "build" approach to a more "challenge" approach. The latter is typically done either quite systematically using the uncertainty grid or more on the hoof with questioning on:

"So, what's the one big thing we have forgotten?"

followed by

"So, what's the second big thing we have forgotten?"

There is always the first and usually there's a second.

The first one was that I asked was:

"Would home-shopping cannibalize the existing business?" It was very obvious. I raised that point and also asked who would be our targeted customers? They said, "Well, Tesco's of course." I strongly challenged this assumption as that would not bring much to the business other than more nonfood sales. I also warned that Tesco's Group FD might challenge a business case, which was significantly value diluting or destroying element through cannibalization. I wasn't sure that they really wanted to hear that at all.

Another unanswered issue was how the logistics would work. In my challenging, I did get them to think about the role that pricing of deliveries would take in the competitive combat. They assumed a round £5 a delivery. Two days later, I was "Dyson-ing" at home and the thought suddenly surfaced: "Hold on, what happens if Sainsbury's deliver for £3 or £2 and free for over £100? Will the margins be blown?"

This underlines the point that developing scenario stories isn't something you do just in a mad workshop hot house, but often by steady infusion in the issues to allow new thoughts to spring up and so you don't overlook issues on the edge of attention.

But the real killer area that I did probe on (but didn't get fully to the bottom of) was logistics. Again, I asked: "So how's the logistics going to work then?" to which I got thoughtful faces but no real answers or suggestions. Probing again, I said: "So, can we assume that we will have a dedicated logistics facility?" Again, I got no clear response. I do wish that I had really dug in here as I often do when I morph into a more "Lieutenant Colombo" detective-type role, famed for his tenacity.

Little did I know that Tesco's then mindset was that they were going to try to pick everything from an existing store, thus replicating the inefficiencies of the customer picking the items for themselves. This meant that there would be errors, gaps in what was picked, and time inefficiencies. Also, how would the financials work out while the fixed costs of the store would be paid for by the usual retail business? Assuming little overall cannibalization effect, would that be sufficient to pay for all these incremental picking costs plus the delivery costs? The lesson is here that in scenarios, operational or tactical details aren't something that can saved for until later.

While my questioning was solid, this just shows that you often need quite a bit more time—a second day was needed here at the very least to do a thorough "deep-dive" into the issues, particularly of the "how" and the way a business or operating model would actually work. The specific options suggested also needed thorough evaluation (Grundy 2018). In scenario work, just like any strategic work, you *need to sometimes dig around the issues here and there a bit more in detail and allow time for reflection and refinement.*

An example of that syndrome of freezing the results too soon was the delivery strategy was nearly skirted over. But fortunately, I had done some preliminary research before the workshop. I went in search or my then wife who I found was putting the washing out in the back garden. She had pegs in her mouth so to speak, had to stop, and take them out before continuing. I asked her: "What would you pay to get the Tesco shopping delivered to our home?" Answer: "I don't know." Next, "what would happen if the delivery were late?" She stopped and thought for a few seconds and then replied: "I wouldn't use them again. If, for example, they were late and it was the school run, then I couldn't be late as your son James would go mental!"

When I challenged Tesco on this imperative later, they admitted that they had not thought at all about the problems of meeting delivery slots. I am told by a manager in a big grocery store in 2018 that such things are a real operational problem even today, especially with returns.

Another area that I tried to probe, which was resisted was whether they should offer part of their range or all of it. I suggested to consider jut a part, but they insisted it must be all. They wanted to satisfy *all of the customers' needs*. It was laudable but would that ever be profitable?

Were you only to have an order for potatoes, for example, would that be a loss-making business? I am not saying I was right and they were wrong to offer everything, but there were other options and business models. Looking back, just talking about the grocery deliveries, the combined effects of doing the whole range, not trying to mainly target competitors' customers, and the heavy costs of picking would almost certainly result in a value-diluting business model. This underlines the point that there is a big need for economic analysis behind scenario development; it's not sufficient just to do the visionary stuff. And psychological input is essential too. Witness my asking my then wife what her needs were and her buying process. Finally economic analysis is needed to assess future *value*.

A final "one big thing that we missed" was the longer term competitive dynamics, which might play out between substitute business models here. Remember that Tesco Non-Food had an edge in some respects like price and convenience versus the high street, for example, on clothes. This highlights the need to reflect sufficiently on the time horizons for the work. Think not just about the time reach of when there is "reasonable foreseeability." But also consider the time horizon over which you will expect returns or maybe even losses, possibly beyond an obvious Future 1 to a Future 2 and so on. *You need to model the game in each time slice to have a joined up longitudinal picture.*

But we then saw that in a workshop only some months later we foresaw the future rise of the Internet and home-shopping. Eventually, after about ten years, this would begin to corrode demand for Tesco Non-Food items such as clothes and electricals, too. So, the "click retailers" and even Tesco.com would actually be eating into Tesco Non-Food! I confess that I didn't get that one, but to be fair, we were certainly not operating with 10- to 20-year timescales that day. With hindsight, one might argue that we should have seen that coming.

Lessons from the Tesco.com case are the following:

- Scenario development can be very enlightening and is especially powerful where a market is latent or emerging.
- The initial process can be surprisingly quick.
- But likely some testing is needed, looking at other angles and other refinements.
- But you really need to do some thorough, detailed investigation with some "deep-dives" when trying to generate strategies and business models out of the scenario exercise; and you may need to allow more time for that.
- You really have to ask sometimes a number of times: "So what is the really big thing that we have missed?"
- Beware assuming then that you have got the complete picture or that once done, you won't have to redo or extend the time horizons, nor that the emerging strategy is then something that never needs to be revisited.
- Economic analysis is essential to model how a market will behave in the future.
- Similarly, future psychology should also be modeled.
- Stretching time horizons may be necessary to do the business case, specially to deal with maturity or change.
- Interactive discussions and debate need some targeted sprinkling of real empirical data; in Tesco's case, quality and richness is preferred to volume, as in the interview with my then wife.

Postscript: By the late 1990s, Tesco had a number of really strong things going for it. Not just its Internet business and new formats like Tesco Express and Non-Food that I also helped to do scenarios with, but with its loyalty Clubcard, Tesco broke through the £1 billion profit barrier around 2004 (see Figure 3.9). At that time, it was said that "Tesco has one foot on the accelerator and the other foot on Sainsbury's throat."

Tesco could seemingly do no wrong. Based purely on data available from the public domain and from general observation to understand the evolution of its business model, I drew a "business value system" specific to the, by now, huge Group . On the surface, this looked impressive in its complexity and clever interdependences, but business and management are conditional on humans and thus behavioral processes that typically once they lose a grounding in simplicity are often very hard to manage.

With any piece of strategy work, after the event, it is essential to ask the question: "So what's the 'so what?'" For me, here it was:

"How hard will Tesco find that to manage, especially with an overlay of international development, competitor imitation, and erosion of those superordinary margin levels?"

In the earliest years of the new millennium, its amazingly talented CEO Sir Terry Leahy was about to step down, creating huge leadership challenges. Just like when Sir Alex Ferguson retired as a manager in 2013, Manchester United landing in a soup. Since then, the club never seems to have found anyone to fill those boots up until 2022. It was all going to be mission impossible organizationally. Tesco ran into serious problems relatively soon after that partially because attention seemed too internally focused. Around the time, I spotted that Tesco were dishing out 20 percent off vouchers on purchases over £40, a "strong signal." Why do that unless sales were flagging? I was in one of their stores and immediately thought "Are they losing it? Margins are 6 percent?" I e-mailed someone I knew well around the very, very top with pages of ideas to rejuvenate its core UK retail strategy and never heard back. The stance was that their UK strategy was okay.

The lesson from this is "like a dog, the scenario process is not just for Christmas, it is for life."

So, the business value system might be another possible tool (although not essential) tool in implementing the process.

CASE STUDY 4

International Strategy

I have taught international strategy at several business schools, in addition to my consulting work. I gained by experiences at BP and the then ICI. So I have insights into uncertainty at an international level of strategy. The first thing to say here is that many of the tools and principles here are very similar, if not identical to, business unit and national strategy. So, we would find the same set of tools applicable.

Analysis

Does that international business have additional things to worry about, which I will describe and explain next? Then I will take a brief look at a couple of additional theories and perspectives.

The first of these the Uppsala model (Johansson and Vahine 1977), which suggests that international strategies evolve through different phases such as domestic, indirect export (via an agent), direct export, licensing of other agreements, or joint venture, and the ultimate, foreign direct investment (FDI). This phased model allows for more opportunity to learn, thus reducing overall uncertainty. Of course, uncertainty is likely to increase over time. This model is simple and intuitive, but it doesn't necessarily surface the critical assumptions that need to be evaluated as these usually need to be done on a case-to-case basis and with the deployment of other tools, for example, a future fishbone analysis to deal with things like an agent going off the rails, or a joint venture party causing quality problems and so on.

The second model is that of OLI, not the catchiest name for a model (Dunning 2001). This stands for Ownership, Locational and Internalization (the latter being) intangible assets like brand that confer special advantages in a particular country, like MacDonalds did until recently in Russia). Probably "intangibles" or "resources" would have been better here. L stands for location, which covers the naturally favorable assets, competences, and skills that could make the location decision more advantageous. Finally, there is internalization, or "I," which could feel rather "the odd man out." This concerns the extent to which there are advantages through insourcing. I do see here the relevance of looking at the economics of investing oneself as opposed to leveraging off buying product in or some form of exporting, but for me the broader criteria might be pitched more as being "economic." So that would not just be looking at insourcing but at the whole gamut of economics including the whole business value system, value chain, and the economics of skills locally. If I were to use artistic license to rename "location," then I will pick "area" suitability.

So, synthesizing this, we have "RACE" analysis for:

- Resources
- Area suitability
- Culture fit
- Economic

Does that feel more memorable, relevant, and complete?

Besides these two theories, there is a third main element of culture fit, which is obviously relevant to international strategy. Textbooks on international business strategy are crowded and rightly so with not just general material about national culture differences for example, between Japan and China and Western countries, but also within Europe for example, Britain, France, Germany, and Italy. *Basically, the greater the cultural differences the greater the uncertainty and risk, not just strategically but operationally.*

Finally, there can be issues from the strategic onion model around:

(a) Country-specific market attractiveness
(b) Country-specific competitive advantage

Where either of (a) or (b) are mistaken or inaccurate, then the overall strategic attractiveness can be misjudged with huge ramifications for financial attractiveness as well.

Once I recall working with the top team of a health insurance company with very strong position in the UK. The company had just acquired a subsidiary in Spain. The Strategic Planning Director took the stance that country- specific competitive advantage was irrelevant as we wouldn't know that until we were actually there. I suggested that was also relevant and important because if our brand didn't fit, that would be a weakness from the start. Also, how amenable would customers in certain countries be to a British brand? How would incumbents take to a new entrant too? Would they counterattack here? While we can't measure potential country-specific competitive advantage, it will play a major role in future performance. So it is still good to try to estimate it.

The bottom line is that there is another level of uncertainty of international business strategies. So uncertainties and risks will be higher, and this will be exacerbated through culture difficulties. These will also be greater with FDI and with acquisitions and alliances. This makes using tools like the uncertainty grid, the uncertainty tunnel with some scenario storytelling even more essential.

Most Common Tools Applicable

These would include:

The strategic onion, Porter's five competitive forces (especially for un the strategic option grid), the difficulty- and value-over-time curves, the uncertainty grid, and scenario storytelling, in addition to OLI or "RACE."

Particularly Sensitive Assumptions and Uncertainties

Some key, sensitive assumptions are:

- We already have a real competitive advantage in our domestic market and there is no big risk of losing that.
- Going international isn't going to overly distract us.
- According to the "RACE" framework, this does seem to give us a competitive edge and positions us in a country's market, which is genuinely strategically attractive.

- We have adequate management resources and appropriate skills to do that.
- We can, and we are honest with ourselves as to what the extra costs are and we are not deluding us about the business case.

Reader Exercise

For an international strategy in your current or precious company, or for one elsewhere that you know enough about, what does the uncertainty grid tell you about its vulnerability?

Applications

Strategic workshops again.

BT Case and Behavioral Uncertainty

This case study highlights not just the significance of using the scenario tools but also the risk of unsurfaced agendas and stakeholder drives easily deflecting and disrupting the process of seeing further into the future.

I was once conducting some research into the behaviors of a team who were tasked to formulate technology strategy (Grundy 1998), which is published in my book *Harnessing Strategic Behaviour—Why Politics and Personalities Drive Company Strategy*. This was a behavioral study into how it influenced the prioritization of technology issues and strategy for British Telecom (BT). This was done as action research, meaning that after surfacing and feeding back the issues, the team had the opportunity of trying out better strategy frameworks and processes and shifts to their team's default style.

During these workshops, the team used the uncertainty grid for exploring future scenarios and during that process, they had one assumption: The Internet was positioned using a Post-it as low importance/medium uncertainty. During the debate, the assumption underwent shifts, first to "more important" and then to "very uncertain," hence into the danger zone. Yes, that was a little piece of history. BT was instrumental in the spread of the Internet, but the Internet and broadband gave BT a massive new lease of life.

But coming back to the stakeholder dimension here in this story, in that team there was polarity and indeed tension between two members that you could feel in the air. Potentially, it could have been a constructive tension, but as I found it on the ground during workshops, it was mainly dysfunctional.

At one point, one of the pairs who was at that time facilitating seemed to have misinterpreted a comment from the other, who we will call Davina, when writing that down on the flipchart. Davina reacted very strongly and I was only told afterward that the team was teetering on the edge of the abyss as this felt a replay of something that had gone down before, which severely disrupted a previous session and there were still bruises all around from that. The team was passionate about the issues and had adversity of views, which was healthy, but to date, they had no real structure or process in how they surfaced and debated their agendas. So their work as a team was frustrating, not fully productive and at times fraught. The interplay of this filled 147 pages of that book!

While my analyses were prolific, it was only later on that I filled in an important gap in the picture. The senior manager who had helped me to get access to the team asked me how it had all gone. I gave him a picture, but flagged up this apparent tension between these two players, both of whom I said played important but differing roles within the team. He did tell me that BT was a very male environment traditionally, so females often felt they needed to fight extremely hard to begin to be heard. On top of that, he mentioned that Davina had gone to private school, which had a very traditional attitude, and Davina had some bad experiences there, especially with male teachers. So very simply, it was not really surprising that Davina felt a strong and driving need to be listened to and at a very detailed level so much so that this could hold the team back in its mission of "being the advanced intelligence of BT." And be at times difficult, too.

Digesting that revelation not only reminded me of the value of stakeholder profiling but also how stakeholder agendas can be the tail that ends up wagging the strategic dog. Had that altercation gone on just before the positioning of the Internet on the uncertainty grid, then BT might have not put it on the agenda for months or even a year! Micro uncertainties can be decisive.

We all have our patterns and most of us have hang ups and knowing them is the clue to how we will behave in certain situations in the future (see the mood-over-time grid). Let's never forget that in our lives and in our actions, we are major players shaping our own worlds.

In summary, the BT case study is useful as it not only highlights team dynamics as a big driver of uncertainty but also the role the individual stakeholders play in that uncertainty soup.

Letter to Boris Johnson (then UK Prime Minister) Regarding His Future and Career

The Right Hon. Boris Johnson
Prime Minister
United Kingdom
10 Downing Street
London SW1A 2AA
April 2, 2022
Dear Prime Minister

Even More Parties! Let's Rename the Conservatives as "The Party-Party"!!

Hi Boris

Since I last wrote, you have been busy beyond belief—inflation, energy prices, a potential third world war, and "Cake Gate," your birthday party! I am surprised that they give the fly overs of No. 10 and pictures of the gardens on TV that we haven't seen pictures of a battery of Vulcan high-velocity, high-caliber, rapid fire Vulcan Phalanx guns to knock down the media missiles coming back from the bad publicity stream of parties over the COVID period.

Maybe these guns have all gone to the Ukraine, instead?

I was watching your interview on TV a week or so ago and it did seem to me and many others that, from the questioning and your demeanor, you had no legs left to stand on. We can apply the same words of Sir Alan Sugar in the *Apprentice*, which summed up the debacle of the timeless

"Chicken Pizza Project" a total disaster: "Once you had bought those chickens [read 'parties'] you were DOOMED."

Only in December when I wrote to you on the 9th, *there might still* have been the possibility of coming clean and limiting the damage. I could have helped with that through helping you formulate a "Detergent Strategy," but now it does seem terminal.

But could there still be a Plan B?

Watching the news yesterday triggered an idea even before I heard that Liz Truss is going to the Ukraine next week. I did a thought experiment, which I hope you will forgive me for .... It is daring and involves you in some personal risk but might pave the way to some personal rebranding.

Suppose you do a press conference saying that you are taking a couple of weeks out on a "special project" in the Ukraine. You initiate a temporary reshuffle and Rishi Sunak can be temporary PM. Liz can do a mini stint in the Treasury as interim Chancellor; you can be acting Foreign Secretary. So you can look really brave and wear a tin hat, which will help all forgive you in the party and maybe some of the electorate (cross fingers).

You go in behind the Ukrainian border as a presence to deter the Russians: how dare Putin invade when you are ensconced and at the ready to be a Western puppet in Kiev as soon as there is an attack? Imagine what drama might unfold so that you get to be in pole position for the lead in Mission Impossible 7 when all of this is over and you get to step down graciously! Plan C?

But wait for it. You then have to go into the Ukraine by parachute. Watch those brittle legs when you land! We don't want to upset the slow rebuilding of your credibility!

Optional is for you to deploy your party organization skills to initiate surprise parties for the Russian troops with the second prong of your attack being hampers of M&S food like Carrie laid on during the famous Cake Gate birthday party and wine supplied from Tesco flown in by RAF Hercules. Not only will the Russians get to live longer as any mobilization will be sluggish but the urge to fight might diminish especially now the army is led from the front-tank division by yourself with your bright hair leading the way, gleaming in the sunlight!

Besides the great media coverage of your campaign, which can do no harm, you can also brush aside in advance any prosecutions by the Met for breaking COVID rules (petty in that context) as you are in effect now doing Community Service anyway *under the most perilous of conditions*. Even grannies in Hartlepool might again croon on the news to see your golden locks!

At a pinch a few weeks almost behind enemy lines might just be sufficient to stop the advance of those who will have you go and neutralize any no confidence vote. Even if you lose either the Ukrainian conflict or the attempts to depose you, you might be able to stay on as Foreign Secretary with Rishi as PM. I am sure his tunnel under number 10 is nearly completed, as his invasion of No 10, financed by the billions of IOUs that were not all really needed for COVID. Maybe you retire peacefully and star in Mission Impossible 7. Your wife Carrie would love that. So, all's well that ends well in Plan B.

Keep in your head! My cunning checklist question number 44:

"How, generally, can you change the rules of the game, and if the rules are changing, how could you bring that forward?"

Best wishes and good luck.

A N Grundy

Dr. Tony Grundy MA MBA MSc MPhil FCA PhD
Director, Corporate Development
33 Heathway
Croydon CR08PZ 07710198462
tony.grundy101@gmail.com
Boris Johnson finally stepped down on September 6, 2022.

CASE STUDY 7

The Random Weekend—a Field Study of Uncertainty

In August 2022, I and my wife Carolina, a clinical psychologist, decided to set off on an adventure—a random weekend to court and experience uncertainty. I had previously seen a TV documentary on "Dice Living" and was familiar with the concept, which had a following in the United States. I had also come across this in a date that I had with a lady I met in Haywards Heath via the Times Encounters page, some 45 miles away.

The date was not a success as the lady seemed scarcely recognizable from her picture and also brought a friend to tag along with her, but one conversation was around their Random Weekends that they did together once a month. They knew I was from Bolton, where they had apparently traveled to not just once but twice consecutively! They didn't like it much and had to grin and bear their second visit (not everyone's taste but I like it there!)

Apart from that, it had been a dead-end trip, but the seed was sown to try it some day with someone much more suitable. In addition, some friends suggested this as a possibility and when we found an opportunity, we were off. It was a heat wave with 33 to 35 degrees across Southern Britain.

We framed this as a "Field Study in Uncertainty" with the deployment of mindfulness through which we studied in real time the phenomenon of how we behaved in dealing with uncertainty as it came at us following our random intervention.

My case study runs as follows:

- Design of the field study
- Implementation
- Insights and learnings

Design of the Field Study

We decided to go by train as that would be easier and our first random decision would be which terminal main line station in London to go to, to start the process. There were 10, including Victoria, Waterloo and London Bridge, Paddington, the Kings Cross stations, and Liverpool St in the East.

Implementation

We jumped on the 194 bus at Millers Pond in Shirley, South London, and got our homemade cards depicting these 10 stations as if we were playing the game of Monopoly. Each had a drawing, for example, Paddington had Paddington Bear and Waterloo had a toilet with a bucket of water going down it.

We decided to take the first train on or after 12:50 a.m. regardless of its destination, but just as we were coming into Waterloo, which was our chosen card, I suggested that we change to 12:45 so we went hanging about. *This adjustment changed the world we were about to enter* as we were no longer going on for example, the Reading line. This demonstrates the impact of a transitional event.

On the way to Waterloo, I had dreamed of going to the seaside, maybe even somewhere like Portsmouth, but we were in lap of the Gods. My wife Carolina was looking for the ticketing office as I scanned the giant board. It was at that point that I emitted a large cry yelp! "Oh! my god, Portsmouth!"

The actual outcome, Portsmouth, was determined by my adjustment of our earlier departure time by 5 minutes, which was akin to the film *Sliding Doors* where a small jump in time set us off on a quite different scenario trajectory.

Carolina jumped thinking that there was some breakdown of law and order and then she realized what had happened; we were both going to the sea, in and maybe out to sea.

After a relaxing journey of one and three quarters of an hour, we arrived and set about finding a hotel. We tried cards again to determine the choice and by searching the Internet, but abandoned the idea as everywhere was expensive and most were booked. But eventually we struck gold with a quirky modern art style hotel called G Boutique, six minutes from the sea. In the 33 degrees heat, we dashed to the sea and braved the cool English Channel. It was time to be exposed to a stream of uncertain events.

As we swam, I began to be aware that the pier had come a lot closer and that as I swum there was a strong tug. Oh dear, a strong tidal current. A scenario story came to me, as the tug was pulling me out to sea, about my getting into difficulties, *resulting in a very sticky ending...* Not entirely fanciful as I hadn't had the results of a heart pumping pressure test back at that point from earlier that week.... So a drowning was on my uncertainty grid! (Five days later, I got the results—100 percent normal but not known at the time.) Suffice to say I swam hard for the shore!

But scenarios should not over dwell on the down sides as there were some very positive stories that were told and that came to pass.

Insights and Learnings

But observing these upside and downside uncertainties and their dynamics made us doubly aware of the way our lives both together and separately are routes through a maze of ever unfolding uncertainty. Events and their consequences are highly sensitive to the timings of events and the structure of human decisions and actions that are like a roulette wheel. There may be a myriad of possibilities, but that doesn't mean that one can't explore a reasonably small number of alternative stories. For example, we might have gone to Bolton, Inverness, or Peterborough.

By charting the structure of possible futures as we did in the chapter of MBA futures, we sketch a range of possible architectures, as if have journeyed to the "crossroads station" of Crewe and been able then to switch to subroutes of Wales, Manchester, Liverpool, Lancaster, Glasgow, or Inverness.

In charting these futures, we would be able to sense dangers and opportunities ahead better, become more agile, and gather resources to become more resilient.

Amplifying the final two points, it really helped having agility and also spare resources to take on uncertainty. We are both financially okay, so it wasn't the end of the world to find budget hotels at the sea in that weather and season coming in at over £130 a night with no breakfast included! If we hadn't been "comfortable," it would have been hard to leave our accommodation up to chance (although thinking "contingent strategy" in that heat, there was always the beach!)

The other thing we noticed ("phenomenologically") is that the exposure to uncertainty and risk gave a sense of heightened alertness, which was stimulating if not actually exciting—as we learned from the core book, sometimes groups undertake more risky tasks than its constituents might undertake solo ("risky shift"). *So rather than see uncertainty as always being your enemy, it can also be your friend, not to mention a stimulus for change and innovation.*

References

"An MBA Has Barely Helped Me to Progress—What Next?" n.d. www.ft.com › content.

"The Global Demand for Graduate Management Education Access Report, Webinar, Blog, and Infographic Application Trends Survey 2020." November 10, 2020. Graduate Management Admissions Council.

"What Do HE Students Study?" 2021. HESA.

Allison, G. July–August 2012. "The Cuban Missile Crisis at 50: Lessons for US Foreign Policy Today." *Foreign Affairs* 91, no. 4, pp. 11–62.

Ansoff, H.I. 1975. "Managing Surprise by Response to Weak Signals." *California Management Review* 8, pp. 21–33.

Berrger, P. and T. Luckann. 1966. *The Social Construction of Reality*. Penguin.

Bywater, H. 1925. "1932 The Great War on the Pacific." Bedford, Massachusetts: Applewood Books.

Cairns, G. and G. Wright. 2011. "Scenario Thinking." Palgrave Macmillan.

Checkland, P. 1981. *Systems Thinking, Systems Practice*. New York, NY: John Wiley.

Coveney, P. and R. Highfield. 1991. "The Arrow of Time." London: Flamingo.

Csikszentmihalyi, M. 1990. "Flow." Harper.

Dunning, J. 2001. "The Eclectic Paradigm of International Production." *International Journal of the Economics of Business* 8, pp. 173–192.

Fine, C.H. 1998. *Clock Speed*. Cambridge: Basic Books.

Gleick, J. 1997. *Chaos: Making a New Science*. Oxford: Heinemann.

Grundy, T. 1993. *Implementing Strategic Change*. London: Kogan Page.

Grundy, T. 1995. *Strategic Learning in Action*. Maidenhead: McGraw Hill.

Grundy, T. 1998. "Harnessing Strategic Behaviour-Why Personality and Politics Drive Strategy." *Financial Times*.

Grundy, T. 2002a. *Be Your Own Strategy Consultant*. London: Thomson Learning.

Grundy, T. 2002b. *Shareholder Value*. Oxford, London: Capstone.

Grundy, T. 2003a. *Value—Based HR Strategy*. Oxford: Routledge.

Grundy, T. 2003b. *Mergers and Acquisitions*. Oxford: Capstone Press.

Grundy, T. 2004. "Rejuvenating Strategic Management: The Strategic Option Grid." *Strategic Change* 13, pp. 111–124.

Grundy, T. 2012. *Demystifying Strategy—How to Become a Strategic Thinker*. Kogan Page.

Grundy, T. 2014. *Demystifying Strategic Thinking- Lessons from Leading CEOs*. Kogan Page.

Grundy, T. 2018. *Dynamic Competitive Strategy—Turning Strategy Upside Down*. Oxford: Routledge.

Hamel, G. and C.K. Prahalad. 1994. *Competing for the Future*. Harvard University Press.

Heidegger, M. 1927. *Being and Time*.

Hertwig, R., T.J. Pleskac, and T. Pachur. 2019. *Taming Uncertainty*. Mass: MIT Press.

Hines, H. and P. Bishop. 2015. *Thinking About the Future*. Houston: Hinesight.

Janis, I.J. 1982. *Groupthink*. Houghton Mifflin.

Jimmy, L. and Sampson. 2020. *How Has the Effects of Social Distancing and Home Working Influenced Work Norms?* [Unpublished MBA Project].

Johanson, J. and J.E. Vahine. 1977. "The Internationalization Process of the Firm." *Journal of International Business Studies* 8, no. 1, pp. 23–32. "Uppsala Model."

Kahneman, D. 2011. *Thinking Fast and Slow*. London: Penguin.

Kaplan, A. n.d. "A School Is a Building With Four Walls With Tomorrow Inside—Towards the Reinvention of the Business School." https://doi.org/10.1016/j.bushor.2018.03.010.

Kotter, J. and H. Rathgeber. 2017. *Our Iceberg Is Melting*. Pan Macmillon.

Levy, D. 1994. "Chaos Theory." *Journal of Strategic Management*.

Madonna. 1984. "Material Girl." Sire label.

Mintzberg, H., J. Lampel, and B. Ahlstrand. 1998. *Strategy Safari*. New York, NY: Simon and Schuster.

Mitroff, I.I. and H.A. Linstone. 1993. *The Unbounded Mind*. Oxford University Press.

Nietzsche, F. 1902. *The Will to Power*.

N.A. 2019. https://find-mba.com/articles/employer-funding-for-mbas-myth-or-reality.

Piercy, N. 1989. "Diagnosing and Solving Implementation Problems in Strategic Management." *Journal of General Management* 15, no. 1, pp. 19–38.

Porter, E.M. 1980. *Competitive Strategy*. Harvard University.

Rumelt, R. 2011. *Good Strategy Bad Strategy*. London: Profile Books.

Schwarz, P. 1996. *The Art of the Long View—Planning for the Future*. New York, NY: Penguin.

Senge, P. 1990. *The Fifth Discipline the Art and Practice of the Learning Organisation*. New York, NY: Doubleday.

Simon, H.A. 1957. *Models of Man; Social and Rational*. Wiley.

Stoner, J.F. 1968. "A Risky and Cautious Shifts in Group Decisions, the Influence of Widely Held Values." *Journal of Experimental Social Psychology* 4, pp. 442–450.

Taleb, N. 2007. *The Black Swan—The Art of the Improbable*. London: Allen Lane.

Taylor, C.W. 1990. *Creating Strategic Visions*. Pensylvania: Strategic Studies Institute, US Army War College.

Tetlock, P. and D. Gardner. 2015. *Super Forecasting—Prediction*. London: Penguin.

Van der Heijden, K. 2014. *Scenarios—The Art of Strategic Conversation*. John Wiley & Sons.

Von Neumann, J. and O. Morgenstern. 1944. "Theory of Games and Economic Behaviour." Princeton University Press.

Wells, H.G. 1895. *The Time Machine*.

About the Author

Dr. Tony Grundy is a prolific management thinker, writer, international strategy consultant, senior executive, developer, and mentor. He has consulted with KPMG and independently in total for 38 years and has held senior positions at BP and ICI. He has taught at 10 major Business Schools including Cranfield, Cambridge, Durham, Henley, Manchester, and Warwick and is now coleader of the UCL MBA Capstone Futures project. His work spans strategy, change, and finance.

Index

OTHER TITLES IN THE HUMAN RESOURCE MANAGEMENT AND ORGANIZATIONAL BEHAVIOR COLLECTION

Michael J. Provitera, Barry University, Editor

- *The Intrapreneurship Formula* by Sandra Lam
- *Navigating Conflict* by Lynne Curry
- *Innovation Soup* by Sanjay Puligadda and Don Waisanen
- *The Aperture for Modern CEOs* by Sylvana Storey
- *The Future of Human Resources* by Tim Baker
- *Change Fatigue Revisited* by Richard Dool and Tahsin I. Alam
- *Championing the Cause of Leadership* by Ted Meyer
- *Embracing Ambiguity* by Michael Edmondson
- *Breaking the Proactive Paradox* by Tim Baker
- *The Modern Trusted Advisor* by Nancy MacKay and Alan Weiss
- *Achieving Success as a 21st Century Manager* by Dean E. Frost
- *A.I. and Remote Working* by Tony Miller
- *Best Boss!* by Duncan Ferguson, Toni M. Pristo, and John Furcon
- *Managing for Accountability* by Lynne Curry
- *Fundamentals of Level Three Leadership* by James G.S. Clawson

Concise and Applied Business Books

The Collection listed above is one of 30 business subject collections that Business Expert Press has grown to make BEP a premiere publisher of print and digital books. Our concise and applied books are for…

- Professionals and Practitioners
- Faculty who adopt our books for courses
- Librarians who know that BEP's Digital Libraries are a unique way to offer students ebooks to download, not restricted with any digital rights management
- Executive Training Course Leaders
- Business Seminar Organizers

Business Expert Press books are for anyone who needs to dig deeper on business ideas, goals, and solutions to everyday problems. Whether one print book, one ebook, or buying a digital library of 110 ebooks, we remain the affordable and smart way to be business smart. For more information, please visit www.businessexpertpress.com, or contact sales@businessexpertpress.com.

www.ingramcontent.com/pod-product-compliance
Lightning Source LLC
Chambersburg PA
CBHW061141220326
41599CB00025B/4311